Missing Links

Missing Links

By
Phillip S. Yarbrough

Missing Links

Copyright © 2021 by Phillip S. Yarbrough

ISBN: 979-8-9857202-7-3

All rights reserved. No part of this book may be reproduced or transmitted in any form or by any means, electronic or mechanical, including photocopying, recording, or by any information storage and retrieval system, without permission in writing from the copyright owner.

The views expressed in this work are solely those of the author and do not necessarily reflect the views of the publisher, and the publisher disclaims any responsibility for them.

To order additional copies of this book, contact:

Proisle Publishing Services LLC
1177 6th Ave 5th Floor
New York, NY 10036, USA
Phone: (+1 347-922-3779)
info@proislepublishing.com

PROISLE PUBLISHING

Dedication

The loving memory of my mother and father,
one brother and sister who have departed this life,
and now rest in peace awaiting their resurrection.

AND

Aubery Fisher Yarbrough
Grandfather

A Baptist preacher known and loved by many

ALSO

Hezekiah Smith
Friend

A solitary man, who knew the Lord

Contents

Preface i

Chapter I: *The Great Debate* 1

Chapter II: *The Theory of Creation* 17

Chapter III: *Mission Debrief and Conclusions* 38

Chapter IV: *Philosophy and Theology* 45

Chapter V: *A Myth Found and the Reality Lost* 62

Chapter VI: *Timeline Prophecies of the Bible* 81

Chapter VII: *Timeline Prophecies of the Bibl*........................... 103

Chapter VIII: *Prime Numbers 1, 2, 3, and 5* 116

Chapter IX: *Doctrines and Traditions of Men* 128

Chapter X: *Delusions and Illusions* 141

Chapter XI: *Badges* 152

Chapter XII: *The Ultimate Reality* 159

Bibliography 164

Appendix I 166

Appendix II 168

Appendix III: *A Lunar Sign* 171

Appendix IV: *Revelation Countdown* 174

Preface

Most people today are concerned about our recent [2008] and ongoing economic crisis. [Still ongoing 2021.] Some may be concerned about the global economy and other world conditions. On Sept. 30, 2008, America's and other global stock markets began a seemingly persistent downward spiral. The economic gurus gave much advice concerning the crisis; however, efforts made seem to be in vain. Our government has injected billions upon billions into its system, yet the more it piles on the greedy beast's economics buffet, the more it demands and consumes. The late 2009 rebound seems encouraging to many, but there are some that see beyond the summit of optimism.

The choices made by today's governing elders will affect future generations. All choices have consequences! When the billions in deficit spending on bank bail-outs, corporate rescues, and the wars in Iraq and Afghanistan by the previous administration is added to the billions in the recently passed stimulus package, ongoing wars, more bail-outs, and numerous proposals of the present administration, our national debt will be somewhere between 15 to 20 trillion dollars by 2012. This does not include the interest that will have to be paid on maintaining the hooked-on steroids, forever growing national debt. Based on an estimated population of 400 million [under-estimated due to abortions over last 13 years], a 15 to 20 trillion-dollar debt (future tax obligation) is 37.5 to 50 thousand dollars **per person**. We are sacrificing our children and our children's children on alters of greed, usury, and taxation. They will have to make a most difficult choice in the tyranny that will soon come concerning their indebtedness. At some point in time, the piper will have to be paid!

By 2012, this nation's indebtedness and economic disparity could be so enormous that a Leviticus 25:10 type of miracle by a Revelation 13 authority may have to be performed in order to heal the crisis. A choice will have to be made! Choices inherently demand options. Without options, the freedom to make a choice is irrelevant. *Freedom of Choice* is a constant theme throughout this book, and we can only thank our Creator for its endowment. (Declaration of Independence)

The topic, freedom of choice, has been widely debated throughout the course of life, liberty, and the pursuit of happiness. It is the presentation of options that is crucial in the debate. What options should or should not be allowed? Whose moral standards should dictate the options? By what authority should the standard of options be based? There are only two realistic choices: good or evil. That is the *duality of understanding*.

Our constitution was designed to guarantee certain freedoms and institute a limited government to protect them. When that government denies options and limits choice, is there loyalty to the constitution? Should a new declaration be instituted? Our forefathers freed us from an oppressive king, but a just and merciful King will soon make His own declaration on this world. That is the heart of this little book.

In 1980, I wrote a poem for a creative writing class while in junior college living near San Francisco. I only got a "C" on the assignment. I've kept a copy all these years. It seems to apply to today's current situation, as it did then. The following is my "Sonnet 1980" revision **40** years later.

"Sonnet 2020"

Minds all too distant - the leaders of the land,
Dissatisfaction! - Truth! Mislead masses demand.
Many fingers pointing - no one takes the blame,
Old clocks ticking - yet times remain the same.

The people crying - tears of distress so pure,
Great hunger and thrust - none see the cure.
Many eyes seeking - someone from the clan,
The forest's desire - a strong oak in the land.

Same sex unions - men's hand upon the hip,
Preachers love preaching - reputations they rip.
Children taken away - authority just and fair,
Hearts of mothers broken - so few really care.

Deceitful seekers seeking - a profitable plan,
Man's dream of Utopia - so far from hand.

All Scripture quotes will be from the Authorized King James translation of the Bible and all Greek and Hebrew definitions from Strong's Exhaustive Concordance of the Bible. The scripture quotes will be written in full in Chapter II; however, throughout the remainder of this little book you will need your own Bible to follow along. There will be many relevant as well as related book, chapter, and verse references given throughout in support of the text. I hope and pray that all readers will take the time to read the Bible with this little book. I assure you that it will be a most unusual, but shockingly revealing Bible study.

[2020 Revision Addition]

Since the week of Passover, I've been busy editing this little book and my spring gardening. I can think of better things to do than staking red solo cups, and several other things as seen on TV. Out of all the things that I have seen people doing with all the spare time on their hands, one is **not** searching the Bible for some answers! It just might be that **The Scripture of Truth** does indeed hold the answers to most if not all of the questions being asked today.

I can assure you that the current situation the entire world is facing now is 100% Scriptural! Yes, it is indeed from China, but not for the reasons that one may think. Ezekiel 38:8-23 makes that perfectly clear; that is if one understands that Gog is China and *The House of Israel* is the United States, Great Britain, Western Europe (the lost ten tribes of Israel), and the State of Israel is *The House of Judah* (tribes of Judah and Benjamin). (Ezek. 37:15-28) The present land(s) of Israel are anywhere on planet earth that both The House of Israel and The House of Judah currently reside and possess.

In the Old Testament times the Lord used King Shalmaneser of Assyria to destroy and take into captivity the House of Israel because of its sins. The Lord used King Nebuchadnezzar to destroy and take into captivity the House of Judah for its sins. (II Kings 17 & 24) The Lord is the same today as He was in ancient times. Prophecy for both houses of Israel in the latter days (years) are no different. The Lord will use whom He pleases to punish His people for their sins. Today, it just so happens to be the King of China and his puppets! Can the Kings of modern-day Israel resist the will of the Lord their God? It is obvious that most of the people just don't give a damn!

Testing is the *hot topic* of the day. (May 7, 2020 – I'm listening to "The View" this moment. Woppi, can you say: "King Trump"?) If people want to know what is really going on – **READ THE WORD OF GOD!** The only respect lacking in America today is the respect for the **LIVING WORD OF GOD!** Yes, all nations of the world are being tested! Judgment is upon us! Take a good look in the mirror. Judge not, least ye be judged. (Commercial)

The only real sacrifice being made today is that made by all the health care workers and frontline responders. The sacrifice that **we the people** need to accept is that made by **Jesus Christ** in 29 AD. We are being judged for our sins, both secular and religious. To repent is to put away sin and the doctrines and traditions of man, then to do the will (desire) and the commandments of the Lord. (John 14:15-21) That is the essence of what this **Little Book** is all about.

The white horse of Revelation 6 has begun its ride. Just as Paul Revere did on April 18, 1775, I hope to be doing soon on the internet, just as soon as I can get it and learn some tech stuff. As an Ezekiel 33 Watchman for Israel today, I must sound the alarm! In the spirit (character) of the late Martin Luther King: **The Lord is coming; the Lord is coming – thank God Almighty – the Lord is coming!**

AMEN!

[2021 Revision Addition]

Revision 2020 was published by the same POD publisher September 2020 as in September of 2008. I was unable to pay for outside promotional services both times and in one year, only two copies sold. (Same in 2008, but only seven copies sold.) Found a crucial mistake the second week of August 2021 in a 2020 revision addition that was cause for the republication. I had not yet called the publisher about the mistake when I received a phone call from another publisher, who claimed to have read one of the two copies and was interested in publishing it. I suppose the Lord does work in mysterious ways! We worked out an agreement to republish and promote with the corrections necessary for republication. Other than a few misspelled words, a couple of mistyped dates and a math error, the one mistake that caused the reason to republish was I used the wrong Strong's number for "bow" in Rev. 6:2. I had published the H5015 definition instead of H5115 in the Chapter VII 2020 revision addition. [Didn't really alter my definition of the white horse (political, economic and religious confusion and chaos) all that much. Never really considered it "False Religion" alone. That's been around for six millennium.] Ops! So I deleted the addition to Chapter VII and Added Appendix IV. I found the mistake when posting "A Sabbath Message 8/14/21 - The White Horse" on my web/blog site. (Got internet and new PC mid July 2020 and learned how to set up a blog/site on April 25, 2021 with Word Press.)

https://theezekiel33watchman.report/

The study and research for this little book itself began back in 1999 and I started writing it in 2001 on an old word processor. The first publication was off the word processor's floppy disk I sent to the POD Publisher in 2008. After publication, I managed to get it reformatted and transferred to my younger sister's hand-me-down 1998 Windows with Word 2000, which is a whole story in and of itself. Around 2010, I transferred it to a hand-me-down Windows HP laptop with Word 2005 my Uncle had given me. He got it from a friend that had upgraded, and he just didn't do computers. [Looking back, that would be like a hand-me-down times a hand-me-down or H-M-D^2.] I added to the 2008 poem and reference paragraph only preface in 2010 and went thru it again numerous times, but couldn't afford to republish, so set it aside. A decade later, I got a wake-up call! (See Appendix III.)

I'm a retired independent small produce farmer for the last 36 years and not an author, but have been blessed with biblical understanding. Sweet in writing, but bitter in getting this little book published has been an ongoing experience for me. Been putting it up on my web site a chapter at a time. Started with Posting Chapter VI on 4/25/21, the first post to the site and first in archives. As of 11/21/21, it has had 165 views. I haven't posted all 12 chapters as yet because I've had to do some upgrade reformatting and format editing. It still has some old dinosaur age Word in it that needs a little updating. I'm no computer whiz! This is my third and last attempt to get this little book published. It is now in the Lord's hand!

LOLGB+

Chapter I
The Great Debate

The most sacred of all our freedoms is the freedom of choice. Although it is only implied and supposedly guaranteed by our constitution, today's young minds are being denied that most scared of all freedoms. How? Choice inherently requires at least two options. Can a person make a choice without options to choose from? When alternative options are denied, so is freedom of choice! In our public schools, the alternative option currently denied is the other theory concerning the origin of man. Did man evolve from apes, a common ancestor, or was all matter and all the life forms composed of that matter, including man, created by a supreme intelligence?

The great conflict began in 1925 when John T. Scopes was convicted for teaching "the theory of evolution" in a public school. Prior to that historical event, creation was the only theory of man's origin that was taught. After his conviction, the state of Tennessee banned its teaching, but the ACLU rushed to his aid defending his right to teach it. Evolution has since become (evolved into) the foundation of all science taught in public schools and universities today, but any theory of creation has become the "forbidden fruit" due to the misunderstanding of separation of church and state. No state can respect a single freedom of religious practice!

The theory of evolution has evolved into a religion. As the only theory allowed explaining the origins of life, it is taught as if a scientific fact. Is a theory a fact? If theory is not a fact, then why can't two opposing theories be equally taught side by side, and then students allowed freedom in choosing the one they deem the most creditable? Isn't the goal of education to expand the intellectual use of the human mind? Can the ACLU set aside its hypocrisy in the interest of freedom of choice and support the equal representation of any creation theory with evolution's, which is currently endorsed by the State? The guaranteed freedom of religious expression is where freedom of choice is implied. Can freedom of choice be truly maintained when an expression of a theoretical option is denied?

There have been efforts to introduce *life by intelligent design* alongside evolution, but the great defender of freedom of choice will not allow it. The ACLU argues that teaching any theory of creation would violate the separation of church and state. It is true that no single theology (theory) can be established or respected by the State. The First Amendment of our Constitution forbids it! Isn't the State's respect of an established theory (evolution) over another (creation) unconstitutional?

The ACLU devoutly defends a woman's right to abortion yet neglects those of the sperm donor. It has defended voting rights for all Americans, except Floridians in 2000 and 2008. It supports the civil rights of alternative lifestyles but opposes a distinct definition of the institution of marriage. It supports sex education and birth control but opposes the teaching of abstinence. It defended John Scopes' right to teach the theory of evolution, but is hell bent on not allowing a theory of creation to be equally taught, thus denying the young minds of this country the same freedom of choice it so relentlessly defends. Is not that the very definition of hypocrisy? Can you have your cake and eat it too? I do know what their letters stand for, but I have a suspicious idea of what they may now actually represent.

Science itself has poked some significant holes in the theory of evolution. The term *evolutionary design* is now used. Doesn't the very concept of design inherently demand that there be a designer? Modern day advancements in genetics strongly indicate an intelligent design in all life forms. Today, we have genetic mapping, DNA finger printing, and genetic engineering. To engineer something is to first design then construct it, and the engineer is its designer. Engineering demands the understanding of its knowledge, which requires intelligence. Gaining knowledge is one thing, but the wisdom to utilize it is another. How many Doctor Frankenstein(s) are working in secret places? How many deadly biologically engineered organisms been created? Is a global beast system being secretly engineered? Who is its designer and engineer?

I think that the scientific knowledge we have today can prove creation, or at least propose a more credible theory. Can our knowledge in science prove the existence of a *Supreme Designer*? Could the Bible be scientifically investigated by setting aside the theological chaos that exists among its various religions? I'd like to suggest that it could be done. We should at least be able to propose a more logical theory than *accidental evolution without intelligent design*. Our increased knowledge was prophesied. (Dan. 12:4)

Which of the two theories, evolution or creation, offers the most hope for man? Can technology solve the planet's problems facing us today? Technology has brought about many luxuries, but usually at great environmental expense. Electrical power and automobiles are ideal examples. Life became more comfortable after the discovery of electricity and much faster with cars, but fossil fuels and coal cause air pollution, and nuclear power plants generate deadly radioactive waste that takes millions of years to decompose. Will hydrogen, wind, and solar technology become mankind's salvation?

Many advances have been made in solar power, thanks to the increased knowledge in quantum mechanics (the electromagnetic qualities of light). We hear much about solar power cells. Solar power is often made available at no cost to some people in remote areas without electrical power; however, homeowners cannot find any reasonably priced systems at our local home improvement centers. Systems are available, but the cost is too high for most people. Why is this technology so costly? If this renewable source of electric energy were suddenly made available at a reasonable cost, what would the CEO's and stockholders of the major energy corporations do? What would happen to their multiple billions in profits?

What about hydrogen for cars? What would it really cost to produce hydrogen? It is part of that thing called H_2O or water. The best way to produce hydrogen is to separate it from oxygen through the electrolysis process, which is the sudden chemical decomposition of the H_2O by a DC electric current. The process is expensive, unless the water is a brine solution (saltwater). Ever get a mouthful of seawater while swimming in the ocean? Since solar panels produce a DC current, and oceans are full of saltwater, we could build hydrogen plants with solar panel roofs, pump seawater into tanks, drop the DC electrodes into the tanks of saltwater, flip a switch, and literally shock the hydrogen right out of the seawater. What would we do with the oxygen byproduct? The biggest obstacle may be the ownership of our inalienable right to the sun's energy and *Charlie's hydrogen of the sea*. They are gifts from our Creator, but he could send us a sunlight and seawater bill. What happens when your light bill is not paid?

Congressional budgets have increased funding for the research and development of ethanol, but cut funding for wind, hydrogen, and solar. If you were a farmer and corn earned the most money per acre, what would you plant? When the price of tortillas, cornflakes, and daily bread gets as high as a tank of gas, blame the government, not farmers! What would happen if our government spent half as much money on the availability of existing solar, wind, and hydrogen technology as it does on trying to democratize Theocratic Islamic countries? We could tell all the oil producing countries in the world to kiss our energy loving asses! Then, we can feed our excess corn to the poor. Think of all the hearts and minds we could win, and never have to drop a single bomb. Smart ones are expensive!

Technology has brought us into the computer age. Advancements in its technology have grown so fast that any product purchased today becomes *Smithsonian* within a year or two. Frequent system upgrades, reformatting, and new adaptability devices are constantly required. Most human beings you see on the street have a gadget of some sort in their hands or pockets. Kids have camped out in front of stores waiting for the newest thing. It's like being addicted to marijuana. I shouldn't laugh, having been once busted for growing four little plants. I bet it is easier to abstain from marijuana than put down a cell phone, Play Station, iPod or blackberry. How often do you see kids reading books? Fingers and thumbs can turn pages too!

Most religions offer hope for a better future, but the multitude of denominational theology and philosophy that presently exists in the world has settled a great fog on the truths that can be found in the Holy Bible. It is the only source of information that fully explains creation, which is a common theme among many religions, but the ACLU will not allow its theory of creation to equally stand side by side with the theory of evolution. Does that defend the equal rights of all taxpayers who fund the free education for all children in public schools, which is the tenth platform of the Communist Manifesto? (See Appendix I) Do all taxpayers funding public education have an equal right in the representation of *the origin of life* curriculum? Both creationists and evolutionists pay taxes. Was not the Revolutionary War based upon taxation without representation? The displays of the Ten Commandments are stripped down from many public buildings. Doesn't the ACLU know the Ten Commandments and many other biblical statutes form the very foundation of our justice system?

The biggest problem with evolution's *Origin of the Species* is the biological fact that an outside ionizing force was needed to begin the formation of the more complex molecules. From my college biology textbook: *"For life to appear, somehow these simpler molecules had to be joined together. The trouble was that the molecules, by themselves, had no tendency to join. They could coexist quite nicely side by side for an indefinite period."* Dinosaurs did not evolve from a chaotic cesspool of biological soup, and neither did the human beings of today evolve from apes, nor a common ancestor with the apes. Today's advancements in genetics can substantiate the creation theory more than the evolution theory. Biological knowledge is the understanding of how any living organism functions, not how they came to exist. Did life begin from a chaotic cesspool of biological soup with no intelligent course of direction or purpose? Is the universe a creation for the liberty of humankind? (Rom. 8:19-21)

I may have discovered the biggest hole in evolution's theory during my search for some chromosome count information. I knew that humans had 46 or 23 pairs. Apes (chimpanzees, orangutans and gorillas) have 48 or 24 pairs. I have yet to find any chromosome count information on the other primates (monkeys and lemurs). I did find the number of chromosomes for sheep, pigs, cattle, chickens, corn, and soybean seeds. Since genetic engineering has supposedly advanced production in agriculture, I suppose that I will just have to wait until there is a demand for monkey and lemur meat. Where will the processors find immigrant workers for those critters?

Taxonomists have divided all the species on planet earth into classifications. Although there are some disagreements among them, the general order of species classification is: kingdom – phylum – subphylum – class – order – family – genus – species. A species is considered as *any organism that can successfully reproduce.*

In the order of Carnivora, dogs and wolves are often considered different species, but that cannot be, because they do interbreed. Dogs are a prime example of *microevolution*, which can happen within a species or genus. In this case, the correct term is really *hybridization*. When man began to live in cities and created garbage piles, some lazy wolves found an easy source of food. After relatively few generations, there were minor changes in their characteristics. When they became unafraid of man and found useful as guard dogs, man began selectively breeding them for a variety of useful tasks. That is why we have various breeds today. Since the 18th century, man has selectively breed dogs simply for their looks, and some are not so pretty. Recently, Poodles and Labradors were interbred to produce Poodledors or Labradoddles. [Is there a Poodle for my chocolate lab – Choco?]

Primata is one of the twelve orders, not tribes, of mammals subdivided into the lemur, monkey, and ape families which includes the human species. Shouldn't the ape family be divided into chimpanzee, orangutan, and gorilla genus? The man family skips genus and is a single species. The missing link between the ape family and the man species is **genus**. Confused? The Bible's book of **Genesis** may hold the answer to that dilemma. Although man is a single species, we have many races, but we all have the same number of chromosomes and do interbreed. Variety is a beautiful thing, as with chickens. They are a single species of domesticated fowl with a variety of breeds that do interbreed. If you were to put Rhode Island Reds, White Leg Horns, and Blue Bantams in the same pen, in time you would have Red, White, and Blue chickens. They could be called *The Star Spangled Bantams* and their eggs used for America's breakfast of patriots.

Any living cell in all living plant or animal organisms contains within its nucleus a specific number of characteristic chromosomes that identifies its species. The number of chromosomes in any species of living organisms is always divisible by two; thus, they are more often called pairs. Humans have 23 pairs, and all three genera of the ape family have 24 pairs. Wouldn't the higher superiority within a genus or family require extra genetic information to be written in its genetic code? I tend to think that an extra pair of chromosomes would be necessary to contain that additional genetic information in order to justify the superiority of the higher species within a genus or family. Can a decrease of information in the genetic code of family – genus – species establish superiority in an evolutionary chain? Did ape evolve from man, but remain inferior? Are apes superior to man? This is what I consider to be the major **MISSING LINK** in evolution.

There are three major religions that hold their beliefs to the same Creator God. Judaism believes God is monotheistic, and most of Christianity believes that God is a Trinity. Islam also believes God is monotheistic, but Mohammed is his primary and last Prophet. All three acknowledge the same Creator God but have killed each other for almost two thousand years over their differences. Some are still at it! During the Protestant Reformation, Christians killed other Christians.

The major difference between the three is the man Jesus. Judaism claims he was just a good teacher, while some of the more radical claim he was crazy. In 29 AD, the Jews insisted the Romans crucify him, and they deny his divinity to this very day, which is technically anti-Christ. Christianity claims that Jesus was the Son of God, crucified by the Romans at the request of the Jews, but resurrected, ascended to his father, and will return at the end of days to *fly them away* from the madness that will take place before the end of the world. Islam claims that he was born of a virgin, a prophet, but not the Son of God; however, he will return to fight the Antichrist. [I don't know if Mohammed is supposed to return and assist him or not.]

The three have their own holy books but share in some of them. Judaism has the Hebrew Bible (Old Testament) and the Talmud. Christianity also uses the Hebrew Bible, but with the addition of the New Testament. Islam has the Koran but share in the books of Moses up to a point, and maybe the Prophets. They claim that Mohammed was the last of a long line of prophets preceded by Adam, Noah, Abraham, Moses, and Jesus. Their other major difference concerns Abraham's first two sons. Ishmael was born first by his wife's handmaid Hagar, and then Isaac was born to him by his wife Sarah in her old age. Abraham went to sacrifice Isaac as a test of faith, but God stopped him at the last second and provided a lamb. Although not specifically stated in the Koran, Muslims believe that it was Ishmael and not Isaac, but the Old Testament states that it was Isaac. (Gen. 22)

All the geological evidence of earth's history dating back millions of years disproves the claim that the earth was created a little over 6,000 years ago. When utilizing the Bible and secular records, we can count from the creation of Adam (4131 BC) to the present (2008) and arrive to a total of 6139 years. Some claim the six days of creation weren't days as we count days because one day to God is like 1000 years to man, and Adam wasn't created until the end of the sixth day. That line of thought adds another 6,000 years, but our planet is billions of years old. Although man is much more recent, Adam did not live with a bunch of nut-cracking and vegetarian dinosaurs as some idiots like to claim.

The confusion can be easily answered. Genesis 1:2 states: *"And the earth was without form..."* The word *was* is from the Hebrew word *hayah* meaning: to be, to become, come to pass, or as a past tense adverb became. The earth was not created in the condition stated in Gen. 1:2. If God is a creator of perfection, then what we really have is a lapse of time between Genesis 1:1 and 1:3. It is often referred to as the MISSING TIME, but to be truly objective and totally honest, let's call it the **MISSING LINK** in creation.

Now that we have evolution and creation on an even platform with each having a missing link, let's discuss the history behind the evolution theory. A French contemporary, George-Louis Leclerc de Buffon (1707-1788) proposed in 1753 *that in addition to the animals of creation there were lesser families conceived by nature and produced by time.* He claimed there were *imperfections in the Creator's expression.* A decade later, Erasmus Darwin, Charles' grandfather, suggested that the formation of the species was also due to *competition and environmental changes.* [Let's keep in mind that all this was mere human speculation with no supporting facts.]

During the days of the French Revolution, Napoleon's General Berthier captured the Pope and imprisoned him to France in 1798. Napoleon had completely dissolved the Holy Roman Empire by 1804, and France had become an atheist nation with the majority claiming that there was no God. It was during those darkest of days that Jean Baptiste de Lamarck (1744-1829) claimed *that not only had one species given rise to another, but man himself had risen from other species.*

In 1831 Charles Darwin sailed to the Galapagos Islands aboard the Beagle as a Naturalist to record various types of life. Prior to his departure, he obtained Charles Lyell's (1797-1875) first publication, "Principles of Geology". Lyell had rejected the commonly held Biblical thesis that the earth had been created in the year 4004 BC, which at that time was the commonly held date. During the voyage, Darwin observed and wrote about many fascinating species living on the islands, which can be observed today. No new ones have evolved, but a Giant Tortoise may remember Charles!

In 1798, the Reverend Thomas Malthus (1766-1834) had published an essay warning of the danger in overpopulation. He had made the assessment that *as man continued to geometrically spread out, he would soon outstrip his food supply, therefore creating a world of misery and vice.* [What would he say if alive today? I think that he could rightfully say, "I told you so."]

In 1858, Alfred Russell Wallace (1823-1913) had outlined his thesis on *Natural Selection* and ready to publish it but waited until Darwin had pulled together all his notes and prepared his paper, *Origin of the Species.* Together, they presented their work to the Linnaean Society of London in 1859. In 1871, Darwin published *Descent of Man* claiming that *man and ape had evolved from a common ancestor.* He recanted before he died. Scientific research has proved many of his concepts wrong, but they are still taught.

It should be noticeably obvious that the theory of man evolving from or with apes has its roots in atheism. There are only two possible positions to choose from: You are an Atheist and your religion is the belief in evolution with no intelligent evolver, OR, you are a Creationist and your religion is the belief in creation by a supremely intelligent creator. Will the ACLU allow both theories to stand side by side with equal rights and let students exercise their own freedom of choice? If not, then take that damn evolution religion out of the schools and let true separation stand! Remember the Stephen King novel, "The Stand"? We are at the closing chapter, and it's time to take one. Is it possible that an intelligent evolution of matter is relative to creation? $E = mc^2$ is the proven equation for all relative mass-energy relationships. Inverted it is: man (matter) = $E \div C^2$.

Although our increased knowledge in science has been utilized to enforce evolution as the sole theory for man's existence, it can also equally support if not prove creation. Knowledge in the biological sciences is very dependent upon the physical sciences, which are the more absolute sciences. The student in a beginning biology class is first taught that man evolved from or with apes, then atoms, ions, electron shells, molecules, ionization, and oxidation are discussed in order to explain the complex processes of the amino acids, enzymes, carbohydrates, proteins, lipids, and peptides. The physical sciences have fundamental laws, and mathematics is its pure language. Can basic physics and math prove creation? Biology can only explain how a living organism functions, but it cannot explain how inorganic matter became organic. It cannot explain how organic matter became intelligent either!

The architecture of ancient Egypt, Babylon, Persia, Greece, and Rome prove there was great mathematical and geometric knowledge during those eras but declines and stagnation had its times as well. Much knowledge was lost during the Dark Ages, but knowledge began to rapidly increase in the late 15th century AD. In 1945 it literally **mushroomed!** (Dan. 12:4) The following list, although not complete, gives an idea of the progression to our present-day knowledge:

1489 - Johann Widman introduced the + and − signs to arithmetic.
1628 - Rene Descartes introduced analytical geometry.
1631 - William Oughtred introduced the × as a multiplication sign.
1642 - Blaise Pascal invented the first calculating machine. [It was a mechanical type and is now in the Smithsonian.]
1656 - Isaac Newton developed the principles of integral calculus and the law of gravity. [Math came first, but gravity's law obviously came to him after the apple fell on his head.]

1703 - Gottfield Leibnitz developed the binary system of mathematics. [It became the language of computers.]

1766 - Leonhard Euler founded the science of pure mathematics. [This is the pure language of the science of physics.]

1785 - Charles Coulomb discovered the rules of electrical force. [This wasn't too long after Ben Franklin flew his kite.]

1789 - Antoine Lavoisier discovered the principles of modern-day chemistry. [It ended the era of wizards. Bye – bye, Merlin Potter!]

1803 - John Dalton explained the atomic nature of matter. [This was the foundation of today's nuclear physics.]

1819 - Hans Christian Oersted discovered electromagnetism and the principles behind magnetic fields. [It is the spirit of energy!]

1821 - Michael Faraday discovered the principle of electromagnetic induction. [Its application was critical to the invention of the electric motor. Ten years later in 1831 he applied the reverse principle for the invention of electric generators.]

1873 - James Maxwell discovered electromagnetic Radiation. [It is the electromagnetic waves that carry energy in the form of oscillating (pulsating) electric and magnetic fields. It led to the understanding of alternating current (AC) that made long distance distribution of electricity to your outlets possible.]

1895 - Wilhelm Roentgen discovered x-rays. [Ever have one?]

1900 - Max Planck originated quantum theory. His concepts were later extended and applied by Albert Einstein, Niels Bohr, and others, which revolutionized the science of physics.

1902 - Pierre and Marie Curie discovered the radiant energy emitted from radium. [Radium is a natural radioactive element.]

1905 - Albert Einstein published **The Theory of Relativity** and the equation $E = mc^2$. [Jewish born, he believed in a creator, but was more interested in the process of creation. If knowledge is indeed divinely revealed, then he was the prophet to physics.]

1913 - Niels Bohr applied Plank's quantum theory to subatomic physics. [This led to **The Big Bang Theory**.]

1925 - Erwin Schrodinger developed the science of wave properties found in atomic particles. Wave mechanics are a form of quantum mechanics. [This is the foundation of solar energy technology. *quantum leap* to energy independence!]

1924 - Thomas John Watson founded IBM Corp. and pioneered its development of electronic computers. [Microsoft came later.]

1927 - Neils Bohr produced the first fission reaction in uranium. [He is considered the father of modern Nuclear Physics.]

1928 - Chandrasekhara Raman discovered particles in visible light. [This was essential to solar energy technology. Why didn't solar energy technology grow as fast as nuclear energy's?]

1929 - Max Knoll and Ernst Ruska invented the electron microscope. [Man can now see **The Real Atom Family!**]

1931 - Karl Jansky developed radio astronomy. [We can now listen to the stars in Heaven - not Hollywood! Is anybody out there?]

1932 - John Cockcroft and Ernest Walton bombarded lithium with protons. [During World War II lithium hydride and lithium borohydride were used as sources of hydrogen.]

1940 - John Randall invented the cavity magnetron. [It was critical to the advancement of radar during WW II.]

1942 - Enrico Fermi, and his team of scientists, achieved the first sustainable nuclear reaction during the Manhattan project.

1945 - J. R. Oppenheimer, Arthur Compton, Enrico Fermi, and Leo Szilard detonate the first atomic bomb. [The rest is history.]

1952 - Edward Teller and Igor Kurchatov invented and built the first hydrogen bomb. [Unlike fission, fusion cannot be contained!]

1962 - Digital Corp. U.S. developed the first minicomputer.

1973 - Trong Truong invented the first microcomputer.

These advancements have only occurred within the last 520 years, a very short period compared to the 6139 years since the creation of Adam. We now live in a computerized nuclear age. [Scary thought when cyber-terrorists are taken into consideration.] The Scriptures tell us that knowledge would be increased in the latter days, and that all things can be used for good or evil. Have greed and the lust for power ever taken advantage of technology? Can today's hi-tech devices be used for evil purposes?

There are three main areas in the physical sciences, which have basic and fundamental laws. They are the energy-mass relationship, electro-magnetism, and gravitational relativity, which I prefer to call the

knowledge of science. The three sciences of Geology (the study of the earth's crust), chemistry (the blending of substances), and biology (the study of life both plant and animal), I call the **understanding** of science. The only laws I can think of that relate to the understanding of science is for the archeologist to not to fall in his hole, the chemist to not blow himself up, and the biologist to not let any dangerous bugs get loose. These are very wise safety rules. The number six is associated with humanity in scripture, and seven is the divine prime number of God's perfection. The thing missing from man's scientific knowledge and understanding is the **wisdom** in its utilization. Why do governments and militaries always get first crack at new knowledge and technology? Why is conservational technology so ignored?

Just what, how, and why is man? What separates us from all the other animals, puts us on top, and gives us dominion over the earth? All animals, including man, have **instinct**. Do they have **intelligence**? Choco, my chocolate Labrador was smart. [I never found him a poodle. He died 08-08-08. I found his six-month-old daughter from a white Pitt Bull. Coco is a Pittador.] PBS aired a special about dogs' intelligence. With training, a dog's sense of smell can be utilized for a variety of useful tasks. Some were being trained to detect cancer. Chimpanzees are intelligent. Some have been taught sign language. If the great apes had evolved into the superior species, would they experiment on humans as we do them? Remember the movies – Planet of the Apes? Would some consider it as *inapeuman*? Do animals have **memory and recall**? Chimpanzees can remember how to arrange geometric shapes with training. Dogs can remember which color ball to retrieve. Instinct and intelligence are directly related to memory and recall, which is what makes dogs and chimps smart.

Do animals have **self-awareness**? I think that all animals are self-aware to some degree. Put a chimp in front of a mirror, and he will reach out to touch the other chimp. When he realizes the other chimp is not there and begins touching himself, he will express curiosity or frustration. Do animals have **emotions**? The higher mammal species express emotion when their young die. Apes cling to their dead babies for days. Ever see a female dog bury her dead pup? Once, I discovered a dead pup and went to bury it. Its mother followed me, watched me bury it, and then spend some time at the site before returning to her litter. I think that emotions are directly related to self-awareness. Do humans become emotional when they look in a mirror?

Those **five aspects** of animal nature, which can also be called *dimensions* or *senses,* can also be considered human nature. They are *the five dimensions* of all animal nature. That brings us to a *sixth dimension* or *the sixth sense*. The biblical number for man is six! What separates man from all the other animals? The only thing man has that no other animal possesses is **the sense of morality**. Animals don't care where they piss, crap, or copulate. You can effectively house train a pup, but you cannot get a male dog to do a damn thing when there is a nearby bitch in heat. [That is how Coco came to pass! Her mother was a mile away. Her owner was pissed off at me. Choco had a damn good sense of smell!]

Morality is simply the knowledge of good and evil. You can call it good and bad, righteousness and wickedness, right and wrong, left and right, up and down, or any other opposing aspects in the prime of two, but it is what it is. No other animal in the animal kingdom possesses this capability. Where did it come from? Did it miraculously evolve, or was it created? It isn't genetic because it is not in our genetic code, and there are no chromosomes for it. We often say to our pets, "good or bad boy or girl", but that is simply a part of the conditioning process in training them.

Morality could not have evolved through natural selection. The only true source to find it is the Holy Bible. Not only did God give Adam and Eve intellect, He gave them *Freedom of Choice*. Did man create or choose the knowledge of good and evil? There is the evolution of morality and/or immorality by the reasoning of man. We have numerous criminal codes that are Biblically based and our prisons are full of murders, rapists, thieves, extortionists, child abusers, but maybe soon some for not having any health insurance. Shouldn't we concentrate on greater moral issues such as teen pregnancy, abortion, cloning, usury, corporate greed, bullying, violence, war, political corruption, bearing false witness under oath, bribery, forcing democracy on others, and using human food for automotive fuel?

Can we come up with a theologically unbiased approach to **The Theory of Creation**? The Bible is the only source of information. Can we devise some rules of scientific investigation, similar to those of scientific experimentation and observation, in order to form an objective scientific method to investigate what the Bible really has to say concerning creation? Let's try to set up some rules that might be satisfactory to the ACLU. The following will be the rules:

(1) The Bible cannot be called the Bible. It will be called *"The Book of Data"* and shall only guide our investigation.
(2) Only the invisible realm will be investigated. The creation of man will be the conclusion of the investigation.
(3) The words God, Lord, Word and/or Jesus cannot be used. Only the corresponding Hebrew or Greek terms will be utilized.
(4) Only the Hebrew or Greek names of spirit beings or angels can be used in Bible quotes and discussions.
(5) If the name of any human being is in a Bible quote, only their Hebrew or Greek word can be used. Information from the passage can be used, but it must not involve human passions or attributes that may infect the investigation.
(6) All Biblical quotations utilized shall be identified by its book, chapter, and verse at the end or beginning of each quote.
(7) God, no, it is the ACLU that forbids the Holy Bible to trespass the boundary of the taxpayers' school property! This investigation will take place outside of the gravitational jurisdiction of planet earth. I don't think the ACLU will mind that!

Does it sound impossible? Before we get started on chapter two, let's first establish the basic terms and their definitions that will be utilized from the Hebrew and Greek dictionaries.

Hebrew:

(1) Elohiym – God(s) – plural in form but pronounced as singular. [...*Elohiym said, "let us create..."*]
(2) Elowahh – God, which is the singular form of Elohiym.
(3) El – God as in *The Almighty*.
(4) Yehovah – Translated *Lord*, it is also the Jewish name for God, and is the speaking part of Elohiym in The Old Testament.
(5) Helyel – Lucifer, who was the anointed cherub.
(6) Mosheh – Moses
(7) Adam – Adam – Hebrew name of first man. Derived from the improper noun: adam – mankind as the human species.

(8) Mal'ak – to dispatch as a deputy – a messenger, spec. of God i.e. an angel

Greek:

(1) Theos – The deity God as in *the supreme divinity*.
(2) Logos – Something spoken as in *the divine expression*.
(3) Michael – Michael, the chief prince or the archangel.
(4) Aggello – to bring tidings; a messenger – an angel.
(5) Archaggelos – a chief angel – archangel

The Authorized King James (AKJ) translation of the Bible will be used because it was translated from the original Hebrew and Greek languages. Strong's Complete Concordance will be used for all Greek and Hebrew definitions because it is indexed to the AKJ.

With the rules above, we can now begin our objective scientific investigation of **The Theory of Creation** from the world's best-selling book, The Holy Bible. I do not know what the ACLU may think about the above rules, but all I can say is that famous line by Clark Gabel in the great classic film – Gone with the Wind: **"Frankly my dear, I don't give a damn!"**

[2020/2021 revision addition]

I heard on "The View" today (June 10, 2020) that Hollywood was going to remove the movie classic just mentioned. I honestly don't know how they could effectively do that, but the idea itself is totally ludicrous. How many downloads have been made and copies possessed? They can stop showing it and nothing more!

If we start removing evidence of the past, then the future has no foundation to build upon. How can it? Society will never learn from its mistakes if the evidence of them or about them are removed. That is why the Jews that survived the Holocaust insisted the camps not be destroyed but remain and be maintained, not as a memorial, but as evidence of the atrocities committed there. That is something all folks in the south may want to reconsider. When it comes down to the removal of Confederate

Monuments, frankly, I don't give a damn. I'm 65 and too old to care about such petty crap, but one cannot change the future by erasing the past! You can only learn from it and move forward, but if you keep looking back all of the time, you'll just run into another brick wall!

A similar problem exists in religion today. The old covenant is polluted by the philosophies adapted over centuries to the new covenant that has perpetually replaced the previous until the whole world is deceived and has no idea of the original truth in both the old and the new testaments of the Word of God. Even its authenticity is challenged by its own supposedly educated scholars. Yes, it was written by men, BUT - by the inspiration of God! It's a miracle that the Holy Bible has been preserved thru the millennium, and for centuries has been available to the common folk, thanks to the invention of the printing press. It is true that definition of terms in the original language have been lost in translation, but another miracle came to pass in the 1800's when another inspired writing was made. The Strong's Concordance, indexed to the KJV English translation, is a dictionary of English terms used in translation of the original languages in which the New and Old Testaments were written.

In the last few centuries, it has been translation upon translation, translations from translations, paraphrase upon translations, paraphrase upon paraphrases, a little philosophy here and a little philosophical theology there, until just about every precept of truth has been mingled with the philosophy of men. (Col. 2:8) "This people draweth nigh unto me with their mouth, and honoureth me with *their* lips; but their heart is far from me. But in vain they do worship me, teaching *for* doctrines the commandments of men." (Matt. 14:8-9)

"And the Jews marvelled, saying, How knoweth this man letters (scripture), having never learned? Jesus answered them, and said, My doctrine is not mine, but his that sent me. If any man will do his will, he shall know of the doctrine, whether it be of God, or *whether* I speak of myself. He that speaketh of himself seeketh his own glory: but he that seeketh his glory that sent him, the same is true, and no unrighteousness is in him. Did not Moses give you the law, and *yet* none of you keepeth the law? Why go ye about to kill me?" (John 7:15-19)

May God have mercy on our stupidity!

Chapter II
The Theory of Creation

Life! The ultimate existence of matter – to go where no organism has gone before. [Has quite a ring to it doesn't it?] The first thing we will need to do is give the definition for (not the meaning of) life. The best scientific biological definition is *the ability to reproduce, whether by asexual or sexual methods*. Asexual reproduction is when an organism self-divides, and then becomes two separate but identical organisms. Sexual reproduction is through the production of seed. Only by one of these two methods can any species procreate. Cloning is not procreation! A species is defined as *any organism with the ability to successfully reproduce*. Most of the species on our planet procreate through seed by the sexual interaction of its male and female counterparts, whether it is a plant or an animal.

Every element of universal matter exists in one of three basic forms: gas, liquid, or solid, and is either inorganic (not living) or organic (living) in its natural state of existence. All living organisms consist entirely of elements that also exist in an inorganic state. All living organisms, both plant and animal, consist of 99% CHNOPS, which in biology represents these six elements: Carbon, Hydrogen, Nitrogen, Oxygen, Phosphorus, and Sulfur. All this is pure basic science without having to get into too much detail. It is not science fiction! If it requires an intelligent mind to understand the complexity of how a living organism functions, wouldn't it require a more superior intelligence to bring inorganic matter into existence, then transform it into organic matter? If so, where and when did it all begin?

Time and space are considered infinite and inseparable. I don't think that any scientist on the planet will disagree with that. At some point in the *space-time continuum*, birth had to be given to all the inorganic matter we call the universe. Let's try to find that point in time and follow it through. We will take this journey in our cozy little space-time ship called the U.S.S. Emeth with the Book of Data at its controls. With its gravity generator and inertia dampeners, there is no need for seat belts. Don't worry; no one else exists to write us a ticket. So, off we go, back in time, into the vast darkness of the great infinite abyss called space.

The Emeth takes us to a point within the mist of the space-time continuum. There is total darkness and no evidence of any matter. There are no stars giving light to see by. The Emeth's Book of Data flashes a message on its viewing screen. *"In the beginning was the Logos, and the Logos was with Theos, and the Logos was Theos."* (John 1:1) This passage states the fact that two entities exist, and the way they exist, but it is somewhat odd. How can two entities simultaneously exist, but be the same? The only possible mathematical explanation is a *unit fraction* where the denominator is in unity with and equal to its numerator. [1 ÷ 1 = 1]

Who is the denominator? Is it the **Logos**, or the **Theos**? The Greek Dictionary defines *Logos* as being something said – the divine expression, and *Theos* as a deity – the divine supreme deity. The term divine is an identical factor in both definitions, which leaves us with expression and supreme deity. Expression is a type of action, as in the denominator that does the dividing; therefore, Logos must be the denominator and Theos is the numerator. What will happen when division is expressed? [1 Theos ÷ 1 Logos = 1 what?]

To calculate any three-part equation (a = b × c) or (c = a ÷ b), we need at least two known factors. The laws of mathematics require us to identify the factors or entities involved and assign quantities. We must find at least two physical characteristics that are associated with the mathematical expression [1-Theos ÷ 1-Logos = 1-what?].

The Emeth's viewing screen flashes, *"The same was in the beginning with Theos. All things were made by him; and without him was not any thing made that was made. In him was life; and the life was the light of men."* (John 1:2-4) We now have the two physical factors **light** and ***all things***. All things are made of matter, including man. With these two identifiable physical factors (light and matter), we can build a mathematical equation from the unity fraction.

Almost everyone knows about dear old *Uncle Albert*. [From a Beatles song] Albert Einstein (1879-1955) published his **Theory of Relativity** with the famous equation **[$E = mc^2$]** in 1905. **E** is energy, **m** mass (any quantitative amount of matter), and **c** the velocity of light. It wasn't until 1942 (first sustainable nuclear reaction) that the equation had any real meaning. The reaction released an enormous amount of energy from a small mass of matter. [If they weren't wearing special goggles they would have been *blinded by the light.*] The whole world realized its significance after the atomic bombs were dropped on Japan in 1945.

Two fundamental laws in physics state: •**Energy is the ability and capacity to do work.** •**Energy cannot be created nor destroyed, but only transformed from one form to another.** Ability inherently requires intelligence and capacity is its quantity. We have identified matter and light, so Theos must be energy. Theos is *the supreme intelligent energy entity* and Logos *the supreme intelligent light entity.* Since light is the transformation of energy and contains energy within itself, they have the ability and capacity to do work. If creating matter is hard work, then creating intelligent matter must be really hard work. Do any intelligent matter entities exist? After transposing [$E = mc^2$] to [$m = E \div c^2$], we get a quantitative amount of matter.

RED ALERT

The Emeth's Book of Data alerts us to, *"In the beginning Elohiym created the heavens and the earth."* (Genesis 1:1) *"And Elohiym said unto Mosheh, <u>I AM (THAT) I AM</u>: and he said, Thus shalt thou say unto the children...."* (Exodus 3:14) [Hebrew: *"aniy hayah zeh aniy hayah"* meaning **I exist (that) I exist**.] This confirms the prime directives of energy.] Also, *"Theos, who at sundry times in divers manners spake in time past unto the fathers by the prophets, Hath in these last days spoken unto us by his son, whom he hath appointed heir of all things, by whom also he made the worlds; Who being the brightness of his glory, and the express image of his person, and upholding all things by the word (action) of his power (energy)..."* (Hebrews. 1:1-3)

The Hebrew term *Elohiym* is plural, but pronounced as a single entity, which is the unity of the two Greek terms *Logos* and *Theos*. Logos is son of Theos because light is the *express image* (duplication by transformation) of energy. Together, they're Elohiym. Logos is both light and energy because energy is in light. We get electrical energy from the suns energy/light through transformation by solar cells. Our sun is a mass of matter from which we receive light and energy. Substituting terms in the John 1:1 data, *"In the beginning was the light entity, and the light entity was with the energy entity, and the light was energy."*

Since light is in as well as of energy, and work will require some type of motion, light must have velocity, which is the universal constant of

186,000 miles per second. When squared, it would be traveling faster than warp-10 on a galaxy class spaceship, much faster that the blink of an eye. Since mass is any quantitative amount of matter, the quantity for **E** and **m** will be infinite with **m** representing all universal matter and **E** infinite energy. With the transposition of [$E = mc^2$] to [$m = E \div c^2$] we can conclude: *All universal matter is the dividend of the supreme energy entity's and the light entity's division.* Can a son be born through asexual reproduction? If not, then mathematics, physics' fundamental laws, Einstein's Theory of Relativity, and the understanding of Biology are all nothing but lies!

Summarizing all the above, Theos is the supreme eternal energy and Logos is the supreme eternal light. Mathematics and the laws of physics are concrete evidence. [Eat that, ACLU!] The entire universe is the dividend of their ability and capacity to do work. There is still one problem that exists and must be clarified. How did they self-divide?

Another law in physics states: •**For every action there is a reaction.** Inverted: •**For every reaction there must be an action.** Suppose that Elohiym (Theos/Logos) is the nucleus of a supreme intelligent atom, and desires to release its infinite energy, light, and mass into the darkness of the great abyss. For an atom to release the energy, light, and internal mass of its nucleus, an external force must penetrate the nucleus shell, but nothing else seems to exist that is necessary for external bombardment. How can our supreme intelligent atom self-divide?

In the understanding of biology, there are three processes in asexual reproduction: budding, sporulation, and vegetative fission. Some organisms can self-divide, and then become two separate but identical organisms. In vegetative fission, the new individual leaves the parent at some developmental state between sporulation and budding. It becomes an identical duplication by the regenerative transformation (express imaging) of its parent. Reproduction through regeneration is possible in a few species that do not normally reproduce by other means. (Flatworms, hydra, and sea anemone) The key word is *fission*, which is one of two types of nuclear reactions. During vegetative fission a small amount of energy-mass is lost during the express imaging process. What happens to it? Where does it go? Can anything come from it? Can it become anything?

Fission is splitting an atom to release its mass-energy, and fusion is by fusing hydrogen nuclei. Both require an external bombardment or trigger and are basically opposite methods in achieving a nuclear reaction, but both obey the mass-energy relationship in Einstein's Theory of Relativity. Fusion is a thermonuclear reaction releasing more energy than fission and lead to the development of the hydrogen bomb. Man has yet to contain or control a fusion reaction. [Man can and does make some really super bombs!] Our nuclear power plants utilize fission reactors. Applying the concepts of vegetative and nuclear fission, our supreme intelligent atom has the possibility and capability for a self-induced fission reaction. But what is the source of external bombardment? Nothing else exists except the atom's electron. Is it intelligent too? [Remember the lost energy-mass above?]

The smallest component that matter can be broken down to and retain its chemical properties is the atom. The atom's three main subatomic particles are: the **neutron** (electrically neutral and the greater mass) and **proton** (positive charge and a mass almost as great as the neutron) in its nucleus, also called nucleons, and the **electron** (negative charge and much less mass than the proton) orbiting the nucleus. A *polarity of understanding* exists between the proton (+) and electron (−). There are other smaller sub-atomic particles within the atom's nucleus, such as quarks (a basic unit of matter − mass). We'll just call all of them family members of sub-atomic particles - **The Atom Family.**

Let's suppose our intelligent atom's nucleons (neutron/proton) are Elohiym (Theos/Logos). They are living in their comfortable atomic nucleus having a cup of tea discussing the Universal Master Plan Called **Creation**. Theos and Logos are the Architects. The plan is a perfect plan with safeguards in case anything may go wrong within the space-time continuum. All members of The Atom Family are in complete agreement with all the plan's aspects. Elohiym is ready to release its infinite mass-energy. Now, why in all the empty infinite abyss would they want to do that? Energy is the ability and capacity to do work. Elohiym (Theos/Logos) as energy/light are relative. By the power of ($E \div c^2 = m$) they are ready to **GET–R–DONE!**

The Emeth takes us to: *"Whereupon are the foundations thereof fastened? Or who laid the corner stone thereof; when the morning stars sang together, and all the sons of Elohiym shouted for joy?"* (Job 38:67) The Hebrew Dictionary defines the following:

(1) morning – *beqer* – dawn as the break of day. From: *baqar* – (primary root) – to plow, or generally to break forth. Figuratively to inspect, admire, care for, and/or to consider.
(2) stars – *kowkab* – a star as in round and shining.
(3) sons – *ben* – a son, as in a builder of the family or its name.
(4) sang – *ranan* – (primary root) – to creak, or emit a stridulous sound, i.e. to shout (usually for joy, but sometimes in wrath).
(5) together – *yachad* – to become one, to join, or unite as one.
(6) shouted – *ruma* – (primary root) – to mar, especially by breaking forth. Figuratively to split the ears with sound, i.e. to shout.

The phrase ***morning stars sang together*** is the birth of our universe and the perpetual motion of innumerable galaxies plowing through space. The phrase ***sons of Elohiym*** are the stars (quarks). The phrase ***shouted for joy*** is a super cosmic boom. The answer to the question, *"Whereupon are the foundations thereof fastened?"* is the inverted relativity equation $E = mc^2$ to $m = E \div c^2$. Through the polarity of understanding, the proton commanded the electron to penetrate the nucleus, thus releasing its infinite mass-energy into the darkness of the great abyss. Ever accidentally short-circuit a 12-volt acid battery by reversing its polarity? Just for the fun of it, let's call it: **THE BIG BANG!**

It was like the atomic bombs dropped on Hiroshima and Nagasaki at the close of World War II. The only difference is those bombs had a finite quantity of mass and energy. This is an eternal reaction of infinite mass-energy transformations with various types of radiation and sub-atomic particles emitted. This first display of fireworks was the best Fourth of July in all the cosmos, and like the famous rock star Jerry Lewis sang many times: **goodness – gracious – great balls of fire!**

Alpha particles are helium nuclei with a low velocity ($1/20^{th}$ that of light). They have a low penetrating capability; however, their ionizing power is very high since they are positively charged. The beta particles are streams of electrons traveling at various high rates of speed, but less than that of light. Their penetrating power is 100 times that of their alpha brothers. Since they have a negative charge, their ionizing power is less than half of alphas. Gamma radiations aren't really particles, but electromagnetic rays traveling at the speed of light. They have no ionizing power within themselves, but their penetrating power is much greater than x-rays. Neutron radiations are heavy uncharged particles that can travel great distances in air at various speeds. They have no ionizing power within themselves, but like gamma, they can make ions when encountering other atoms. All four are produced during both fission and fusion reactions and can be considered as brothers like *the sons of Elohiym*.

In order to properly explain the short-circuit concept of our self-induced fission reaction, we will need to utilize Planck's Quantum Theory developed in 1900. All sub-atomic particles have mass and energy and obey the mass-energy relationship laid out in Einstein's Theory of Relativity. Scientists considered Einstein a crackpot, and he couldn't get a job until Max Planck, a German physicist asked him to work with him. Their theories were in harmony like Theos/Logos. [Isn't Jewish and German harmony in the early to middle 1900's a bit ironic? Remember Hitler and Nazi Germany?]

When an electron jumps from one remoter orbit to one nearer its nucleus, it loses potential energy and emits a light wave or light quantum. Its kinetic energy (work) is equal to its lost potential energy (rest) transformed by the jump. The electron travels to or near the nucleus, and the proton then shares its own energy-mass. This mass-energy transfer occurs when the electron is accelerated to a high velocity, then collides with, or passes near the nucleus of the atom. The electron's energy is transformed into a gamma ray or an impulse radiation (high-energy photon). It is at this point only that the positive electron **(positron)** has the same electric charge and infinitesimal mass as the free negative electron **(negatron)**. The positron and negatron become **identical twin photons**, except for their electrical charge. Photons are light particles within an electro-magnetic field.

Remember the tea party? We now have contractors as well as a labor force to assist in the plan. These contractors and laborers have various degrees of ability, capacity, power, and rank. They are the *sons of Elohiym* and members of **The Atom Family**. They were born free to begin assisting in the work of the Universal Master Plan. The song they sang may have been: **"Free at last, free at last – thank Elohiym almighty – free at last."** [I'm willing to bet that the ACLU thought I would slip on myself and use their forbidden word there. I think that I may have a better understanding of separation than they do. No pun intended!]

Members of The Atom Family are like a construction crew. Their power, ability, rank, and capacity vary like those in trades of construction. The chain of command in a major construction project is Architects,

General Contractor, Job Superintendent, Job Coordinator, Subcontractors, General Foremen, Foremen, Supervisors, Leadsmen, Journeymen, apprentices, helpers, and laborers. If all personnel involved are in complete harmony with the design, a perfect plan becomes a perfect creation.

The Emeth's Book of Data now informs us: *"Who is the image of the invisible Theos, the firstborn of every creature: for by him were all things created, that are in heaven, and that are in earth, visible and invisible, whether they be thrones, or dominions, or principalities, or powers: all things were created by him, and for him: And he is before all things, and by him all things consist."* (Colossians 1:15-17) The Greek Dictionary defines the following:

(1) thrones – *thronos* – a stately seat, a throne, as with power.
(2) dominions – *kuriotes* – mastery, rulers, a government. From: *kuros* – supremacy, or a controller with authority.
(3) principalities – *arche* – a commencement or chief in various applications of order, time, place, or rank.
(4) powers – *exousia* – in a third person sense of ability: subjective force, capacity, competency, freedom, or objective mastery as in a magistrate, superhuman or potentate – delegated influence.

These four terms characterize the heavenly hierarchy, and there are four types or ranks of invisible entities (mal'ak or aggelos) that are found in the Emeth's Book of Data, which are cherubim, seraphim, elders, and aggelos or mal'ak. One is designated as the Archanggelos. Cherub is singular for cherubim. The four types of invisible radiation emitted from our intelligent atom's self-induced fission reaction (alpha, beta, gamma, and neutron) represent the four types or ranks of the invisible entities and their thrones, dominions, principalities, and powers.

Let's return to the point of the **BIG BANG**, and travel around this newly created cosmos. Our space-time ship does come with a reverse mode. There are constellations of stars of various sizes and colors, and nebula joined into united galaxies that are plowing through space as if dancing to a systematic choreography. There are billions of stars dancing around their dark centers of thick clusters of matter called *black holes*. As we begin to approach the *event horizon* of our own galaxy's black hole, the Emeth's early warning system sounds.

Yellow Alert

The Emeth has automatically changed course away from the black hole due to excessive gravitational forces, and has flashed the following on the viewing screen: *"Canst thou bind the sweet influences of Pleiades, or loose the bands of Orion? Canst thou bring forth Mazzaroth in his season? Or canst thou guide Arcturus with his sons? Knowest thou the ordinances of heaven? Canst thou set the dominion thereof in the earth?"* (Job 38:31-33) That was a close call! Who knows what would have happened if we would have entered the event horizon? The key Hebrew definitions are:

(1) sweet influences – *maadannah* – a bond: i.e. group by influence. A transposition of: *anad* – (primary root) – to lace fast, bind – tie.
(2) ordinances – *chuqqah* – appointed custom, manner, ordinance, site, or statute. The Feminine of: *choq* – an enactment, hence an appointment (of time, space, quantity, labor, or usage) – an appointed boundary, commandment, decree, law, or ordinance.
(3) dominion – *mishtar* – jurisdiction. From: *shoter* – to write, as a scribe. By implication: superintendent, magistrate, or overseer.

From the definitions above, the appointed binding ordinances are the laws of gravitation, and the jurisdictional boundary is the space-time continuum in which the entire universe resides. Gravitation is the result of the gravity that all mass bodies in the universe possess. The various degrees of gravity and gravitation are dependent upon mass and distance. What would happen if our mass bodies did not gravitate toward the earth's center as a result of its gravity? Gravity is the work of invisible magnetic energy, which has a theoretical unit value of magnetic moment called a **magnetron**.

Magnetron is the entity unit and overseer of the jurisdiction of universal gravitation and the Archaggelos (chief prince) and defender of the space-time continuum, which is Elohyim's eternal domain. Gravitation is an energy transformation of magnetism. All mass bodies, including that of man, have potential energy because they are a transformation of energy and revolve around its central source. [All entities including matter-man have free moral agency or freedom of choice to remain in the central source's realm of influence. Think about that ACLU!] Universal gravitation is the *sweet influences* or bond that binds all mass bodies to their perspective positions in accordance with the appointed custom of their mass density. What is the primary form of pure energy? Could it be magnetism?

The Emeth's Book of Data asks us the (predefined) questions: *"Who can (could) number the clouds (galaxies) in wisdom? Or who can stay (lay down) the bottles (nebula) of heaven, when the dust (atoms) groweth (placed firmly) into hardness (fusion), and the clods (molecules) cleave fast together (adhere)?"* (Job 38:37-38) The Geological Time Chart begins with Precambrian, which began 4.5 billion years ago with the earth as a cosmic ball of dust. All it needed was an intelligent entity to direct the various sources of ionization. Basically, ionization is the process that makes stuff happen. Simple molecules form quite nicely without assistance, but the more complex ones, especially those of living organisms, needed a source of intelligent instruction. All the members of The Atom Family have various ionizing capabilities and intelligence. Were they the source?

From the Book of Data: *"Thou art the anointed cherub that covereth; and I have set thee so: thou wast upon the holy mountain of Elohiym; thou hast walked up and down in the mist of the stones of fire."* (Ezekiel 28:14) The Hebrew dictionary defines:

(1) anointed – *momshach* – in the sense of expansion: outspread, as with outspread wings. From: *mashach* – (primary root) – to rub with oil, to anoint. By implication to consecrate – to paint on.
(2) covereth – *sakak* – (primary root) – to entwine as a screen. By implication to fence in and cover over. Figuratively, to protect – cover, defend, hedge in, join together, set, and shut or close up.
(3) Holy – *qoesh* – a sacred place or a thing – holy.
(4) mountain – *har* – a mountain or range of hills. Sometimes it is used figuratively with a sense of promotion.
(5) stones – *eben* – to build, a stone + (carbuncle + mason + plummet) as in building blocks. From the root of: *bahah* – (primary root) – to build (literally or figuratively).
(6) fire – *esh* – (primary root) – fire, in both the literal or figurative sense – burning, fiery, fire, or flaming hot

The ***anointed cherub*** is an expanded and promoted entity like the electron in the self-induced fission reaction. All sub-atomic particles have mass and a unit of value (atomic mass unit). The electron's (.000549 amu) is significantly less than the proton's (1.007277 amu). The proton expanded and promoted the electron to an identical twin photon status by sharing its mass-energy. [That's one heck of a promotion!] The phrase ***thou wast upon the holy mountain of Elohiym*** was the electron orbiting the atom's nucleus and its participation in and after The Big Bang. The phrase ***thou hast walked up and down in the mist of the stones of fire*** is traveling around the cosmos as well as working with highly radioactive matter. Planet earth began as a fiery ball of radioactive cosmic dust. ***Covereth*** is the ability to entwine, cover over, defend, hedge in, join together, set, and close up. Doesn't that sound like genetic engineering? Can gamma radiation alter living cells or DNA? Too much will kill you!

The anointed cherub now ranks third in the heavenly hierarchy and was given intellectual power over gamma radiation. [Gamma is the third letter of the Greek alphabet.] He was consecrated king over our sun's solar system and given charge over a number ($1/3^{rd}$) of the other ionizing entities with varying degrees of ionizing power. He was also given the position and responsibility of General Contractor to implement the Universal Master Plan. Is it possible he started with the fourth cosmic ball of dust from the sun – Mars? Its elements would have cooled sooner, and it is an appropriate distance from the sun for possible life, but we are concerned with the third dust ball from the sun – Earth.

It isn't necessary here to go through the entire Geological Time Chart. Most earth science books should have one beginning with Precambrian 4.5 billion years ago with earth as a cloud of cosmic dust that supposedly *self-evolved*. When the earth began to cool, the simple molecules formed and could coexist side by side for an indefinite period with no tendency to join. They needed a source of ionization, and the alpha, beta, gamma, and neutron members of The Atom Family were well equipped for the job.

The Universal Master Plan that Elohiym (Theos/Logos – the two Architects) devised and was agreed upon by everyone begins to be implemented. The anointed cherub with his gifts of gamma power and intellect (knowledge – understanding – wisdom) begins to coordinate his brothers. The perfect cosmic ball of dust with all the elements required for the formation of inorganic matter and organic life begins to yield its fruit. Utilizing all our knowledge of biology, chemistry, mathematics, and physics, we can climb the geological ladder of our planet's development.

Over the course of 4.5 billion years, The Atom Family ionized and genetically engineered many things.

The Emeth moves us forward in time to: *"And the earth was without form, and void; and darkness <u>was</u> upon the face of the deep. And the spirit of Elohiym moved upon the face of the waters."* (Genesis 1:2) The English translation of this data passage has misled many for centuries. The Hebrew language has no primary articles or conjunctions; *a, an, the, and, but* are always added in translation. The verb <u>*was*</u> is an addition by the translators, but the other *was* is in all the ancient manuscripts. Its Hebrew term is mostly used to place emphasis on other verbs, but as a verb it has no tense, neither past, present, or future. The Hebrew Dictionary defines the following:

(1) was – *hayah* – (primary root) – **to exist** or **to be**. As an adverb: to become, come to pass, or became. **[Used as a verb in Ex. 3:14.]**
(2) without form – *tohuw* – to lay waste, a desolation of surface, or desert. Figuratively, a worthless thing. As an adverb: in vain.
(3) void – *bohuw* – to be empty, a vacuity, i.e. an indistinguishable ruin, to be good for nothing, or useless.
(4) darkness – *choshek* – the dark. Literally, darkness. Figuratively, misery, destruction, death, ignorance, sorrow, or wickedness.
(5) face – *paneh* – the face, as the part that turns. From: *panah* – (primary root) – to turn, to face, i.e. appear, or to look.
(6) deep – *tehum* – an abyss, usually considered endless. From: *tehuwm* – to make an uproar, or to agitate greatly.

Utilizing the above definitions with no conjunctions and only one article, let's rephrase the data: *Earth became a wasted, desolated, deserted, worthless, dead, indistinguishably ruined, and a good for nothing useless thing.* Is this the condition it was originally created? It was a beautiful ball of cosmic dust ready to be transformed into a beautiful creation under the guidance of an intelligently designed plan. All its matter was useful and had great value. It had great potential! Something had to disrupt the plan. Darkness (no sunlight) upon the part that turned (earth) was the result. Something terrible happened! What could it have been? Before we look for that answer, let's first verify this data with more evidence from the Emeth's data bank.

The Book of Data's voice mode speaks: *"For thus saith the Yehovah that created the heavens; Elohiym himself that formed the earth and made it, he created it <u>not in vain</u>, he formed it to be inhabited: I am the Yehovah; and there is none else."* (Isaiah 45:18) The word **vain** in this data is from the Hebrew *tohu*, the same as **without form** in Genesis 1:2. This verifies our previous conclusion. It also states that the creation, both heavens and earth were created for the purpose of being inhabited. The verbs **created, formed,** and **made** refer to both nouns **heavens** and **earth,** and the adverbial phrase <u>**not in vain**</u> modifies all three verbs. Elohiym did not create the earth in the condition stated in Genesis 1:2. So, what in the heck happened?

The Emeth's Book of Data returns us to: *"Thou art the anointed cherub that covereth; and I have set thee so: thou wast upon the holy mountain of Elohiym; thou hast walked up and down in the mist of the stones of fire. Thou wast perfect in thy ways from the day that thou wast created, till iniquity was found in thee. By the multitude of thy merchandise they have filled the mist of thee with violence, and thou hast sinned: therefore, I will cast thee as profane out of the mountain of Elohiym: and I will destroy thee, O covering cherub, from the mist of the stones of fire. Thine heart was lifted up because of thy beauty, thou hast corrupted thy wisdom by the reason of thy brightness: I will cast thee to the ground, (earth) I will lay thee before kings, that they may behold thee. Thou hast defiled thy sanctuaries by the multitude of thine iniquities, by the iniquity of thy traffic; therefore, will I bring forth a fire from the mist of thee, it shall devour thee, and I will bring thee to ashes upon the earth in sight of all them that behold thee."* (Ezekiel 28:14-18) *"And there was war in heaven: Michael and his aggelos fought against the dragon; and the dragon fought and his aggelos, and prevailed not; neither was their place found any more in heaven."* (Revelation 12:7-8) *"How art thou fallen from heaven, O Helyel, son of the morning! How art thou cut down to the ground, which didst weaken the nations! For thou hast said in thine heart, I will ascend into heaven, I will exalt my throne above the stars of El: I will sit also upon the mount of the congregation, in the sides of the north: I will ascend above the heights of the clouds; I will be like the Most High."* (Isaiah 14:12-14)

The anointed cherub is now identified with the name **Helyel**, which means **bright and morning star**. It seems that our General Contractor decided that his position wasn't good enough. He wanted more than what was given him, along with that which he engineered with all his knowledge. He rebelled against Elohiym (Theos/Logos) the Architects because of pride, envy, and jealousy. He attempted to elevate his position to a higher one within the chain of command. He disrupted the Universal Master Plan with rebellion and war. **Michael** is the Archaggelos (first chief prince – Magnetron) and General of the defending army. It was a failed family COUP D'ETAT!

In a major construction project, the Architects have total control over the design and plans. The General Contractor agrees to them and establishes a contract (covenant). This begins his obligation. Under him are his Superintendents, Coordinators, and Subcontractors. What happens when the General Contractor decides to not do the work according to the plans thinking that his ideas and methods are better than those of the Architect? He is most assuredly fired! He might try to dispute his firing by going into a court of law to sue, but the rights of the Architect will be upheld. The legal battle would be like the war in heaven and the Magnetron Michael the Attorney for the Defendant. The judge will uphold the rights of the Defendant, thus dismissing the case. The only difference in this case is the Defendant; Yehovah Elohiym (Logos) is the son of El (Theos), the Highest Supreme Judge! [We are not talking about the Chief Justice of the Supreme Court of the United States of America!]

The players in any game of sports must obey the rules and authority of the umpire. Likewise, the General Contractor must obey the **Universal Master Plan (UMP)** and authority of the Architects. If a player is called and penalized and argues with the UMP, you can bet your sweet ass he is immediately ejected from the game. The worst penalty in any game of sport is an ejection from the game. If you blow a second and/or third chance, it is total suspension from the sport. **YOU ARE OUT!**

That brings us to two points made in the passages from the Book of Data already quoted: *How art thou fallen from heaven!* And *I will cast thee to the ground*. World War II was the most destructive in human history. Imagine what an all-out thermonuclear World War III might be like. The war in heaven would have been trillions of times more destructive. [As the growing national debt will be!] The earth became an indistinguishable ruin totally devoid of life!

Have you ever wondered what happened to the mythical Lost City of Atlantis? It was supposed to have been a magnificent civilization. Much has been written about what it may have been like. Some have supposed that it might lie under the Mediterranean Sea off the coast of Tyre, which is in present day Lebanon. Most have supposed it lie under the middle of the Atlantic. What about those ancient batteries that have been dug up by archeologists and can't be explained, but thought to have come from space aliens? There are many things that have been dug up, and dated to be millions of years old, but can only be speculated upon. There was the woolly mammoth found frozen with fresh vegetation still in its digestive tract as if fast-frozen from an unexpected and sudden **immense ice age (darkness)**.

Then the Emeth takes us back to: *"...the spirit of Elohiym moved upon the face of the waters. And Elohiym said, Let there be light: and there was light. And Elohiym saw the light, that it was good: and Elohiym divided the light from the darkness. And Elohiym called the light Day, and the darkness he called Night. And the evening and the morning were the first day."* (Genesis 1:2-5)

Helyel's rebellion and cosmic war must have been so cataclysmic that it not only brought the earth to a total ruin, but darkness to the entire solar system. Could the uncontrollable fusion reaction of our sun come to a sudden stop? Can energy control matter? Is the dividend "matter" greater than its divisors "energy/light"? Without the sun's light, earth would have instantly become a ball of frozen water. The entire universe may have come to a standstill. The fusion reaction of the sun and the earth's rotation on its axis were restored by the express command of Elohiym, the supreme intelligent entities.

Again, from the Book of Data: *"And Elohiym said, Let there be a firmament in the mist of the waters, and let it divide the waters from the waters. And Elohiym made the firmament, and divided the waters which were under the firmament from the waters which were above the firmament: and it was so. And Elohiym called the firmament Heaven. And the evening and the morning were the second day."* (Genesis 1:6-8) The Hebrew Dictionary defines:

(1) waters – *mayim* – (dual of a primary root, but in the singular sense) – water. Figuratively, juice of any type.

(2) firmament – *raqiya* – an expanse, firmament, or apparently, visible arch of the sky. From: *raqa* – (primary root) – to pound the earth, as a sign of passion. By analogy, to expand, as by hammering. By implication, to overlay, as with sheets of metal: beat, to make or spread broad, forth, over, out, as into plates.

The earth was passionately beat back into shape. Most of the waters are the oceans, some the firmament or visible arch of the sky, which is the atmosphere. The ***dividing of waters*** is the making of the atmosphere as well as the pounding back together of the earth's tectonic plates. Helyel's rebellion must have really messed earth up!

Again, from the Book of Data: *"And Elohiym said, Let the waters under the heaven (sky) be gathered together unto one place, and let the dry land appear: and it was so. And Elohiym called the dry land Earth; and the gathering together of the waters called he Seas: and Elohiym saw that it was good. And Elohiym said, Let the earth bring forth grass, the herb yielding seed, and the fruit tree yielding fruit after his kind, whose seed is in itself, upon the earth: and it was so. And the earth brought forth grass, and herb yielding seed after his kind, and the tree yielding fruit, whose seed was in itself, after his kind: and Elohiym saw that it was good. And the evening and the morning were the third day."* (Genesis 1:9-13)

The rising of the dry land separated the seas, and the dry land was seeded with all manner of plant life. There are millions of species in the Plant Kingdom that reproduce from seed. Taxonomists have spent lifetimes classifying the plant species of our planet. They are still doing so to this very day, not only with plants, but animal life at earth's greatest depths.

Again, from the Book of Data: *"And Elohiym said, Let there be (come to pass) lights in the firmament of heaven to divide (separate or distinguish) the day from the night; and let them be for signs, and for seasons, and for days, and years: and let them be for lights in the firmament of the heaven to give light upon the earth: and it was so. And Elohiym made two great lights; the greater to rule the day, and the lesser to rule the night: <u>he made</u> the stars also. And Elohiym set them in the firmament of the heaven to give light upon the earth, and to rule over the day and over the night, to divide the light from the darkness: and Elohiym saw that it was good. And the evening and the morning were the fourth day."* (Genesis 1:14-19) [The <u>**he made**</u> was added by the translators.]

Lights and firmament in this data passage are the visible lights of stars, constellations, and galaxies, which are seen from earth. The rotation of the moon around the earth gives us our months, and the earth's rotation around the sun our seasons and years. It is possible that the war in heaven caused so much destruction that the entire universe may have come to a standstill and had to be restored. Orbital motion was restored to the earth, moon, and solar system as well as the rest of the universe. Also, the clearing of heavily condensed fog within the newly created atmosphere would have made the stars visible from the earth. [*Let there be* is from *hayah* modifying the action *to divide*.]

Again, from the Book of Data: *"And Elohiym said, **Let the** waters bring forth abundantly the moving creature that hath life, and fowl that may fly above the earth in the open firmament of heaven (sky). And Elohiym created great whales, and every living creature that moveth, which the waters brought forth abundantly, after their kind, and every winged fowl after his kind: and Elohiym saw that it was good. And Elohiym blessed them saying, Be fruitful, and multiply, and fill the waters in the seas, and let fowl multiply in the earth. And the evening and the morning were the fifth day."* (Genesis 1:20-22) [There are no Hebrew words for ***Let the***. *Hayah* is not used in this passage. The command was given directly to the ***waters***!]

This is the recreation of new animal life in the oceans. Some are mammals like the whales and dolphins, while others are fish and all sorts of creatures. There is also a blessing to *be fruitful, and multiply, and fill the waters in the seas*. Some of this life has been harvested and killed to the point of extinction. Efforts in preservation and conversation are taking place today, but only a few have proved truly successful. The fowl of the air were also created and given the same blessing. Is it possible that the newly created life forms were similar in design to the former life forms? [This is what is meant by the expression *"...after its kind..."*]

Again, from the Book of Data: *"And Elohiym said, **Let the** earth bring forth the living creature after his kind, cattle, and creeping thing, and beast of the earth after his kind: and it was so. And Elohiym made the beast of the earth after his kind, and cattle after their kind, and everything that creepeth upon the earth after his kind: And Elohiym saw that it was good. And Elohiym said, Let us make man in our image, after our likeness: and let them have dominion over the fish of the sea, and over the fowl of the air, and over the cattle, and over all the earth, and over every creeping thing that creepeth upon the earth. So Elohiym created man in his own image, in the image of Elohiym created he him; male and female created he them. And Elohiym blessed them, and Elohiym said unto them, Be fruitful and multiply, and replenish the earth, and subdue it: and have dominion over the fish of the sea, and over the fowl of the air, and over every living thing that moveth upon the* *earth. And Elohiym said, Behold, I have given you every herb bearing seed, which is upon the face of all the earth, and every living tree, in the which is the fruit of a tree yielding seed; to you it shall be for meat (food and medicine). And to every beast of the earth and to every fowl of the air, and to every thing that creepeth upon the earth, wherein there is life, I have given every green herb for meat: and it was so. And Elohiym saw everything that he had made, and behold, it was very good. And the evening and the morning were the sixth day".* (Genesis 1:24-31) [*"Let the"* is the same as in Genesis 1:20-22.]

Just as the *waters* were commanded to bring forth marine and fowl life, the *earth* was commanded to bring forth new life on dry land. Man was created and given dominion over the entire earth and everything on and in it. Remember dominions? Adam is now the new General Contractor entrusted to continue implementing the Universal Master Plan. Man (male and female) was created in Elohiym's *image* and *likeness*. Remember the unity fraction and the intelligent atom dividing by self-induced fission?

From the Book of Data: *"And the Yehovah Elohiym caused a deep sleep to fall upon Adam, and he slept: and he took one of his ribs, and closed up the flesh instead thereof; And the rib, which the Yehovah Elohiym had taken from man, made he a woman, and brought her unto the man. And Adam said, This is now bone of my bones, and flesh of my flesh: she shall be called Woman, because she was taken out of man."* (Genesis 2:21-23)

The word *"ribs"* is from the Hebrew prime word *tsala*, which means *curved as in one-sided*. Does that not resemble the loop-shaped chromosome that contains the genetic information of human DNA – the code of life? A chromosome pair was split as in fission, but not self-induced. Human chromosome number 2 is two that were fused together (fusion). This intelligently controlled fusion explains the phrase *closed-up the flesh instead thereof. (biological fusion)*

The members of the ape family have 24 pairs of chromosomes. Humans have 23 pairs. No fused chromosomes exist within the ape family. The fusing of two human chromosomes has caused many evolutionists to claim it as evidence that man evolved from or with apes but cannot explain how or why they became fused. The fact that chromosomes are counted as pairs means that the total number in all living organisms must be divisible by two. Are there any species on the planet with X½ pairs? Viruses exist with single and double strands of DNA or RNA, but many biologists debate if they are indeed alive. Like parasites they need a host to reproduce, but can remain proactive for a period of time outside a host.

If we do some simple arithmetic, we may learn something! When Yehovah Elohiym took one of Adam's chromosomes, it left 47, which cannot be evenly divided by two. When He *"closed up the flesh instead thereof,"* it fused two chromosomes and Adam had 46. Eve was genetically duplicated from a single chromosome to be Adam's sexual counterpart.

Yehovah Elohiym is the Logos and son of El, who is the Theos. Elohiym is a *single atomic nucleus* (Theos/Logos) and in their image and likeness, mankind is a *single adamic nucleus* (man/woman). Both are two separate entities, but one unity (family nucleus). The purpose of Elohiym (Theos/Logos) is the work of creation. The purpose of adam (man/woman) is procreation. [Marriage] Could the Ultimate Goal of The Universal Master Plan be the building of an energy-mass (matter) family through the light? What happened to the rebellious Helyel?

From the Book of Data: *"And the Yehovah Elohiym planted a garden eastward in Eden; and there he put the man he had formed. And out of the ground made the Yehovah Elohiym to grow every tree that is pleasant to the sight, and good for food: the tree of life also in the mist of the garden, and the tree of knowledge of good and evil."* (Genesis 2:89) *"And the Yehovah Elohiym commanded the man (male/female), saying, Of every tree of the garden thou mayest freely eat: But of the tree of the knowledge of good and evil, thou shalt not eat of it: for in the day that thou eatest thereof thou shalt surely die."* (Genesis 2:16-17) [This is true **freedom of choice** or free moral agency!] *"Thou hast been in Eden the garden of Elohiym; every precious stone was thy covering, the sardius, topaz, and the diamond, the beryl, the onyx, and the jasper, the sapphire, the emerald, and the carbuncle, and gold; the workmanship of thy tabrets and of thy pipes was prepared in thee in the day that thou wast created."* (Ezekiel 28:13) *"And the aggelos, which kept not their first estate, but left their habitation, he hath reserved in everlasting chains under darkness unto the judgment of the great day."* (Jude 1:6)

We have seen the fall of the rebellious anointed cherub – Helyel, and now see an even greater description of him prior to his fall. After the war in heaven, Helyel was cast to the ground. After the earth was remade, he was bound to the tree of knowledge of good and evil, which became his prison. His ionizing brother entities were placed in everlasting chains under his darkness, which are the ones that kept not their first estate (earth). The fallen Helyel and his rebellious ionizing brothers are bound to or imprisoned by the tree of the knowledge of good and evil. The Hebrew Dictionary defines:

(1) good – *towb* – (as an adj. or noun, singular or plural) – good, a good thing, a good anything. From: *towb* – (primary root) – to be. Transitively, to do or make good, well, and/or better.
(2) evil – *ra* – bad. As a noun, evil, whether naturally or morally: adversity, affliction, bad, and/or calamity. Amplified by misery, sorrow, mischief, and/or distress. From: *raa* – (primary root) – to spoil. Literally, by breaking to pieces. Figuratively, to make good for nothing, as in the sense of becoming worthless.

Helyel is now the Adversary. The knowledge of good now has an opposing counterpart. Whatever existed prior to Helyel's rebellion and fall was destroyed by it. A new earth age has begun. Adam and Eve now have dominion over a freshly recreated earth. They have the **purity of innocence.** They also have free moral agency, which is symbolic of the two trees in the mist of the garden representing two options. Adam and Eve have freedom of choice. What will they do?

This is as far as we can go in our investigation. To go any further requires making a moral decision. We will now end our scientific investigation of **The Theory of Creation**. If you are interested and would like to know what happens next, you will need to search the Book of Data! Then and only then, you will have – as the dear old radio commentator Paul Harvey used to say for many years: **"The rest of the story".**

[2020 Revision Addition]

Is the COVID-19 virus alive? Do the professionals truly understand it? All respiratory viruses should be considered airborne. Cold and flu viruses are considered airborne! Droplets are compressed moisture vapor molecules (particles) formed when coughing and sneezing and a heavy mist when talking and singing. Breath on a mirror and you can see moisture vapor in the form of fog. If you squeegee (compress) it, you form a droplet. If the droplet tests positive with COVID-19 virus, which moisture vapor molecule (particle) in the fog was it attached to before being compressed (squeegeed)? Moisture vapor is naturally in the air. It is called humidity! The medical professionals now use the term aerosols (a colloid system of solid or liquid particles dispersed in a gas: fog or smoke). The medical professionals and mainstream media should be screaming **AIRBORNE**! Would the public take that word more seriously? Most people think aerosol is a spray you get from a can of deodorant which meets EPA standards. If one sprays themselves with deodorant, can another person wearing a mask smell the scent in the aerosols of the deodorant? Is common sense getting hard to find? Seems wisdom is totally lost. Could the whole sum of it all be some sort of morbid conspiracy?

[2021 Revision Addition]

Now there is a vaccine! It was rushed! What normally takes 7 to 10 years to develop and longer to truly test was fast tracked by someone that was mocked by those saying it couldn't be done. Then one of the mockers took his place and took credit of it, then began doing his damnedest to mandate the vaccination on all, while the one who had it fast tracked has said "let the people choose". Even the top scientists in the various fields of its development are in disagreement over the effectiveness and safety of it! The controlling powers (government, mainstream media, Giant Pharma and egotistical and/or duped medical professionals) are pushing it and the need for more and on a continual basis. The only thing being neglected is trust in God's created natural design! Does mankind think itself a better designer? Who do you trust? God over man or man over God? The truth will be in the pudding when it's all poured out! **And now in late November 2021, a new variant has emerged. OMICRON (The 15th letter of the Greek alphabet.) The first variant was called ALPHA! Then there were others, one being DELTA. The new variant of flu is called influenza-covid. Now we have a new variant of FLU and this new variant of SARS!** What does **OMICRON** stand for? **OM**EGA **I**nfectious **C**oro**n**avirus? The last letter of the Greek alphabet is Omega. What happens when we get to it?

What comes after ALPHA and OMEGA?

May the Lord grant us wisdom!

Chapter III
Mission Debrief and Conclusions

Wasn't that one heck of a ride in our little space-time ship? I believe we may have scientifically proven **The Theory of Creation**. Isn't it amazing how the knowledge in physics, mathematics, and biology can be applied to Biblical understanding? Maybe we should try applying Biblical wisdom to science before man clones a monster or integrates an evil human brain with a master computer. Knowledge and technology can do many wonderfully good things, but man also has the tendency to utilize it for a host of evil purposes.

Many of the questions about creation should be answered, and this chapter will briefly discuss what we have discovered. We will also expand on some of the concepts discovered during our little journey. For the remainder of this thesis, I will release myself from the rules of scientific investigation and use some of the ACLU's forbidden words, although the utilization and association of the various Hebrew and Greek terms for God better clarify the duality of the Godhead. [The Trinity Godhead or God in three persons is a Pagan concept! It is not Biblical! Remember the fallen Lucifer? He wasn't satisfied being number 3 in the chain of command.]

We have found the missing time (Gen.1:2) between Genesis 1:1 and 1:3. God created the heavens and the earth billions of years ago. (Job 8:8, 36:26) Earth Science divides the earth's development into three eras: Paleozoic, Mesozoic, and Cenozoic. The Bible has three earth ages. The first came to a complete ruin (pre-adamic). (Gen. 1:2) We're now quickly approaching the close of the second (present-adamic). (Rev. 6:12, 8:1, 20:4) The third is yet to come (post-adamic – KOG). (Is. 45:18, 66:22; Rom. 8:19-22; Rev. 21-22)

We have also proven the divinity of Jesus Christ. Can you now understand how the Father and the Son are one? Jesus often said, *"I and my Father are one. I am in the Father as the Father is in me, and that which I do is the will of the Father."* (Jn. 5:30, 6:38, 10:30, 14:10-11) The Father and Son are the creators of everything. A brief general summation of the scientific story of creation is as follows: *At the commencement of creation was the Light, and the Light was with the Energy, and the Light was Energy. The Light is of the Energy, as the Energy is in the light, and that which the Light does is the will of the Energy. Then the Light said, "Let there be matter", and there was matter, and they saw that it was good. Then the Light said, "Let matter become life, and bring forth children", and it was so, and shall continue to be so!*

Christ created Lucifer like an identical twin to help begin the creation. When the proton (Christ) shared his mass-energy with the electron (Lucifer), he became a high-energy photon (light). (2Cor. 11:14; Lk. 10:18; Is. 45:7) [Both words *create* in Is. 45:7 are from the same Hebrew term *bara* meaning: (as a formative process) – to create, form, make, or choose. Formatively, Isaiah 45:7 should read: ***I formed the light, it chose darkness; I made perfection, it chose adversity. I the Lord will deal with this.***] Human identical twins are a single conception beginning with one sperm and one egg, then self-divides and becomes two identical individuals in appearance. It is difficult to see the difference between most twins, but once you get to know them, you can see a difference in their character. Christ's **first sacrifice** was by which all things were made. Lucifer was created and made perfect, anointed, and then given the job of General Contractor to complete the earth. He forfeited his position by his rebellion! God changed his name to Satan (The Adversary). (1Pet. 5:8; Job 1:6-12, 2:1-7; Rev. 2:24, 3:9, 12:9, 20:12; 2Cor. 11:14)

Two examples of twin relationships are in scripture. Cain and Able were identical twins. Cain revolted against Able, just as Lucifer attempted to ascend above Christ. (Gen. 4:1-8; Is. 14:12-14) Cain means *quick to strike*. After Father God changed Lucifer's name to Satan, he lost his identicalness and became the adversary. He sold and forsook his birthright just as Esau sold and despised his. (Gen. 25:31-35; Ezek. 28:12-16) The fullness of wisdom given to Lucifer when he was elevated to twin status was first possessed (purchased) by the Lord. (Ezek. 28:12-15; Prov. 8:22-23) After the rebellion, Satan was bound to the tree of the knowledge of good (perfecting) and evil (adversity). He had a chance to repent by <u>not</u> tempting man, but his anger, pride, jealously, greed, and lust for power was too great. **"The rest of the story"** is Adam's fall by his own freedom of choice, which brought about the curse of death. The Father's free choice was to give his only begotten son. (Jn. 3:16) The resurrections (regeneration of dead matter) became possible by Christ's **second sacrifice**. He was twice sacrificed! (Job 33:14; Num. 20:11; Jude 11-12;

Ps. 62:11) The first sacrifice began the creation and after the rebellion and Adam's fall, the second redeemed it. **[$C^2 \geq$ creation × crucifixion]**

Most of our science is left intact. The Geological Chart only needs minor editing. Just take the part with modern man evolving from or with the apes out, and insert Lucifer's *evolution by intelligent design,* his rebellion, and the recreation. We now have the MISSING LINKS in both evolution and creation. Are both relative? The first Biblical earth age is the Geological Chart representing the scientific methods (genetic engineering) employed by Lucifer and his ionizing angels. Biology now has its true source of ionization that was necessary to join the simpler molecules into the more complex ones.

It is possible that we may have theoretically discovered the mythical Lost City of Atlantis. Look at Lucifer's description in Ezekiel 28:12-19 and Isaiah 14:12-20 closely. By understanding the principle of duality in scripture, you can see how his rebellion and fall caused the total destruction of the earth. His *merchandise* was the civilization he built and raised to great heights. He *defiled his sanctuaries* by being a god over his evolutionary achievements and *opened not* the truth about the true Father and the First Son to the *house (inward place, i.e. the mind) of his prisoners (evolutions).* He became proud, lustful, and jealous of his primary (first in origin) brother and father, attempted to usurp their authority, but was cast back to the earth causing its total ruin. It became necessary to restore the earth and create new life on it in order to continue the Universal Master Plan, which is to bring many eternal mass-energy sons into the everlasting glory of the Almighty Father. Man was created in the *image* and *likeness* of God and given dominion over the earth to take over the position of General Contractor. What has he done with that position and responsibility?

Atlantis could have been the location of Lucifer's throne and seat of authority prior to his rebellion. He could have been cast down from heaven to the very spot of his seat, and it was pushed so far into the depths of the earth that no man will ever find it. [Read Ezek. 26:19-21, Jude 13, and Job 8:8 as relating to the first earth age.] When God reshaped and remade the earth during recreation week by pounding back together the tectonic plates, he may have made sure that no one could physically find it. God only knows why Plato was caused to write about it. Plato's doctrine of *the immortality and transmigration of the soul* is accepted by most religions, but **it is not in the Bible!** The Atlantis myth has much more biblical creditability than the reality of man philosophically or theologically having an immortal soul.

After Lucifer became adversary to God, his name was changed to Satan, and then he was bound to the tree of the knowledge of good and evil. Later, he was **cast out** *(adventured forth)* from his **grave** *(repository)* when Adam and Eve yielded to his lie. Adam chose the curse of death when he released Satan (death and hell i.e. the grave) from its repository. The old serpent is now the dragon, Devil, and ***prince of the power of the air***. (Ezek. 28:13; Gen. 2:17, 3:1-5; Is. 14:19; Eph. 2:2; Rev. 20:2,10,14) Adam also fell, but the Father and Christ established a backup plan at the tea party. Only the creator could redeem the fallen state of the created, and that is what the first advent of Christ was all about. His second advent is soon to come! [C^2]

Man has always reached out for the stars, even from his earliest days. Pagan religions associated with sun worship, astrology, and nature worship the creation, not the creator, but astronomy and cosmology are areas of science that study the heavens in hope of understanding the universe. With the invention of the radio telescope by Grote Reber in 1937, we were able to look further than the optical types. The Hubble Telescope has reached out even farther, yet we still cannot see the boundaries or the ends of our universe. There's an excellent and a **very, very** true reason for that. **The Creators (Energy/Light) and their creation (matter) are infinite!** (Job 22:12, 38:6,33,37; Dan. 2:44, 7:18; Rev. 19:6, 21:1-5)

Man has discovered small heavenly objects in our Milky Way called pulsars that emit radio pulses on a regular basis, which are constantly recorded in the hope of receiving a message. This is the creation calling for the reveling of the sons of God that man has the potential to become, but the message is not understood because the existence of the radio operators are not acknowledged. (Rom. 8:16-22; Ps. 8:5; 1Cor. 15:40) The Milky Way is our galaxy, and only one out of the thousands discovered so far. God, space, time, and all universal matter are infinite (eternal). Man has the potential to become eternal if he'll acknowledge and except that which is written in the Scripture of Truth. **We have the entire universe to populate, but only as the children of the Almighty God that made it. He made it for us!**

It was prophesied that knowledge would be increased in the last days. (Dan. 12:4) How much more scientific knowledge will God allow man to discover? Much of it has been utilized to make the most destructive weapons ever know, and some underutilized to keep us hooked on oil.

Where is man's wisdom in the use of his knowledge? We can hardly feed the world population now. Should we clone more humans while many starve as we grow corn to fuel our cars? Grow corn to feed the hungry!

Many may ask, "What is God's purpose and plan for mankind?" God's purpose is to build a family he can depend on to bring life to his infinite universe for all eternity. Mankind dreams of going to other planets and colonizing new worlds. It will never happen under man's present mental condition of hate, war, greed, lust, and perversion. Will NASA ever receive enough funding to do it? [2020 insert: Our current national debt was 26.06 trillion dollars on June 13th 3:12 PM, and rising so fast that it will be about 2 to 3 billion higher when I end this sentence! If we were to prorate our birth rate to the speed of the rising National Debt, we would be producing billion-dollar babies. What this nation needs to abort is its spending, not its babies! This country will need them soon as more taxpayers!] God's universe will be one of peace and prosperity as it becomes his **Eternal Eden** while governing from Earth, its central headquarters. (Gen. 13:16, 15:5, 22:17, 26:4; Ezek. 37:21-28; Rev. 7:9, 21:1-4; Rom. 8:21; Eph. 3:9)

Many await the second advent of Christ. The Lord and his saints will reign on earth for 1000 years restoring the government of God on earth, which is the first resurrection. The second resurrection will be after the millennium. It will be the judgment of the rest of the dead, and the second death (eternal death) will have power. (Rev. 20:6)

Jesus told us there are *many mansions* in his *Father's house*. (Jn. 14:2) The Father's house is the universe, and the many mansions are the stars and planets waiting for the *manifestation of the sons of God* to refashion them and make them new for the glory of God. (Rom. 8:19-22; Rev. 2:28, 21:1-7) [In Rom. 8:19-22, the same Greek word *ktisis* (original formation) is translated *creation* once and *creature* three times.] The **new heaven and new earth** that will follow the second resurrection is when immortal man will have the entire infinite universe to populate for the glory of the Father. Yes! He wants to build a perpetual family of children for all eternity. (Gen. 22:16-18; Ezek. 37:26; Rev. 21 & 22) That is the unified theory of $E = MC^2$ and the second book of the two books of life. (Rev. 20:12 & Rev. 21:2)

There are three ages of the earth and universe. The first earth age came to a total ruin by Lucifer's rebellion and the universe to a state of disruption. The black holes in the galaxies may be evidence of the creation's *bondage of corruption*. These great gravitational fields that hold the galaxies into spirals will come under the control of Christ and the Saints in the third age. Their matter can be widely dispersed and rearranged to support all manner of life for the children of God. The second earth age began with the creation of Adam and will end with the Second Advent of Christ, his millennial reign, and the judgment. The third earth age is when the Father and the great city, Holy Jerusalem comes after the judgment. That will be the new beginning after God has restored law and order to the entire universe. **There will be one universe, under God, indivisible, with liberty, justice, and righteousness for all his children's - children's children for all eternity!**

Can all nations and their various religions, including those that acknowledge the same creator, ever set aside their pride and live in peace, or will God have to literally beat their pride out of them? That sounds rough, but as the old saying goes, *spare the rod – spoil the child*. The **Almighty Energy Source** is a loving **Father**, but he is not going to have a bunch of spoiled rotten, lawless, rebellious matter brats running around his universe! [Like some stars in Hollywood] Some people of faith will disagree with certain aspects of my understanding of things, but I dare not place limits on the love, mercy, justice, or power of the **ALMIGHTY GOD!** Some will say, *"he isn't going to do this, that, or the other."* **That would be very, very foolish!** (Duet. 32:1-43; Rev. 15:3)

The Bible states that God wants his children to come out of Babylon (confusion). Most of the Christian theologies today are the doctrines and traditions of men polluted with ancient philosophy and mysticism. We have been hooked on the doctrines and traditions of men for so many generations, we don't know what to trust as truth, but the Word of God is truth. You can't trust the shepherd that might be the wolf in sheep's clothing, but you can trust the Word of God. Open, read, study, and earnestly search it with a *broken heart and a contrite sprit,* then you will feel the presence of the Father. (Is. 66:2; Ps. 34:18) He will draw you unto himself through the light that is Christ. You can become Christ's brother and friend by accepting his love and sacrifice and obeying his holy commandments. The Father (energy) and Son (light) created and sustains all matter and all life!

I'm just a flesh and blood human being like every person on the face of this planet. We all struggle with the understanding of truth, except for those who just don't give a damn. The writing of this book has been a great learning experience for me. When I began to see the pure mathematics and physics in scripture, the Mystery of God started to become clear. I had to review my old college physics and biology textbooks. [Now I know why I've kept them for the last 30+ years.] Science would be more interesting if we would let God have his rightful place in it. (Job 37:16; Dan. 1:4; 1Tim. 6:20; Prov. 1-6)

God gives all mankind freedom of choice; each to make their own decisions. It is unfortunate there are so many wanting nothing else but their own ideology to prevail while oppressing and denying the right of peaceful expression to others. Children worldwide are brainwashed by their various schoolteachers, preachers, and elders while their parents, politicians, and judges approve, or stand idly by while certain truths found self-evident are blotted out and prohibited as options.

American's public schools teach children that we are nothing more that the product of biological evolution and living life to its fullest before death our only purpose. Humanism and socialism have almost replaced math and pure science. The evilest parts of man's past are edited out of history books or softened by the concept of progress and the ideology of the righteousness in the American way.

We are told about certain rights. Between life and death, we have the right to fight and die for our freedom, other's freedom, freedom of free flowing oil, Wall Street greed, allowing gay marriage, and any other perverted thing deemed acceptable. It is now required that alternative lifestyles be taught as acceptable. High School Biology classes have become more about evolving from or with apes and sex education than the function of living organisms. Maybe they should rename the biology course and call it, *Jungle Love, Sex, and the Art of Having Orgasms without Getting Pregnant, and if you do and don't want it, just choose to destroy it.*

If the ACLU would allow **The Theory of Creation** to be equally taught in our public schools, then freedom of choice would be truly upheld. If they cannot allow the other option of man's origin, then the ACLU is really **Anti-Choice Liberty Undermined**. That, along with all their other anti-God and anti-religious activity, has surely established them as adversary to universal truth: **Anti-Christ Lucifer's Understudies!**

Chapter IV
Philosophy and Theology

Philosophy and Theology can be considered as evolutionary twin brothers. The modern-day theologies that are held by mainstream Christianity, Judaism, and Islam have been greatly influenced by ancient Greek (Ionian) philosophy. Before proceeding any further, let's define these terms as given in the Standard English Dictionary.

* **Philosophy - 1.** The theory or analysis of the principles that underline the conduct, thought, knowledge, and/or the nature of the universe. **2.** The general principles in the field of knowledge. **3.** The love of wisdom, and the leading in the continuous search for it.
* **Theology - 1.** The study of God, religious doctrines, and matters of divinity. **2.** The philosophy of religion.

Many ideas of the ancient Greek philosophers were written down and preserved, and throughout the centuries have played a significant role in the scientific knowledge and religious theology we possess today. (Col. 2:8, Acts 17:16-30) They introduced the idea that atoms were the small invisible particles that make up all universal matter. The ancient Greeks also conceived the idea of the *transmigration and immortality of the soul*, in that the soul was a separate entity within the body or being of man and transmigrated after death. The knowledge in nuclear physics has proved their theory of the atom; however, man having an immortal soul that transmigrates to some other place of existence after death, such as heaven or hell, is not scriptural. Man having an immortal soul cannot be found in the Bible. Immortality is something that will be ***put on*** in a resurrection. (1Cor. 15:51-54; 1Tim. 6:15-16)

Greek philosophy has an interesting history. Some of its earliest thinkers are long forgotten because their ideas just did not stand the test of time. The following is a chronological history of some of the most famous

Greek philosophers. [Personal comments and scripture quotes added in brackets.]

* **Thales of Miletus** (636-546 BC) Regarded as founder of Ionian natural philosophy, he believed water to be the basis of all things in the universe. [It is a biological fact that water is necessary for life. Pure water is necessary for eternal life. (Rev. 21:6, 22:1; Jn. 4:7-14)]
* **Anaximander** (611-547 BC) He was the second Thales of the Ionian school of philosophy and believed the universal basis to be the boundless and indefinite. He is ascribed with the invention of geographical maps and the introduction of the sundial. [Life cannot exist without light, and procreation requires energy, which are biological facts. God the Father is the *boundless source of energy*, and his Son (Christ) the *indefinite source of light*. (Jn. 1:1-3; Heb. 1:1-3)]
* **Anaximenes** (6th century BC) He was Anaximander's pupil and believed that one type of substance underlies the diversity of all observable things. He held that air was the universal substance, but in different degrees of density. [All plant and animal life require air but are not made from it. Plants take in carbon dioxide and give off oxygen, while animals take in oxygen and give off carbon dioxide, which is a divine arrangement by intelligent design. After Adam was formed from the dust (elements) of the earth, the Lord God performed *divine CPR*. (Gen. 2:7) The **breath** *(n^{e}shamah)* is defined *intellect* or *spirit*. Adam became a **living** (*chay* – raw, fresh, strong, alive, life, a living thing) **soul** (*nephesh* – a breathing creature, i.e. animal, vitality in a figurative sense, both bodily and mental – mind). *Chay nephesh* is translated **living creature** in Gen. 1:21, 24; 2:19, 9:10, 12, 15, 16, and Lev. 11:46. *Nephesh* is also translated **mind**. Adam became a living breathing creature with a mind (intellect) – a human being.]
* **Pythagoras** (582-507 BC) Philosopher and mystic, he founded the religious brotherhood that believed in the concept of the *immortality and transmigration of the soul*. Also, a mathematician, he was first to assert that numbers constitute the true nature of all things. [He was right about numbers, but not the concept of man having an immortal soul. The Bible does not teach man as being or with an immortal soul. When man dies, he returns to dust and his intellect sleeps until a resurrection. (Gen. 2:17, 3:19; Dan. 12:2; Ps. 31:12, 88:5, 115:17, 143:3; Eccl. 9:5; Is. 26:19; Luke 8:52; Rom. 6:7, 8:11; 1Cor. 15:51-54; 1Th. 4:14-18; Prov. 6:9-11; Rev. 20)]

* **Heraclitus** (535-475 BC) Opposed to the idea of a single ultimate reality, he believed that all things were in a constant state of change. [Energy-mass transformation is a *state of change*. Other changes are like the definitions of some words, such as *gay*. The Flintstones and Rubbles had *a gay ole time* but were not homosexual. Is *pregnant man* a reality? If so, burn every damn dictionary and biology book on the planet!]

* **Parmenides** (5th century BC) He is often considered the founder of western metaphysics, which is the philosophy concerned with the ultimate nature of reality and existence as a whole. It also includes the study of cosmology, which is the study of the origin and structure of the universe as a whole and philosophical theology. This Pre-Socratic thinker held that *being* is the basic substance and the ultimate reality of which all things are composed, and that motion, change, time, difference, and reality are illusions of the senses. The term *being* has a special meaning in philosophy and is frequently used in metaphysics for contrasting appearance and nonexistence. It is often synonymous with an unchanging substance, ultimate reality, God, infinity, or all that exists. Aristotle held that *being* was the subject matter of meta-physics. [If motion, change, time, difference, and reality are illusions of the senses, then his being was an illusion. If you hold your hand in a fire, you will know it is not an illusion because you can sense the flesh burning, but if you insist the fire is an illusion by continuing to hold your hand in it, you will no longer have a hand. That is the ultimate reality of changing flesh with fire! (Rev. 20:11-15)]

* **Anaxagoras** (500-428 BC) He supposedly made Athens the center of philosophy and been Socrates' teacher. Rejecting the *four-element theory* of Empedocles, he suggested all things were composed of an infinite number of particles (atoms). [Today, we know that all things are composed of atoms. (Job 38:38; Gen. 2:7; Ps. 44:25; Eccl. 3:20)]

* **Empedocles** (495-435 BC) He believed the universe consisted of the four elements: air, fire, water, and earth, and the interaction between love and hate caused the mixing of them. [He must have been Parmenides' son. Air, water, and earth do consist of elements, but fire is not an element. If these where to constitute human beings, then the person made of air would be the *air head*, the person of fire the *hot head*, the person of water the *diplomat* to cool down the *hot head*, and the person of earth the *hard head* since earth's crust is mainly rock. The *pregnant man* would be a *hardheaded air head*!]

* **Zeno of Elea** (490-430 BC) A disciple of Parmenides, he argued that motion, change, and plurality are just logical absurdities, and only an *unchanging being is real*. [Tell that to the *pregnant man*!] He attempted to demonstrate that notions of time and motion are erroneous. [Physics prove that time and motion dictates mass-energy conversions. An evil person can change to good and vice-versa, but all people (good or evil) are real beings. (Ezek. 33:11-20) Good (righteousness) or Evil (wickedness) are the only two options which determine eternal life or eternal death. The choice is yours! That is why the Eternal **(El)** gave it to us!]
* **Socrates** (464-399 BC) He was the Athenian philosopher who never recorded any of his views because of his belief that writing distorts ideas. He would question the Athenians about their religious, political, and moral beliefs through a technique called *dialectic*. He is alleged to have said, *"The unexamined life is not worth living."* He was charged and brought to trial for corruption of the youth and religious heresy, then sentenced to die, but drank poison. Plato was his student, and the main source of what is known about him. [He must have really pissed off the *Athenian Cultural Lawyers Union*. If the ACLU had existed during his time defending evolution over creation, I suppose they would be charged, tried, convicted, and sentenced for the same charges. The Greeks loved their Gods, and would not have withstood efforts to remove them, or their philosophical and theological concepts of them from the public arena. Would they have drunk poison? It is a wise idea for people to examine their lives and consider their destiny. (Ps. 8:4-5; Heb. 2:6-7; Eph. 3:11; Ecclesiastes)]
* **Democritus** (460-370 BC) He proposed the mechanistic theory of a world that *required no supernatural forces* and held that the constant motion of indestructible atoms was the composition of all things, perception was unreliable, and knowledge could only be obtained through reason. [Is this view atheist? Why wasn't he charged with religious heresy? The Greeks worshipped 48 Gods and had a statue for one unknown, but he said that *none were required*. All knowledge is a gift from God. (2Chr. 1:7-12; Acts 2:38; Is. 11:1-4; Prov. 1:7) Although acquired by human perception and/or observation, scientific knowledge can also be a gift, as God's to Einstein. Man didn't invent but only discovered knowledge through understanding his observations, and along with controlled methods of experimentation gained even more. (Job 38:36; Prov. 8:12; Dan. 12:4)]

* **Plato** (428-348 BC) Considered the Athenian father of Western Philosophy; he traveled widely after Socrates' death. Upon his return to Athens, he founded an Academy and taught until he died. His writings preserved many of the dialogues between Socrates and other Athenians. Many of Plato's views are recorded in his most famous book, The Republic. He described an ideal state that postulates philosopher kings specially trained at high levels in moral and mathematical knowledge. His other works analyze the morality of man, nature of knowledge, immortality of the soul, and cosmology. All his works have influenced both science and religious theology over the last two thousand years. [Plato is usually considered the source of the *immortal soul doctrine*, but it first originated with Pythagoras. Although camouflaged with Greek mythology, his description of the Lost City of Atlantis may have been a stealthy gift from God for a latter day understanding. The *scientific method* of today can be attributed to the *dialectic method* of Socrates' questioning, but aided by observation of methodic experimentation.]

* **Diogenes** (400-325 BC) As the founder of cynicism, he rejected social conventions, defied traditional comforts, and allegedly lived in a tub. He founded a school for Cynics, and according to legend, he walked around night and day looking for an honest man, but never found one. Cynics believe man should live in a simple state of natural being with few desires and needs. They advocate the moderation, self-discipline, and training of the mind and body. [I know there were schools for Monks, but not for hermits. He would have definitely wasted his time on Wall Street and in Washington DC! A hot bath is relaxing, but I would not want to live in the tub.]

* **Aristotle** (384-322 BC) He was a scientist, logician, and student of many disciplines. He studied under Plato and later became tutor to Alexander the Great. In 335 BC he founded the Lyceum in Athens, a major school for the study of philosophy and science. He emphasized the observation of nature and analyzed everything in terms of four causes: *material cause* – the substance a thing is made of, *formal cause* – the design of the thing, *efficient cause* – the maker of the thing, and *final cause* – its purpose of function. In the field of ethics, he believed virtue to be a means between extremes and man's highest goal should be to use his intellect. [From his four causes, we find substance (man created from the elements of the earth), design (the most complex form of life with intellect), maker (The Creator), and purpose (that which is

found in the Scripture of Truth). These constitute the true analysis of the ultimate reality. If wisdom is to be found in philosophy, it is found here. Man's highest goal should be to know his maker!]

* **Epicurus** (341-270 BC) A follower of Democritus, he founded the *Epicurean Philosophy*. Most of his writings have been lost. Epicureans taught that the supreme goal of man should be pleasure and happiness. Early Epicureans sought mental pleasures (knowledge, understanding, and wisdom) over bodily ones. [That line of thought did not gain a general popularity. Man's great quest for pleasure and happiness has been more bodily that mental. The philosophy of most people is to *eat, drink, and be merry, for tomorrow we may die*. The mental pleasure writings were most likely the ones that were lost!]

* **Zeno (of Citium) the Stoic** (334-262 BC) Born in Cyprus, he founded Stoicism. He believed that man should submit to natural law, man's primary duty is to conform to his destiny, and the soul is a form of matter, not immortal. [He was right about the soul being a form of matter. We all submit to the *natural law of gravity,* and all organic matter returns to its inorganic state. The Ten Commandments (spiritual law as expansively taught by Jesus Christ) are what we should submit to so that we may conform to our potential destiny. (Ex. 20:1-17; Prov. 3:1, 4:1-7; Matt. 22:37-40; Jn. 14:15,21, 15:10; Rom. 12:2, 8:29; Rev. 12:17, 14:12, 22:14; Ps. 78:7, 103:17-19)]

* **Lucretius** (99-55 BC) He was a Roman Epicurean poet and philosopher who depicted the entire universe, including the soul, as being composed of atoms. According to his doctrine, the world arose from atoms moving through space, and a god did indeed exist, but not to interfere in human life. [This was long before The Big Bang Theory based on Einstein's Theory of Relativity and the world's most famous equation $E = mc^2$. It was far beyond any scientific knowledge at the time. The first hydrogen bomb was detonated in 1952. Roman philosophy and theology were much the same as the Greeks. His theory of universal atoms being the foundation of everything is correct, but God does care about mankind and often intervenes in its affairs. The greatest intervention was 50 years later (55 BC − 50 yrs. = 5 BC) when The Eternals' Word became flesh. (John 3:16) The number 50 also represents Jubilee in Scripture and is also important for counting.]

That list brings us to half a century before the birth of Jesus Christ in 5 BC. Judaism had already become influenced by Greek philosophy following the conquest of Jerusalem by Alexander the Great in 333 BC, then Rome in 37 BC. The Pharisees, Sadducees, scribes, and religious lawyers had made a mockery of the Mosaic religion. It was time for the first advent of Christ to prepare the way for the reconciliation of man back unto God, and to do intellectual battle with the religious elite. (Matt. 23, 21:12-16; Luke 19:39-48; Jn. 8; Dan. 9:24; 2Cor. 5:18-19; Heb. 2:14-18)

Some of the philosophers, to put it in everyday language, just didn't know their butt from a hole in the ground. Others formed the foundation for the scientific knowledge that we possess today, which should give us a better understanding of the *ultimate reality*. Some erroneous philosophies were adapted to the understanding of scripture and became the doctrines and traditions of men. After Christ's first advent, many philosophers and theologians of various backgrounds and nationalities greatly influenced the modern theologies in Judaism and Christianity. Islam was founded in 632 AD by the prophet Mohammed, which was supposed to fulfill the hope of Abraham. (Gen. 17:18-21) Islam has also fell victim to the philosophy and theology of men. The following is a list of philosophers and theologians who have greatly influenced modern day religious thought of the three great creator religions:

* **Epictetus** (50-138 AD) As an Epicurean and Stoic philosopher, he founded a school of philosophy after being freed from slavery. His book, The Manual, taught that only by detaching ourselves from what is not in our power to control could we attain inward freedom. [He may have been a young child who was an indentured servant/student among the philosophers that approached the Apostle Paul. (Acts 17:18-21,33-34) Scripture teaches that liberty is the acceptance of Christ's sacrifice, and through a *living faith* we can detach ourselves from sin and its bondage. (Jn. 8:34-36; Rom. 3-8; 1John; 1Cor. 15:56; Jas. 1-2; Rev. 14:12; Acts 26:18; Heb. 11)]

* **Marcus Aurelius** (121-180 AD) He was Roman emperor from 161 AD until his death. As a proponent of the Stoic philosophy, his book, Meditations, claimed that birth and death are natural, and the world is rational and orderly. He was considered a humanitarian, but did persecute the Christians. [The world could be considered as rational

and orderly if the few who control it want to see it that way. Most leaders today only see and hear what they want to! How could a person be considered a humanitarian, but be a persecutor at the same time?]

* **Plotinus** (205-270 AD) Egyptian born, he founded *Neoplatonism*, which synthesizes the ideas of Plato and others. He believed that all reality is caused by a series of outpourings called emanations from a divine source. He established a school of philosophy that flourished from the second to fifth century, and Neoplatonism was influential for the next thousand years. He was not a Christian but was a major influence on Christianity. [When the philosophical thought of a non-Christian philosopher influences Christian thought, the door is wide open for apostasy. The scriptures state that there would be a *falling away* of the faith once given. (2Th. 2:3) I believe it happened long ago. Today, we are trying to come out of centuries of accumulated confusion called *Babylonian captivity* by the great captivator **MYSTERY, BABYLON THE GREAT, THE MOTHER OF HARLOTS AND ABOMINATIONS OF THE EARTH**. (Rev. 17)]

* **Augustine of Hippo** (354-430 AD) Considered one of the greatest among the Latin Church fathers, he emphasized man's need for grace. His most popular works were Confessions and The Holy City of God. [The Roman Empire acknowledged and accepted Christianity as an official state religion in 321 AD. His writings have greatly influenced both Catholic and Protestant Dogma.]

* **Boethius** (475-535 AD) He was a Roman statesman, philosopher, and a translator of Aristotle's works who wrote The Consolation of Philosophy while in prison. His work was widely read throughout the Middle Ages. Addressing reason's role in the face of misfortune, he established the link between philosophy and Scholasticism. [The term *Scholastics* was adopted by *Christian Philosophers* during the Middle Ages as their descriptive title. They followed Aristotle's empiricism using his logic and linguistic methods of argumentation.]

* **Avicenna** (980-1037 AD) An Islamic medieval philosopher born in Persia, his Neoplatonist interpretation of Aristotle greatly influenced medieval philosophers for over 300 years, including St. Thomas Aquinas. He was also a physician, and his medical writings were influential for nearly 500 years. [Aristotle's work influenced Islam, Christianity, and Judaism. His major works were unknown to Europe until the 13th century but became known through Arab philosophers in Spain. Thomas Aquinas adapted the Aristotelian philosophy to his own

but had to defend his Christian Aristotelianism against many bitter conservative attacks while a professor of theology in Paris (1268-72). This is a link between Islam (HQ in Baghdad or Babylon) and Christianity (HQ in Rome). The Roman Catholic Church has already announced that the various terms for God, including *Allah,* are beautiful names for the universal God. Beware of the association and application of linguistic terms to the unknown name of God!]
* **Saint Anselm** (1033-1109 AD) This Italian monk and Scholastic became archbishop of Canterbury. Considered as the founder of Scholasticism, he integrated Aristotelian logic into theology and believed that reason and revelation were compatible. He is most famous for the ontological argument proving God's existence. [A revelation from God is a gift and cannot be achieved by the *logical reasoning* of man. Daniel, John, and the prophets did not *reason out* their writings. Is man's reasoning and God's revelation compatible? (Is. 55:8; Ezek. 36:32; Luke 5:18-26; Mark 8:14-21; Eph. 1:17; Col. 2:8)]
* **Averroes** (1126-1198 AD) Born in Cordoba, Spain, this Arabian philosopher's views of compatibility were similar with those of St. Anselm and he wrote detailed commentaries on Aristotle that were influential for centuries. He believed that faith and reason were compatible, but philosophical knowledge was derived from reason. The Church condemned his views. [Why would the Church (Rome) condemn his views if they were similar with Anselm's? The Christian theologians adapted the Aristotelian philosophy that the Muslim philosophers had shared, and then evicted them and the Jews. In 750 AD the Abbasid family led a coalition defeating the ruling Umayyad family, but Abd Ar-Rahman I escaped the general massacre and fled to Spain. He became the emirate of Cordoba in 780, and Islam's western caliphate persisted until 1031. Following the conquest by the Moors in 711 AD, Muslims, Jews, and Non-Catholic Christians lived harmoniously until the Catholic conquest. The era was known as *The Golden Age.* The Spanish Inquisition under Ferdinand and Isabella expelled most of the Jews and Muslims, confiscated their property, and murdered others unwilling to convert to Catholicism.]
* **Maimonides** (1135-1204 AD) He was the Spanish born Jewish philosopher that synthesized Aristotelian and Judaic thought. His works had enormous influence on Jewish and Christian thinking. [Again, we find evidence of Aristotle's works influencing Judaism. So

far, we have seen his works having great influence on all three major religions holding a belief in the same Creator God.]

* **John Duns Scotus** (1266-1308 AD) Like others before him, this Scottish born Scholastic integrated Aristotelian ideas into his own Christian theology. He taught that all things depend on the divine will as well as God's intellect. [This is the last philosopher/theologian that mentions the works of Aristotle. St. Thomas Aquinas developed the official *Roman Catholic Philosophy* in 1259. The Western Roman Empire had been under Papal control for a little over 700 years. The Eastern Orthodox Church had finalized its split from the Western Catholic Church in 1054, which began after the fall of Rome in 476 AD and progressed through the Byzantine period. The Protestant reformers would soon make their mark in history with their dissent and separation, but the relationship between Catholics and Protestants have greatly improved since Vatican Council II (1962-65) and the election of John F. Kennedy, America's first Catholic President.]

* **Sir Thomas More** (1478-1535 AD) A very prominent Renaissance humanist, statesman, and Lord Chancellor of England, he was beheaded for refusing to accept the King of England as *Head of the Church*. He believed in social reform and the ideal peaceful state, and authored the book, Utopia. [Jesus Christ is the only **Head of the Church**. The last days may resemble the Dark Ages, and God's people may face the same dilemma as More did when he refused to acknowledge a mortal man as the *Head of the Church*.]

* **Thomas Hobbs** (1588-1679 AD) This English materialist, empiricist, and founder of modern political philosophy argued that man is selfish by nature. His famous book, Leviathan, suggested: *a powerful absolute ruler and a social contract with man giving up much personal liberty would be necessary to establish peace on earth.* [Known anybody who is selfish? Hitler must have read his book. **When Jesus Christ returns as King of Kings and Lord of Lords, He will be the powerful absolute ruler, but it will be divine rule under divine law. There will be no social contract!** The word *leviathan* is found in Ps. 74:13-14, 104:24-26, Is. 27:1, and Job 41, and comes from the Hebrew word: *livyathan* – serpent, sea monster. Derived from: *layah* – to entwine and unite. LINK the following: anointed cherub – fallen Lucifer – cast back to the earth – Satan – dragon – serpent – sea monster – dreadful diverse beast – rising from the sea – Lost City of Atlantis (Dan. 7:7; Rev. 13:1; Is. 43:16, 11:12; Job 41:25,31; Rev. 8:8; Ezek. 26:19-21)]

* **Benedict (Baruch) Spinoza** (1623-1677 AD) This Dutch born philosopher was expelled from his Amsterdam Jewish community for heresy in 1656. Then, he was accepted by Christians, but attacked by theologians 14 years later. In his book, The Ethics, he presented his views in a mathematical system of deductive reasoning and concluded that mind and body are aspects of a single substance called God or nature. He declared: *Besides God no substance can be granted or conceived.* Through mathematics, he set forth geometric proof of the union of man, God, and universe. [The human mind (brain) and body (flesh) are two aspects of the single biological entity that is called the soul (nephesh) that was created in the image (body) and likeness (mind) of God. Man disobeyed his Creator and brought death upon himself. It is human nature for man to be hostile toward his creator and in need of reconciliation, which became possible by the second sacrifice of Christ. I do not know if my understanding is the same as Spinoza's, but both Jews and Christians had rejected his wisdom. His work was during the peak of the reformation. Why did theologians reject his philosophical wisdom that has so much scriptural support?]

* **Gottfried Wilhelm Leibniz** (1646-1716 AD) Considered one of the greatest minds of all time, this German mathematician, philosopher, and diplomat believed that *the entire universe is one large system expressing God's plan.* **[AMEN!]** Leibniz and Sir Isaac Newton discovered calculus and are considered as the forefathers of modern mathematical logic. [The pure language of science is mathematics. When Christ returns, man will be given a pure language. (Zeph. 3:9) As a mathematician, he truly <u>summed</u> up the *ultimate philosophy.*]

* **George Berkeley** (1685-1753 AD) He was an Irish philosopher, Anglican Bishop, and a British empiricist who embraced subjective idealism, and believed that everything which exists is based on perception. According to his view, material objects are collections of sensations or ideas in a person's or God's mind. This is the bases for subjectivism, which is the theory that all moral values are completely dependent on the personal tastes, feelings, or inclinations of the individual and has no source of validity outside of the human subjective state of mind. [That is the very source of the Anglican problem today concerning sexuality. There are some Bishops that acknowledge their own homosexuality and claim that it is compatible with scripture. They may need to actually **read** The Holy Bible and stay the hell out of gay pubs! (Lev. 18:22; Rom. 1:24-27)]

* **Francois Marie Arouet Voltaire** (1694-1778 AD) He was a French philosopher, essayist, historian, and one of the major thinkers of the *Enlightenment*. A Deist and anti-Christian, he advocated the tolerance of liberal ideas, and called for positive social action. A Deist is a practitioner of deism, which is the philosophical viewpoint that although God may have created the universe and its laws, he removed himself from any ongoing interactions with the material world. [This atheist's *tolerance of liberal ideas* continues today with gay and lesbian rights, same-sex marriage, abortion, and other issues. His *positive social actions* are the laws passed or judiciously legislated from the bench requiring *the tolerance of liberal ideas* regardless of how contrary they are to those of the community. Free moral choice is every individual's right, but to force a whole community to accept ideas contrary to their ethical standards, moral beliefs, and religious practice is a violation of their first amendment rights. If homosexuals and lesbians want *civil unions*, they can exercise their common law right to contract, which is protected by the 9th and 10th amendments of the Constitution. They can call it anything they want to, **except marriage!** Heterosexuals have abused that sacred institution enough with divorce. *"What God has put together, let no man (lawyers, judges, and politicians included) put asunder"*. (Matt. 19:3-9)]
* **David Hume** (1711-1766 AD) This British empiricist's arguments against the proofs for God's existence are still influential today. He held that moral beliefs have no basis in reason but are solely based on custom. [If custom is the foundation for moral beliefs, then that explains the greed and corruption that exists in today's governments and corporations. The custom of corporations is to exact its bottom line by laying-off workers, cutting pay and benefits, or relocating to other countries with lower environmental standards and wages. It is the custom of governments to exact its ideological policies on people. The custom of both has neither regard for the human suffering caused, nor the ultimate consequences of their actions. If the conquest of economic philosophy by greedy corporate policy and political ideology by military might is a good thing to do, regardless of how right it may seem in the eyes of men, then – *I don't want to be right*.]
* **Immanuel Kant** (1724-1804 AD) He is the German philosopher, possibly the most influential of modern times, who synthesized Leibniz's rationalism and Hume's skepticism into his own critical philosophy that: *ideas do not conform to the external world, but rather,*

the world can only be known insofar as it conforms to the mind's own structure. He also claimed that morality requires a belief in God, freedom, and future immortality, although these cannot be scientifically or metaphysically proven. [Morality does require a belief in God, and it is outlined in his Ten Commandments. Man does have *freedom of choice*, and his future immortality is a gift as stated in John 3:16. The critical truth (not philosophy) is that only by God's mercy and by the blood of Jesus Christ can the possibility of eternal life even exist, but without or the rejection of God is eternal death.]

* **Auguste Comte** (1798-1857 AD) French founder of Positivism and a social reformer, he invented the term *sociology*, which brought the world the religion of humanity that replaces God with mankind as a whole. [This is the fruit yielded from atheist France after the French Revolution. The human potential and ultimate destiny of man is laid out in a divine plan by a divine creator, which can only be found in the Scripture of Truth. It is not *social evolution*! We now have another OLOGY that is manmade.] * **Soren Kierkegaard** (1813-1855 AD) This Danish philosopher and religious thinker founded the religion of *Existentialism*, which holds that truth is subjectivity, religion a personal matter, and that man's relationship with God requires suffering. Modern Existentialism holds: *since there are no universal values, then man's essence is not predetermined, but based only on free choice, and that man is in a state of anxiety because of free will, and there is no objective truth*. [Man's relationship with God does not require suffering, although it can bring a closer relationship. This modern philosophy proves that by *free choice* man took upon himself the knowledge of good and evil; however, without *universal values* or *objective truth* in knowing God, His truth, and His plan for all mankind, his *predestination* is *a state of anxiety*, but only by his own *free will!*]

* **William James** (1842-1910 AD) He was an American philosopher and psychologist who was among the early founders of Pragmatism, and greatly influenced thinkers of his era. He viewed consciousness as actively shaping reality, defined truth as the expedient way of thinking, and believed that ideas are tools for guiding future actions rather than reproductions of our past experiences. Pragmatism is an American philosophy developed in the 19th century with the help of Charles Sanders Peirce (1839-1914) and elaborated on in the 20th century by John Dewey. Its central precept is that thinking is the primary guide to action, and that the truth of any idea lies only in its practical

consequences. [Philosophy has now evolved into Psychology. I think I'll just keep my butt on the farm and not get into that *loony-ology* subject. I've done some stupid things in the past but learned from them by thinking that it would be a good idea not to do them again! The ultimate *practical consequence* will follow the judgment of the *truth of ideas* on the Last Great Day. (Rev. 20:11-15)]

* **Friedrich Wilhelm Nietzsche** (1844-1900 AD) He was a moralist, German philosopher, and poet who rejected all Christian values. He championed a superman who would create a new, life-affirming, heroic ethic by his will to power. [Hitler surely read and believed in his philosophy! Satan will cause to rise up and maybe even possess a **Superman** that through a new, life-affirming and heroic humanistic ethic will deceive the whole world in the last days. **Jesus Christ SUPERSTAR** will come and whoop his ass! Again!]

* **George Santayana** (1863-1952 AD) He was a Spanish born American philosopher, poet, and student of William James, who attempted to reconcile Platonism and materialism by studying how reason works. He found *animal faith* or *impulse* to be the basis of reason and belief. [The roaring twenties was a time when people did things on *impulse,* and that line of thinking persists today. If *doing things on impulse* is *animal faith,* then today's society has *gone to the dogs.* I'm glad that Choco didn't, and Coco doesn't understand philosophy or theology, but if they could, then they would probably take that statement as an insult.]

* **George Edward Moore** (1873-1958 AD) He was a British philosopher who emphasized the common sense view of the reality of material objects. In the field of ethics, he believed that goodness is a quality known directly by moral intuition, and to try to define it in terms of anything else is a fallacy. [We have finally found a modern philosopher with some *common sense* in material objects; however, moral goodness can only be learned through an upbringing with family values, education, and the respect and love for others. The intuitiveness of good moral judgment does not come by the power of reason, but only by the accumulation of knowledge in the understanding of wisdom. The best-selling textbook for intuitive moral goodness is The Holy Bible, which I call The Scripture of Truth.]

* **Martin Buber** (1878-1965 AD) This German-Israeli philosopher was influenced by Jewish mysticism and existentialism, and a major force in 20th century Jewish thought and philosophy of religion. His *I and Thou* held that God and man could have a direct and mutual dialogue.

[That is so true! The quest for truth (seeking) in devoted study of the Holy Scriptures (knocking) with sincere prayer (asking) will bring about great understanding, knowledge, and wisdom. (Matt. 7:7-8; Prov. 9:10; Dan. 2:21) It is also true that a person can have a three-way conversation with our Father and Christ. Conversations in public, when no one can see who you are talking to, might get you put in a straight-jacket and locked up, but if you are truly in the spirit, be confident of your conversation. And praise the Lord!]

That brings us to where the world is today in the religious arena of philosophy and theology. The reasoning of men has polluted Judaism, Christianity, and Islam. The philosophies and theologies of men have blinded most if not all of mankind to the truth. There are truths that can be found among all three of the major creator religions, but their many fundamentalists and extremists have all but destroyed any possibility for peace and harmony in the unity of understanding.

Some philosophers and theologians seemed to be on the right track; few indeed were. Others *created theologies by philosophical design* and *vice versa*. If *natural selection and origin of the species* is true, it is only in *the evolution of religion*. Philosophy and Theology are two close relative species that evolved from the common concept of human reasoning but interbreed and made a hybrid – Philtheology. Today, we still have the two species of foul characteristics, but its many breeds have interbreed and inbreed to the point that our barnyard of philosophies and theologies are nothing more than a compost pile of a vast variety of crap! (Col. 2:8; Lam. 4:4-5; Matt. 15:7-20) We could use its methane gas for our cars and save the corn to feed the poor!

There are some that consider Jesus a great philosopher. That is an insult to Christ! He is the teacher of truth, and there is no reasoning with what he teaches. He is the truth and the light. The Word that became flesh in John 1:1 is the same voice that speaks through the Old Testament Prophets. He is the King of Salem and the High Priest Melchizedek in Genesis 14:18 and the book of Hebrews. He is the voice that spoke to the children of Israel in Exodus 20. He is the Yehovah Elohiym that breathed the breath of life into Adam in Genesis 2:7. *"All things were made by him, and without him was not anything made that was made."* (Jn. 1:3) [$m = E \div C^2$] Christ is Lord! He is the possessor of wisdom, and the sons of men are his delight! We can become his brothers if we trust in him and keep his ways. (Prov. 8:22-36; Jn. 14:15, 15:10; Matt. 12:48-50; Mk. 3:33-35)

I must call myself a Christian because there is no other word in the English vocabulary that is appropriate. The blood of Jesus Christ's sacrifice is the one and only hope for our species. That is not mere human reasoning, philosophy, or theology. It is the one, and the only, **critical truth in the ultimate reality of the great human potential.**

[Revision 2021]

Love them ___ology words! Well, kinda? But they are necessary in the use of language. Biology is the science in the understanding of how living organisms function. It has no damn business in how they came to exist! That's a matter for another ___ology word. Psychology is the understanding of the mind and thought processes, and I'm not so sure that it is a science, but more like medicine, which is a practice. Seems there is a lot of that going on these days by a bunch of moronic-demonic politicians with some sort of medical degree hell bent on tyranny over all.

A sports team can practice all spring and never win a game. I've seen a few over the years. Others have gone to the super series. Faucinsten and his gang of Igor's just can't make up their minds as to what is good for the health of the masses that they practice their dictates on. But so far, they're ahead. Just hit a home goal. RBI mandates are mounting up like baskets of balls. The covid-ball is being run to the end zone. Touchdown!

WHO rides the white horse? Does its rider have a sidekick? Must be, since this type of insanity abounds in other ___ologies. Biology and Psychology have interbred and transformed. **Psycho-bio-trans-ology+**

It is biology that determines the sex of an individual. There are only two sexes - male and female. The evidence is between one's legs. It is not what one thinks it is in between the ears! That is a matter of psychology. I am sticking to the biology of the matter. The actual process of sex determination is the prize to which swimmer that reaches the finish line first. How the race begins was designed to be a wonderful physical function between a man and a women united as one in the likeness and image of their creator. Anything outside of that is a matter of several ___ology words. Now, to the biological facts of the procreation of sons and daughters.

Chromosomes are a thread-like complex structural design that are made up of a combination of DNA and protein found in the nuclei of cells. In humans, each cell contains 23 pairs of chromosomes. Of these 23 pairs,

22 pairs (44 chromosomes) are non-sex chromosomes, also known as autosomes and a single pair makes up the sex chromosome. A cell that contains two complete sets of chromosomes is called a **diploid cell**, and that which contains only one set is called a **haploid cell**. Only egg and sperm cells contain one set, whereas all the other cells of the body contain two sets. Chromosomes that determine the sex of an individual are known as sex chromosomes.

A single human sex chromosome is labeled either **X or Y**, and these chromosomes pair up as either **XX** or **XY**. An **XX** designation signifies that the person will be a female, while an **XY** pair will be a male. This is determined by which sperm cell wins the prize! Chromosomes come in pairs and **there is no third** sex chromosome **Z** - nor any other letter of the alphabet plus mathematical signs that can form a transgender+ pair. That's the difference between being a **hap** or a **dip - loid**.

I have recently learned that Facebook now recognizes 53 different transgender classifications, whether they be pronouns, nouns, adverbs or adjectives. Hell, maybe even a few verbs, prepositions and conjunctions too. Sure aren't no 53 pronouns in the English vocabulary! There is one pronoun for them all, except male and female: **IT**! Remember cousin **IT** on the Adams Family? Couldn't see any legs. **IT** was all hair with a hat and a pair of sunglasses occasionally smoking a cigar. I have just one question. How in the hell can one get 53 different genders when there are only 46 chromosomes in the human species? **And**, they are paired up in 23 pairs with only **one** being a haploid. When **two haploid cells** come together in the unity of love, the parents are **hap**py with the outcome whether son or daughter. Mr. **Loid** was happy with all of his daughters that were the outcome of all those XX combination **haploids.**

Another thing about chromosomes. Humans have one chromosome that is fused, which has been a mystery. Why? Human chromosome number 2 is a fused chromosome. How it got that way is unknown to science. They don't look in Genesis! Most think and some claim that it is proof man evolved from apes. **How foolish!** Think it may have something to do with the creation of one sex then the making of the other?

[The above addition is the text portion of "What Is One's Sex? - Biology or Psychology" a blog on my website.]

https://theezekiel33watchman.report/

Chapter V
A Myth Found and the Reality Lost

It was suggested in chapters II and III that there might be a Biblical explanation for the mythical Lost City of Atlantis. Plato wrote the oldest and fullest account of the rise and fall of the great island city – continent. He beautifully described its layout and compared the city's gardens to that of Eden's. [Plato must have known about the book of Genesis.] The golden laden temples with its brilliant and illuminate copper finished walls, precious stones, and marbled floors would have been a beautiful sight to behold. He wrote of many kings and princes that ruled throughout the glorious era of Atlantis.

Their first king was to have been Atlas, son of Poseidon (Greek god of the sea). The illustration of the temple in the Time Life Book, Mystic Places, shows a chariot with Poseidon holding his three-pronged trident in his left hand and the reins of six horses with wings in his right. All were to have been made of pure gold.

The people of Atlantis and their surrounding neighbors, the ancient Athenians to the east, and the legendary Mayans to the west, were a peaceful people sharing a world of peace and prosperity. It was the Utopia that man dreams of today. The Atlanteans were supposedly the more technologically advanced, but the Athenians and Mayans were also culturally and technologically endowed. The three superpowers shared in much of their knowledge. [Does this sound like China, Russia, and the United States?]

The Atlanteans were thought to have had flying machines, and a mysterious energy source made from a glowing rock. On April 12, 1939 Edgar Cayce, known as the sleeping prophet, reportedly went into a trance like state. While in one, he is recorded to have said, *"In Atlantis, when there was the breaking up of the land, came to what was called the Mayan land or what is now Yucatan – entity was the first to cross the water in the plane or air machine of that period."* The aircraft and nuclear technology we have today sounds very much like that era, except there is no peace on earth and the sharing of technology is usually through bribery or theft.

Plato also describes how the Atlanteans became *puffed-up* in the pride of their wealth and prosperity. They had become greedy and lusted after more power, wealth, and pleasure in various vices. They became arrogant, and then began oppressing and enslaving their neighbors. They went to war with the Athenians in conquest of more wealth and dominance. They also attacked the Mayans and became their oppressors. There was basically world war on the planet, then one day Zeus, who was the king of the gods delivered a blow of his own. A great earthquake caused the entire continent of Atlantis and all its inhabitants to be swallowed up by the sea.

The ancient Mayan legends also state that their civilization and The Land of Mu disappeared into the bowels of the earth. Zeus was only to have spared the Athenians, who were supposedly his favorite people. Since Plato was a Greek from Athens, and Zeus was the King of the Gods in Greek mythology, it is clearly obvious why he selected the Athenians as the only survivors on the earth. (Source: Time Life Book – Mystic Places)

If we were to take out all the Greek mythological bias of the story, could there be a Biblical version told? There is a story in the Bible that could be a mirror image of this greatest of myths, but the outcome is not quite the same. We now know there are billions of years of time between Genesis 1:1 and 1:2. The creation week beginning at Gen. 1:3 is a recreation of the earth that was completely and totally destroyed. Could the story of The Lost City of Atlantis be a part of the missing time in creation between Gen. 1:1 and 1:2 and the missing link in *evolution by intelligent design*?

Most professing Christians today claim The Holy Bible as being **The Book of Truth**. That is absolutely and positively true, and more so than most people think. We will not have to change the name of the guilty party in order to tell the Atlantis story from a Biblical perspective. God did that! Scripture will not be quoted throughout the story. For a close approximation of the time sequence of events, read the following scriptures: John 1:1-5; Heb. 1:3-5; Col. 1:15-17; Gen. 1:1; Job 38:6-7,31-33,37-38; Ezek. 28:12-19; Rev. 12:7-9; Ezek. 26:19-21; Is. 14:12-17; Luke 10:18; Jude 6; Gen. 1:2; Is. 45:18.

Since no man really knows God's Holy Name, my Lord has given me permission to substitute different English names for the Godhead (Logos and Theos) in the spirit of humor. God does have a unique since of humor, although some people might not think so. God is not boring! I dedicate this story to Larry the Cable Guy, and the rest of the *Blue-Collar Tour* gang. I hope they get a chance to read it. [Larry, ease up on them thar little Pigmies. They never got to the fifth grade, can't read signs, and never tasted tatter salad.]

So, gather around the camp fire, kick off your shoes, fire one up, pop a top if you choose, for I'm about to tell you a little story about how man once was, then suddenly man was not, yet man now is, but not from the man that once was.

The Story of the Billy Creators Inc.

In the beginning was Billy Joe, and Billy Joe was with Billy Bob, and Billy Joe was a Billy. Now Billy Bob was the daddy, and Billy Joe was the son, and they were liv'in together in the Big House called **Atomonos Nucolos**. They lived in the Big House with all the other little billies Billy Bob and Billy Joe made to help out with Billy Bob's and Billy Joe's **Grand Plan of the Universe**. Billy Joe was in complete agreement with the plan, and even volunteered to step up to the plate in the event anything went wrong. All the other little billies liked and agreed with the plan. There was one special itty-bitty little billie that became the smartest, prettiest, and brightest of all them thar other little billies. Billy Bob and Billy Joe called him Lucifer Luke because he was a *bright and morning star*.

Now, Billy Joe would have liked to have had first crack at the Grand Plan, but Billy Bob had to test Lucifer Luke's loyalty to the family business because he was elevated to number three in the family chain of command. Billy Bob was a real smart and wise daddy, and he wanted to teach his only begotten first-born and all the other little billies about that thing called *freedom of choice*, along with patience, humility, and submission. Billy Bob desired to let Billy Joe take over the family business someday, and they had a Plan B just in case Lucifer Luke screwed up Plan A. The first part of the plan was to do some real serious landscaping all around the Big House. Noth'in was in it. It was a big old empty dark abyss full of noth'in.

Now, Billy Bob and Billy Joe were in total agreement about the family business. Lucifer Luke was too, and real sure of himself. All them thar other little billies were ready to be set free and do some serious galactic landscaping in that big old dark empty abyss.

Now, Lucifer Luke stayed outside and was a running in circles around the Big House, because he was a guarding and protecting **Atomonos Nucolos** from all them thar spooks in the darkness of the great abyss. There was really noth'in out there. Old Lucifer Luke had a wee bit of what some like to call *a dark imagination*. He also had a big old firecracker attached to his necklace, and he was always a bit curious about what that dadburn thing was for.

Billy Joe yelled out to Lucifer Luke, "Put that firecracker in the hatch hole and fire her up!" So, Lucifer Luke put the firecracker in the hatch hole, snapped his finger, because he had a bic lighter for one of his fingers, then lite that big ole firecracker and ran around back of the Big House yelling, "Yawl stand clear, she's about to blow!"

Billy Bob and Billy Joe were kicked back on the Big Couch on the top floor of the Big House, and all them thar other little billies were lined up like the Carolina Panther's defensive line ready for a quarterback sack attack, then **KABANG!!!!!!!!!!!!**

That hatch was blown to smithereens. Then, all them thar little billies came a rushing out, and they were a hollering and a singing for joy. I tell you what, that was the happiest bunch of little billies I ever did see, and you know what they was a singing? They were a singing, **"Free at last, free at last, thank Billy Almighty, free at last."**

Now, there was noth'in in that big old dark abyss, *yeah, absolutely noth'in,* and you know why? That's all *it was good for, absolutely noth'in.* Billy Bob and Billy Joe knew that because that was what the big plan was all about. They wanted to let all them thar little billies go free in that big old dark abyss to distribute that stuff called matter, and plant their little billie star candles to shine their little billie bright lights so that *some... day... over the rainbow...* a whole bunch of organic little man billies can say: *Look at that big beautiful heaven Billy Bob and Billy Joe made for us.*

When all the excitement was over and all them thar little billies had finished planting their little star candles in space, they rode their little star horses back to the Big House and gathered in front of the Big Couch for a big meeting with their daddy. Then Lucifer Luke approached Billy Bob to get his work assignment.

Billy Bob said, "Lucifer Luke, I want you to take a third of them thar little billies with all this biology and science knowledge I'm a giv'in you and get on down to that star of yours. I want you to start bringing about some organic life on that third dust ball from your star. Now, when you get some little man critters looking a bit like us, you yourself become like them for a spell, and tell them about me and Billy Joe. Tell them little man critters that they can become billies too, and tell them about eternal life and the Great Universal Plan. Tell them that the Billy Boys made everything that they are made of, and then you can have credit for putting them together and be their king, that is if you are willing to give yourself for them. Be sure to remember that on the seventh galactic day of the galactic week to take a rest from all your work, and come on up here, and we'll watch the football game. I got all them thar other little billies divided up into little billie teams, and they'll be playing a schedule the remainder of the week so that they can praise me with the big game on the Sabbath Day."

Now, Lucifer Luke was real excited about this job of his, and he went to work right away. He had a third of all them thar little billies with all kinds of skills to work for him while he was a thinking about doing that intelligent selectivity nature thing with all his know how, but he wasn't quite sure about that little man critter thing.

Anyhow, this was about the middle of the second galactic day, because the first one was a special jubilee holiday that they spent a shouting for joy and a singing praises to the Billy boys. It was their birthday party called First Fruits, and I tell you what, it was a **Big Bang** of a party. Anyway, it took about half a galactic day to get all their assignments, and instructions, and commandments to work by. Billy Bob also explained what it meant to PACE one's self with the prime responsibility of those things we call *the freedom of press, association, choice, and expression.*

Now, a galactic day on Billy Bob's watch was like a billion years of time to us, and Lucifer Luke had only 4.5 galactic days until the big game. Lucifer Luke worked real hard evolving all kinds of critters using his gamma powers to write and rewrite DNA instructions. Then there was one morning he ended up with a bunch of big old dinosaurs and saw that wasn't gonna work out gett'in that thar little man critter thing a going. So, he grabbed one of them thar big old asteroids from the asteroid belt, and then sent it a sailing into the earth. It killed off all them thar big old dinosaurs, and you know what? That's what them thar scientist fellers call *total extinction*. There was a couple of other times too that he had to back up, rethink his science, and start over again. That's what them thar scientist fellers like to call *near extinction*. Anyhow, when he finally got them thar ape critters a going, he knew he was a gett'in real close to that thar little man critter thing Billy Bob and Billy Joe was a talking about.

About two thirds of the way through the sixth galactic day, Lucifer Luke had got some of them thar ape critters a standing up, walking on two feet, and later – learning all kinds of things, and you know what? They even learned how to make fire without a match or any kind of a lighter. All they had to do was grab hold of a rock and beat the fire right out of another rock. It's true! Them thar scientist fellers said so. And if it ain't true, neither is this story. And you know what that would make it and them thar scientist fellers'? *Tall tale tellers!*

A little later, Lucifer Luke had them thar man critters a walking, and a talking, and a looking a whole bit like me and you, and a whole lot of smarts too. Then he got the best of them divided up into three groups. One group was the Mayans who lived on the west continent, and the Athenians lived on the east continent. The third group he called Atlanteans, and they lived on the middle continent called Atlantis, and he liked them the best. They had a big beautiful city by the same name, and they had flying machines and everything.

Now, them thar little man critters only lived a short time like you and me. In galactic time their life span was quicker than the blink of an eye, and that made Old Lucifer Luke upset. He wanted them thar little man critters to live a long time like him and his little billie brothers. So, he went to ask Billy Bob how he could do that because that was the only thing that he couldn't do. He couldn't make them immortal and get them thar little man critters to become little man billies. You see, Old Lucifer Luke had done and forgot what his daddy told him from the very get-go about that thar little man critter thing and how he could get them to become little man billies.

So Old Lucifer Luke got into his big old golden horse buggy pulled by six big old horses, and you know what? Them thar horses had wings, and they could fly! He also had a big old three-pronged pitchfork he always carried in his left hand, and you know what? Today, he still uses that dad-burn thing to poke Billy Joe's little man critters around and trying to make them mean and evil like him, but Billy Joe gon'na bust his butt for good one day real soon. Anyhow, the late afternoon of the sixth galactic day he asked his daddy how he could give his little man critters immortal life. Then Billy Bob told him, "Son, first you got to tell them about me, that I'm really their daddy. Didn't me and Billy Joe create all the stuff you made them from, and give you all the know how to make and elevate them?"

Then Old Luke said, "But daddy, I made them, let me have more power, so I can make them immortal, then – then – then, I promise I will tell them the truth about you and Billy Joe."

Then Billy Bob said, "Not so son! I gave you everything to make them; therefore, they are mine. You knew that from the get-go. First, you must become like them! Then tell them about me and Billy Joe, and to give us the glory for their being, and then die their death. After that, I will raise you and them up. Then, you can be Lord over them, and build more worlds for Billy Joe. Now go, do this quickly because the Sabbath will be here soon. Don't worry, all things are under my control. Don't forget the big game. Looks like it might be the Aquila Eagles vs. the Delphinus Dolphins. Go on now, honor your father!"

Now, Lucifer Luke was a bit angry about all that, so he turned his back on Billy Bob and Billy Joe, and then went on back to that third rock from the sun. He was a gripping and a grumbling the whole way. There were only a few hours of galactic time left before the Sabbath, but there was plenty of earth time for Old Luke to do what he needed to do. Old Luke was a gett'in angrier by the microsecond, and the more he thought about what he had to do, the angrier he got. He became so jealous, that all he wanted was that power all for himself, but he didn't want to give himself for his little man critters.

All the time that he was boiling in anger, jealousy, and lust for that power, all them thar little man critters were picking up on that same kind of thoughts. You see, Old Luke had radio wave power, and all his thoughts were being received by them thar little man critters. Then, they began to a gett'in the same kind of thoughts, and they began a lust'in for more power. They started a lie'in, and a cheat'in, and a steal'in, and a kill'in, and all other kinds of evil and wicked things. Everything that Old Lucifer Luke was a thinking about, them thar little man critters got to thinking and doing the very same thing.

Old Luke got all his little billie brothers together and began to plot against their daddy. He conned them into thinking that they could go up to the Big House, knock Billy Bob and Billy Joe off their Big Couch, and search under the cushions to find that power he coveted. Yeah, he got evil headed about the whole thing and told his little billie brothers, "I'm not gonna become like these dirty little man critters that I evolved from pooh!

I'm gon'na get that thar power for myself! Me, as beautiful as I am, set all my beauty aside, even for a little bit, just to offer them immortality and to be like me! Daddy's crazy if he thinks I'm gon'na do that! He can take his Sabbath, and his big game, and he can shove it! When that big game starts, we'll charge right on up there when they ain't thinking we're a com'in, and we'll take over the Big House, then **I will sit on the Big Couch!**"

Now, Old Lucifer Luke had done and lost it now. What he forgot was that Billy Bob and Billy Joe could see and hear everything in the whole universe, and that they had x-ray vision, and Billy Bob could see right through his wicked old heart. Billy Bob and Billy Joe didn't make Old Luke that way. He got that way by his own choosing. You see, he tripped and got out of PACE with the prime directive.

Billy Bob asked Billy Joe, "Do you see all the pride, selfishness, jealousy, lust, and greed in Old Luke's heart?"

Billy Joe replied, "Yes Father. You know that I would have become like them thar little man critters and done as you asked."

Billy Bob said, "Yes, I know son. We discussed that possible situation from the very get-go. Next time around, you know that you might have to do that very thing. We got to ready ourselves now, for that evil old **DOG** thinks he's gon'na come up here and knock us off our throne and be the **GOD**, but he's just a fool'in himself."

Now, Billy Bob and Billy Joe knew what was about to go down, so they canceled the big game, and you know what? That game hasn't been played to this very day, but it was rescheduled, and it will be played. Billy Joe got Big Mike the Archbillie to muster up all them thar other little billies. Half stood by the gate of the Big House by Billy Joe, and the other was Big Mike's army, but they got behind the big house. You see, Billy Bob is a fair daddy, and he wanted the odds to be even. Billy Bob just sat on the Big Couch and waited.

Then, Old Lucifer Luke and all his little billies went a charg'in toward the Big House. Then, Big Mike came from around back with his army of little billies. They began to butt heads, rip and rare, knocking each other down, and just a hurting each other real bad. You know, some of them thar little billies even broke their little horns, and that's what them thar scientist fellers like to call *dwarf billies*. I tell you what, that show down was a whole lot worser than the Hatfield's and McCoy's. It was tee-total Galactic War.

When all the ruckus was over, Big Mike went up to the gate of the Big House and told Billy Joe that Old Lucifer Luke and all his rebellious little billies had had the shine whipped right out of them, and are now called *dark stars*. Billy Joe went inside and asked his daddy what to do. Billy Bob said, "Son, I'll handle this one myself!"

So, Billy Bob went out in the front yard where Old Lucifer Luke was and looked around at all the chaos that the S.O.B. (Son of Billy) had just caused, and with a little tear in his eye, he just shook his head in disappointment. It must have broken Billy Bob's big old heart to see his beautiful little billie get that way. Now, all the good little billies stood way back. Billy Joe stood in the gate of the Big House just a watching to see what his daddy would do next.

Billy Bob grabbed Old Lucifer Luke by the head with both his big old hands, looked Old Lucifer Luke right in the eye, and sang him a song, and it went a little something like this: Y*ou SOB, I'm number one from beginning to the end – you've messed up my universe by bringing in that thing called sin – now don't you think I understand this little critter that's called man – for it was my will from the very start of the Great Universal Plan. – Now I'm changing your name you old dragon and Satan it shall be – I'll cast your rebellious butt back to the earth and cover you with the sea.* [Remember the Charlie Daniels tune and fiddle playing? Sing it again!]

Now when Billy Bob finished singing his song, he swung that old dragon around and around and around. All that swinging around made his tail real long, and it scooped up all them thar rebellious little demon billies right up off the front yard of the Big House. Then when Billy Bob let him go, it cast Satan's evil butt along with all them thar little demon billies right back to the earth.

Now, all that evil thinking that them thar little man critters tuned in to had caused them to kill each other off by global war'in – right down to the last one. He was so lonely and soar that, well, he just conceded to the supreme consequence of the inconvenient truth. All that evil thinking of Satan got into their brains. They just went totally nuts, and you know what? Lucifer Luke never did let his poor little man critters ever know who their real daddy was. When that old dragon crashed into the earth, it came to a tee-total ruin. It wasn't worth a hill of beans. Noth'in was left alive. *Absolutely noth'in!*

Now, all them thar good little billies in heaven were real sad about all the ruin and chaos that Satan had caused. They were all a crying and broken hearted about the whole thing, then Billy Bob said, "Cheer up little billies! I have a backup plan!" So, they began to wipe their little billie tears from their little billie eyes, and later, a little billie smile began to glow up on their little billie faces. They were all just a standing around to see what would happen next.

Then Billy Bob headed for the Big House and called out to Billy Joe, "Go fetch the Book marked Plan B." Then, Billy Bob and Billy Joe kicked back on the Big Couch, and all the other good little billies rested and slept for the remainder of that first galactic Sabbath day.

[To be continued!]

Most everybody left before the story was finished, but there were four good old fellers still left. They were blue-collar types like myself that liked sitting around a campfire while having an ice cold one, and just telling stories about life and all kinds of things. The chubby feller in a sleeveless red flannel shirt asked, "What was Plan B?"

Then the red headed feller spoke up and said, "I bet Plan B is the Bible, and everything that's in it."

Then the slim feller asked the red headed feller, "How do you know that? What was the sign?"

Then the feller holding a glass of bourbon spoke up, and said, "Cause he's soooooo much smarter than a fifth grader, and he can actually count to seven."

Then I said, "Plan B is the Bible, and to pick up where the story left off, just start at Genesis 1:3. Seven is your sign."

Then the feller in the red flannel shirt stood up, through his shoulders back, and with a great big smile said, **"GET-R-DONE!"**

I had absolutely no idea how to tell the Atlantis Story from a Biblical perspective. I worked on the other chapters and didn't even know the chapter arrangement at the time. I asked the Lord for some help because I just didn't know how to explain what I've come to understand. One morning I got up laughing and just started typing away. I must thank the Lord because there is no way that I could have conceived and wrote that story out of my own imagination.

Plan B is the Bible beginning at Genesis 1:3. The condition of the earth stated in the 2nd verse is the condition it ***became (come to pass into)*** because of Lucifer's rebellion. Absolutely nothing survived! What Lucifer brought into existence in 4.5 billion years came to a total ruin by his rebellion. God remade the heavens and the earth, then created new life on it in six rotations (days) of our planet earth. That is the testimony of the Almighty God's majestic power.

It doesn't make any difference what you may think about this Atlantis story, but it does explain the missing links in evolution's theory and the missing time in Genesis' creation. Man's tendency is to see some physical evidence of reality and has little or no desire to accept things on faith alone. Of all the things that man can see on this planet, there are three just as mysterious as the myth of Atlantis.

The Great Pyramids of Giza

The Great Pyramids of Giza are probably the most mysterious structures on the face of our planet. Men have beheld them from afar and traveled to them in hope of finding some long-lost truth that may have been hidden inside and/or incorporated within their geometric design and dimensions. Will a day come when the knowledge and wisdom within their design come to man's understanding?

They have been explored for centuries. Many have contemplated their significance wondering who the architect was and the methods utilized in their construction. There have never been any absolute answers to the many questions that ever meet a unified satisfaction of the thousands of curious minds that have beheld them. The best of theories have been dismissed by many considered to be professionals, yet they themselves will admit to knowing little or nothing.

They were built during what is commonly called the Fourth Dynasty. Beginning with the largest, they are believed to have been constructed between 2613 and 2494 BC. (Time-Life's Mystic Places – Mysteries of the Unknown) The largest of the three was supposed to have been for the tomb of Khufu (The Great Pharaoh of Egypt), the second largest for Khafre (Khufu's brother), and the smallest for Menkure (Khafre's son).

Egypt's history of pyramid building began after the sun cult emerged as the official religion. Many collapsed and successful ones were too small to attract much attention. The Giza group would have required a great Architect with an immense knowledge in geometrical design, mathematics, physics, and astronomy. One of his friends said, *"Remember that thou magnify (to grow, enlarge) his (God's) work (an act, work, or deed done systematically), which men behold (through the idea of strolling, turning, traveling). Every man may see it (to gaze, mentally perceive, contemplate, have a vision of prophecy); man may behold it (to look intently) afar off (to remotely widen in any direction of place or time)."* (Job 36:24-25)

Many have traveled to study them or *gazed upon them from afar* with amazement and *prophetic curiosity throughout the ages*. Today, we have the centuries old greatest mystery: Who built them and why? Many Mathematicians, Architects, and Engineers have explored a variety of possible methods employed in the building of the Great Pyramid. Some observers doubt that the three were built merely for the purpose of housing royal mummies. It is a fact that no mummies or great treasure have ever been found in them. Many mathematicians have long believed that the Great Pyramid's Architect possessed a geometrical wisdom that became lost to the world. Could Job have been the great Architect? We found **The Big Bang** in Job 38:6-7, and **earth as a cosmic ball of dust** in Job 38:37-38. The entire Book of Job has an architectural overtone to it. Could this *systematical great work* have been the work of God through Job?

The historical record of curiosity began with Herodotus, famous fifth century BC Greek historian who was the first to visit, gather, and record information about them. The methods of their construction he recorded were mainly based on his conversations with the local Egyptians. He never did find the entrances to see their interiors.

During the ninth century AD, the Arab caliph Abdullah Al Mamun, whose interest in astronomy drove his desire of mapping the earth and charting the heavens, sought to find the entrance to the largest. Being unsuccessful, he had his fellow explorers bore through solid rock by heating the limestone blocks with fire, then dousing them with vinegar until they cracked. They found a small passage after 100 feet of boring, then the entrance 49 feet [7 x 7 or 7^2] above the base. Other passages were blocked with large granite stones, so they bored around them. They found the burial chamber empty of treasure, and the huge granite sarcophagus was also empty. In disappointment, the laborers destroyed the floor and walls hoping to find some treasure. Who knows what knowledge was lost from any inscriptions that may have been written on the walls? If earlier robbers had already raided them, how did they get around the granite barricades? Why were the burial chambers blocked off and sealed without their intended mummified corpses?

Eight hundred years passed before British mathematician John Greaves visited Egypt in 1638. His interest was in finding the unit of measurement employed by its builders. Most of the data he presented proved to be incorrect by those that followed. In 1798, Napoleon Bonaparte conquered Egypt. After the Battle of the Pyramids, the French scientist, Edme-Francois Jomard, and a work force of 150 Turks cleared tons of sand and debris from the northwest and northeast base. He noted the depressions in the base rock where the original corner stones had rested but were carried off centuries earlier. His base measurement of 757.5 feet has proved to be the most accurate. He also measured the blocks and calculated the height at 481 feet, but the capstone had long been removed. He calculated the slope's pitch angle at 51 degrees and 19 minutes. The famous Rosetta Stone, which was the key to interpreting Egyptian hieroglyphics, was also discovered. This began an explosion of European and American interest in Egyptian things during the nineteenth century.

John Taylor, a mathematician and theologian, never visited the Great Pyramid himself, but built a scaled model from acquired data to aid in his studies. He discovered that the perimeter divided by twice its height was nearly equal to pi (3.14159+). In 1859, he authored the book, The Great Pyramid: Why was it built? And who built it? He suggested that *divine intelligence* was at work in its design.

Charles Smyth, an astronomer from Scotland, became interested in Taylor's work. In 1844, he left for Egypt with trunks of up-to-date instruments. The pyramid's perfect north-south alignment, interior passages' pitch angle of 26°, and its intersection at 30° North and 31° East have greatly astonished astronomers for centuries. He devised his basic unit of measurement called the *pyramid inch*, which was 1/25th of a cubit and within 1/1000th of a British inch. He concluded that his 365,200-pyramid inch base perimeter divided by 1000 was equal to 365.2, the number of days in the year. He authored the book, Our Inheritance in the Great Pyramid. He concluded, as Taylor had done before him, that only God could have been the author of its design. [Job was a saintly servant. (Job 1:1; Ezek. 14:14)]

Neither Smyth nor Taylor had offered any evidence of the great pyramid being mentioned in the Bible, but both agreed that in times past God had imparted wisdom and metrical instructions for building to a chosen few for some special or unknown purpose, just as Noah was given instructions for the Ark. Smyth and his followers viewed the pyramid as immutable evidence of a divinity who created the earth in 4004 BC as computed by James Usher, a seventeenth century Irish churchman. Both had suggested that the year of Christ's second coming be hidden somewhere within its geometric dimensions.

In 1877, American churchman Joseph Seiss wrote, "Its stones harbored one great system of interrelated numbers, measures, weights, angles, temperatures, degrees, geometric problems, and cosmic references." Pyramids have five sides (including the base) and five corners (including its pinnacle). Seiss became intrigued with its unique *fiveness*: five corners, five sides, and a pyramid inch as 1/5th of 1/5th of a cubit. He asked, "Was it only coincidental that we have five senses, five fingers, five toes, and that there are five Books of Moses?" [Five is also considered the biblical number for grace.]

In 1880, William Petrie set out for Egypt after reading the works of Taylor and Smyth and confirmed most of their work. He came up with a different base perimeter dimension that refuted Smyth's pyramid inch. Later, British engineer David Davidson discovered that Petrie didn't extend his computations to the outer casing, thus reconfirming Smyth's measurements. In 1924 Davidson published a book that concluded the Pyramid was *truth in structural form.*

In 1925, the Egyptian government completed its own survey of the Great Pyramid and published their official data: south side – 756.1 ft, east side – 755.9 ft, west side – 755.8 ft, north side – 755.4 ft, and height – 481 ft. The angle of the slopes was measured at 51 degrees and 52 minutes. Their side dimensions were within 8 inches of each other. The Lord is a designer of perfection; therefore, the sides would have been equal when originally built. (Ex. 27:1, 28:16, 37:25, 38:1; Ezek. 40:47, 43:16, 48:20; Rev. 21:16)

The variations in the measurements can be attributed to the effects of wind erosion. North winds are usually the strongest, with the eastward and westward much less abrasive. The southern side would have received the least severe winds, hence the variations in the dimensions of the four sides. Is there a practical mathematical method to compensate for the erosion?

With today's computer technology and sophisticated measuring devises, you would think that if the year of Christ's return or the year pointing to His return was hidden somewhere within its dimensions, that theologians and mathematicians would have figured it out by now. It is said that the Lord himself doesn't know the day or hour, but I don't think that is the case. The two are one in mind and character. He did say, *"Now, learn a parable of the fig tree".* (Matt. 24:32-36) Since there are four seasons in a year, the season and maybe the year or years, since winter splits the years, could be known, especially with an understanding of the timeline prophecies in the Book of Daniel. The seasons of the year average 90 days, or 2,160 hours. Could we possibly find at least the year(s)?

Taking into consideration the erosion of the original dimensions, let's try to reconstruct the Great Pyramid utilizing our prophesied increased knowledge with Biblical assistance. The Biblical standard of measurement is the cubit, which is 1.5 feet or 18 inches. Since Noah built the Ark in cubits, Job would have also used the same system of measurement. God is consistent in his ways.

The total of the variations in the four sides minus 755 feet for each side is 3.2 feet. [1.1 + .9 + .8 + .4 = 3.2] Since there are three sides more heavily eroded, let's take the 3.2-foot total and divide it by three to get a 1.0667-foot average erosion factor. When added to the least eroded south side dimension we get a 757.1667-foot dimension for each side. [756.1 ft +1.0667 ft = 757.1667 ft] Now, convert that to cubits. [757.1667 ft ÷ 1.5 ft/cu = 504.7778 cu] When we use this corrected dimension and multiply it by the four sides, we get 2019 cubits when rounded off. [504.7778 cu × 4 = 2019.1112 cu]

The design would more likely have been an even number of cubits, so round off the 504.7778 to 505 cubits, which would be in line with the *fiveness* thought. It would also be the same as Jomard's 1798 measurement. [757.5 ft ÷ 1.5 ft/cu = 505 cu] [Very interesting! Remember Laugh-in?] Multiplying the 505-cubit dimension by 4 we get 2020 cubits. [505 cu × 4 = 2020 cu] If we substitute **year** for **cubit**, could Christ's return to reign on earth be in the year 2019 or 2020? Could these years even point to the year of his coming? If these are the years, what calendar should we use?

The Egyptian calendar is no longer used. The Jewish civil and scared calendar is used only by the Jews and very few Christians. Our present-day Gregorian calendar is a corrected version of the Julian calendar, which was based on 365.25 days to the solar year, and every fourth year an extra day was added to the month of February, just as we do today. In the year 1582 AD the Julian Calendar was reformed by Pope Gregory XIII after astronomers realized that the solar year was 12 minutes and 14 seconds shorter (365.2415) than 365.25 days. The Julian Calendar had advanced ten days from 45 BC to 1582 AD. The British countries rejected that until 1752. When they finally realized the error, they had to drop 11 days to correct their calendars. The sequence of days remained, only the numbered day was advanced. Ex: Tuesday was October 11 and Wednesday was October 22.

Due to erosion of the exterior blocks, the pyramid's pitch angle measurement of 51 degrees and 52 minutes (51.8667°) would also need to be corrected. There are 60 minutes to a degree in nautical plotting and surveying. There is an 8-minute shortage to a full degree in the measured pitch angle. Utilizing the erosion factor 1.0667 and dividing it by the 8 short minutes of a degree, we get a .1333 erosion factor for the transit's pitch angle measurement. When added to the angle measurement, we get an even 52 degrees. (51.8667 +.1333 = 52) [It is the number of weeks in a year.]

An erosion factor of .1333 degrees would have reduced the overall height by .1333 cubits or .19995 feet (.1333 degrees × 1 cubit/degree = .1333 cubits × 1.5 foot/cubit = .19995 feet), which is not all that much considering 4,500 years of erosion and all the picking and prodding over the recent centuries. An even angle of 52° would also render a simpler trigonometric right angle when laying it out on a scaled drawing. [The upper portion was exposed to the elements more that the lower portions that remained buried and protected by sand until its removal beginning in the 18th century.] Utilizing 52° as the pitch angle and 252.5 cubits (half of the 505-cubit base dimension) to form a right-angle triangle, the height calculates to 323 cubits or 484.5 feet. The hypotenuse of the right angle, which is the slope's linear dimension, calculates to 410 cubits. [Basic Trigonometry]

With much searching in the Bible, I found that the number 15 has great significance. The 15th day of the first month is the first annual Sabbath following the Lord's Passover. The 15th day of the seventh month is the Feast of Tabernacles, which is symbolic to Christ's return and reign on earth. The 15th year of Tiberius Caesar's reign was the year Christ began his earthly ministry. (Lev. 23, Luke 3) **The hangings** in the Court of the Tabernacle were 15 cubits (Ex. 27:14-15, 38:14-15). The *hangings* from the pinnacle of a pyramid are its four slopes. There are three sides to a triangle and five corners to a pyramid, and three Giza pyramids with five corners each. (3 x 5 = 15) If we take the 410-cubit slope dimension and multiply it by 15, we get 6150 cubits. Subtracting 2019 or 2020 from 6150 we get 4131 or 4130 cubits respectively. According to the Bible, the foundation of mankind is the creation of Adam and Eve. The **foundation** for salvation is our creator who **hung** on a pole and is the **Chief Corner stone.** (Is. 28:16-18; 1Pet. 2:6) The *foundation* of a pyramid *hangs* by the slopes from its pinnacle, which is its *chief cornerstone*.

Was Adam and Eve created in the year 4131 or 4130 BC? From those dates to the present (2008) are 6139 or 6138 years. How did the early church historians calculate the creation as having taken place in 4004 BC? I honestly do not know, but the number of years from the creation of Adam to the present time can be accurately counted from the Bible and verified by dependable historical records that are acknowledged by many historians. The following list is from the Bible:

(1) Adam to Noah/flood – 1656 years (Gen. 5:3 thru 7:22)
(2) Noah/flood to Abraham – 292 years (Gen. 11:10-26)
(3) Abraham to Isaac – 100 years (Gen. 21:5)
(4) Isaac to Jacob – 60 years (Gen. 25:26)
(5) Jacob to his death in Egypt – 147 years (Gen. 47:28)
(6) Jacob's death to the Exodus – 430 years (Ex. 12:40)
(7) Exodus to the first temple – 480 years (1 Kings 6:1-38)

[1 thru 7 totals 3165 years. See Appendix II for more detail.]

From dependable historical records, King Solomon reigned from 970-930 BC and began building the first temple in his fourth year or 966 BC. (1 Kings 6:1) King Nebuchadnezzar destroyed it in 587 BC (2 Kings 25:8-9). During the reign of King Darius I (521-486 BC), the second temple was built in 515 BC. (Ezra 6:15) It was destroyed by Rome in 70 AD. Adding the 3165 years from 1-7 above to 966 BC when Solomon started the first Temple, we get 4131 total years BC, or the date of Adam's creation – 4131 BC. Adding 4131 BC years to our present 2008, we get a total of 6139 years. When 2019 AD is added to 4131 BC, we get 6150 years, or the same 6150 cubits from our corrected pyramid dimensions. **Very interesting,** Arte Johnson routinely said. (See Appendix II)

The last Giza pyramid built was the smallest one with a completion date of 2494 BC. (Mystic Places) The great flood in 2475 BC would have been 19 years after that date of completion. Nineteen years is the time cycle in which the sacred calendar (lunar type) is corrected seven times to keep it correct to the solar year's spring equinox.

Although unlikely, some claim the Great Pyramid was built in about 20 years. Job lived 140 years after the Lord restored him. He would have died just prior to the flood in 2475 BC, but his three daughters would have been about the same age as Noah's three sons. (Job 42:13-17; Gen. 5:32, 7:6-7) The **work** that Job **magnified** was the Great Pyramid and finished prior to, or during the late stages of its construction, to his run-in with Satan. [2475 BC + 140 yrs = 2615 BC] The work would have been finished by 2615 BC, and various sources place the work from 2700 to 2600 BC. [Pre-flood biblical people lived to be hundreds of years old.] Job's three daughters' names are unique and found nowhere else in scripture. When tracing the definitions for their names to the prime root words, I found them descriptive of the three general races within the human species: Caucasoid, Negroid, and Mongoloid. Although Anthropologists may or may not find that interesting, I surely do.

I have absolutely no idea how Smyth came up with his *pyramid inch*. If it is 1/25 of a cubit and within 1/1000 of a British inch, then how in the hell do you get 25 British inches in an 18-inch cubit? The astronomical aspects of the pyramid's design would play the critical role in keeping a correct calendar. But just for fun, there are 360° in a revolution (rotational and orbital). We could subtract 50 from the 52° of our corrected pitch angle and add *pi* to get the days in a solar year. [360 + (52 − 50) + 3.1415 = 365.1415] Why subtract 50? It's only the number for jubilee. (Lev. 25) It is also 5 pyramid corners times the 10 Commandments. But that leaves us .1 or 1/10th of a day short in the solar year. How can we fix that problem?

Well, since there are only two members in the Godhead (Father and Son) government of the universe and their tax rate is only a flat 10% (1/10th or .1 or tithe), let's just add .1, then, low and behold, we get 365.2415 solar days to the year. [Isn't the **US** (Unified Supremacy) in the **"...let US make man in our image and likeness..."** tax rate more reasonable than what is currently in the good ole **U.S.** of A. today (Federal, State, Sales, Property, Gas, FCC, phone service, electric service, water service, etc. − ∞)? We the people, especially the working class, are definitely overtaxed; however, I don't think that we all are equally represented by those who tax us!] We could drop the pitch angle part and just add 360 degrees to 2.1

(Godhead and tithe) and 3.1415 (pi) and get the same thing (365.2415). Piece of Pie!

There are several other interesting aspects about the layout of the three pyramids. The southwest corners of all three pyramids align to the bearing of northeast. In the scriptures, it is stated that God resides in the *sides of the north*, which would be northeast. (Is. 14:13) There are many references to north and east in the Bible.

The three different sizes of the pyramids offer some insight into scriptural truth. There are three ages of the earth: pre-Adam, present Adam, and post-Adam. Pre-Adam would be the smallest pyramid, representing Lucifer's handy work prior to his rebellion and present-Adam the middle size pyramid representing man today while under the influence of Satan. [Let's ticket this pyramid with a D.U.I. (Destruction under the Influence) and lock that old dragon up.] Post-Adam would be the largest, representing **The Kingdom of God**. Scripture tells us that Christ is *the first and the last* and *the first shall be last, and the last shall be first.* (Rev. 1:11, 22:13; Matt. 20:16; Luke 13:30) The largest to smallest is the north-to-south order in size. Lucifer's world was first, then ours, and soon God's Kingdom will be established on planet earth. Man's present world under the influence of Satan has exceeded Lucifer's first earth age, but The Kingdom of God will exceed anything man could ever possibly conceive. **[Think about that!]**

I'm neither a *Pyramidologist* nor any other kind of a __oglogist. I'm not a theologian either. The year 2019 or 2020 is only 10 years in the future, *"...and except those days (dimensions) should be shortened..."* (Matt. 24:22) The only way to verify the pyramid's geometric year of 2019 or 2020 is from the **timeline prophecies** in the Holy Bible.

Chapter VI
Timeline Prophecies of the Bible

One of the most fascinating subjects in the entire Bible is prophecy and its predictions of future events. When the Lord selected the children of Israel to be his representative nation on earth, he raised up many prophets to warn and redirect them. The children of Israel were a *stiff-necked* people who were constantly turning their backs on The Eternal, breaking his commandments, and polluting his Sabbaths. God's children aren't all that much different today, but a better English word would be *hard-headed*. People like to do things their own way in accordance with manmade traditions. The Lord God sent many prophets to the children of Israel to warn them of their sins, preach repentance, and to return to God's ways. Those prophets still speak, but through their written word that was preserved for centuries, forewarning of God's judgments for rejecting his ways today.

Many of the prophecies in the Holy Bible refer to the last or latter days. That is why they have been preserved throughout the ages. Most prophecy refers to the *House of Israel* or *House of Judah* separately, and some to the *House of Jacob*, which is both houses jointly. Some *House of Israel* prophecies can include both houses. Some prophecies pertain to other nations by name, the earth or worldly system, the *Land of Israel*, and the *City of Jerusalem*. Also hidden deep within prophecy are the missing links to earth's distant past.

There are seven **timeline prophecies** in the Old Testament having a preset amount of time with a beginning and ending point. The most crucial six were revealed to the prophet Daniel. History vindicates the first six, and the seventh will begin in the very near future:

(1) The seven times or 2520 years found in Lev. 26.
(2) The 3.5 times or 1260 years found in Dan 7:25.
(3) The 2300 days or years found in Dan 8:14.
(4) Seventy weeks – 490 days or years found in Dan. 9:24-27.
(5) The 3.5 times or 1260 years found in Dan. 12:7.

(6) The 1290 days or years found in Dan. 12:11.
(7) The 1335 days or years found in Dan. 12:12.

In the New Testament's book of Revelation, both the 3.5 times and 1260 day prophecies are the same timeline as in Dan. 7:25, but expanded in explanation and detail. Revelation 13 picks up where Daniel 7 left off with the fourth beast prophecy. Secular history validates these prophecies in The Scripture of Truth. (Dan. 10:21)

There are hundreds, even thousands of years outlined in only a few passages of scripture. It is like a fast forward of history with centuries happening in the blink of an eye. The Scriptures state that one day to God is as (about) a thousand years to man. (2 Peter 3:8) Time is infinite with God; therefore, prophecy in the Scripture of Truth can relate to the past, present, and/or the future. The future seventh timeline prophecy could not be calculated until the latter days when the previous six were fulfilled and historically understood.

The basic mathematics for understanding prophecy is found in Num. 14:34 and Ezek. 4:6. These two verses give us the **day to a year** principle. **(1 day = 1 year)** Some prophecies are given in days while others are given in *time* and *times* and *dividing of time*. A *time* is one cycle, *times* are two cycles, and the *dividing of time* is 1/2 cycle – totaling 3.5 times or cycles. A cycle is one complete revolution, as in the earth on its axis **(day)** and the earth around the sun **(year)**. This corresponds to the day to the year principle. Mathematically, one complete revolution is 360 degrees. The prophetically set period for one-time cycle is 360 days. [360° × 1 deg/day = 360 days] The 3.5 times is 1260 days and the year to a day principle makes it 1260 years. [360 × 3.5 = 1260]

The only timeline prophecy given in weeks is the seventy weeks prophecy. [70 weeks × 7 days\wk = 490 days or years] The timeline prophecies have a single fulfillment and verifications, but the seventy weeks has two. This is based on the two advents of Jesus Christ and the two weeks of years fulfilled by Jacob to his Uncle Laban for the hand of marriage to Rachel. After fulfilling the first seven years, his uncle tricked him by slipping Leah into his tent on the wedding night. The next morning, he agreed to fulfill another week and serve a second week of years, then straight away married Rachel. (Gen. 29:15-30) The first fulfillment was Christ's first advent. The second fulfillment verifies the seventh timeline in Dan. 12:12 and only points to Christ's return. The *two weeks of years* begins at the seventh timeline's conclusion, which begins the seven seal years of Revelation. [1 week = 7 days or 7 seal years]

The Seven Times Prophecy

This prophecy is found in Leviticus 26 and the *seven times* are mentioned four times. (Lev. 26:18, 21, 24, 28) There are seven churches, seals, trumpets, and plagues in Revelation. [Lev. 7777 to Rev. 7777] Leviticus 26 discusses the promise of blessings for the children of Israel if they keep the commandments of God and walk in his statutes. The Lord warned them of the withholding of blessings and the terror and sorrow they would experience if they would not keep all his commandments. The *seven times* is a period that the promise of blessings would be withheld as well as the intensity of judgments for their disobedience. The blessings and promises given to Abraham, Isaac, and Jacob, and then passed to his sons were also a prophecy for their future generations. The two key aspects became separate covenants: the national birthright blessing of prosperity to the two sons of Joseph, and the sceptre promise that included sovereign kingship over the Promised Land to Judah. (Genesis 48-49)

The blessings and promises began with Abraham in Genesis 12, and then passed on to Isaac, then Jacob, then Judah and the two sons of Joseph. The national prosperity birthright blessings were passed to Ephraim and Manasseh, the two sons of Joseph. Both lads were given Israel's name. Jacob adopted them as if his own. Ephraim would **become a multitude of nations** and was **set before** his older brother, Manasseh, who would **become a separate great nation**. Together, they would become the stone (builder) and the glory (magnificence) of Israel. (Gen. 49:24; Duet. 33:17) The sceptre promise **shall not depart from Judah**. (Gen. 49:10) Genesis 49:1-28 is a prophecy for all the children of Israel as to what form of nationality their descendants would become in the latter days.

From Lev. 26, you follow the history of Israel to the time of King Solomon when he sinned and turned from the Lord. The Prophet Ahijah tells Jeroboam that God will take the kingdom out of the hand of Solomon and give him ten of the tribes. (1 Kings 11:29-32) The Kingdom of Israel became two separate nations, kingdoms, or houses. The sins of Solomon, his death, and the division of the kingdom are found in 1 Kings 11 and 12. From this point you follow the histories of the northern and southern kingdoms in the remainder of the Kings and Chronicles, as well as Ezra and the other Prophets.

The northern kingdom (House of Israel) turned away from God, and their nation was destroyed in 722 BC. The remaining people of the ten northern tribes were taken captive by the King of Assyria into the land of Assyria. (2 Kings 17) In 609 BC Assyria was defeated and divided by Nabolpolassar, King of Babylon. Many Assyrians and most if not all the remnant of the northern ten tribes fled, thus beginning their migrations northward and westward. The descendants of Ephraim and Manasseh with their national birthright were among them. They became known as **The Lost Ten Tribes of Israel**.

Whether deserved or not, God keeps all his promises! They were made to Abraham, Isaac, and Jacob (Israel). Ephraim did not become a *company of nations* and Manasseh did not become a *separate great nation* in the Old Testament Bible. These promises were withheld for seven times or 2520 years. [360 × 7 = 2520] and [2520 yrs − 722 BC = 1798 AD] England continued expanding its global colonization. The British Commonwealth is a company of nations. The United States had recently won its independence from its older brother and established its Constitutional Republic. Eli Whitney had just invented mass production and Robert Fulton the steam engine. The industrial revolution was well underway.

When reading the books of prophecy in the Bible, the *House of Israel* refers to the United States, Great Britain, and the other eight lost tribes. The *House of Joseph* refers to the United States and Great Britain. (Amos 5:6,15, 6:6; Obad. 18; Zech. 10:6; Ezek. 37:16,19, 47:13; Ps. 80) The other eight lost tribes of Israel are: Reuben – Netherlands, Simeon with Levi – Spain with Portugal, Gad – Finland, Zebulun – Norway, Issachar – Sweden, Asher – Belgium, Naphtali – France, and Dan – Denmark. (Gen. 49; Deut. 33) Benjamin is a part of The House of Judah. (1 Kings 12:2124) Out of the lost ten tribes, only the United States has not joined the European Union. Will the US lose its superpower status to the EU? Could the Euro replace the dollar as the global dominate currency? A numerical significance in prophecy is linking the lost ten tribes to the ten toes, horns, and ten kingdoms with the breaking of the Ten Commandments. (Dan. 2 & 7; Rev. 13 & 17) [10 + 10 + 10 + 10 = 40, which will prove to be another significant number in scripture.]

The southern kingdom (House of Judah) also turned from God and was punished for seven times. The Jews did not lose their identity but lost the sovereignty and kingship over their land when King Jehoiachin surrendered to King Nebuchadnezzar (606-562 BC) and was carried away in captivity to Babylon in 598 BC. (2 Kings 24:8-12) This ended the independent Kingdom of Judah and the sovereign control of the land by the Jews. Adding 2520 years to 598 BC we come to 1922 AD. The League of Nations (now United Nations) made Palestine a British Mandate to set up a homeland for the Jews in 1922. It followed the Balfour Declaration of 1917 by Great Britain supporting a Jewish National Homeland. The British were harsh in their implementation of the mandate. The Jews began fighting the Arabs around 1947 and in 1948 the mandate ended. The Jewish leaders proclaimed the **State of Israel** with David Ben Gurion as their first Prime Minister. [The movie "Cast a Giant Shadow" starring Kirk Douglas and John Wayne was based on this period in history. Douglas played the American Jewish Colonel who went to Israel to help the Israelis. It was a great movie!]

When reading the books of prophecy in the Bible, the *House of Judah* refers to the State of Israel. All Jews are Israelites, but all Israelites are not Jews. All New Yorkers are Americans, but are all Americans New Yorkers? Also, the twelve tribes intermarried among themselves and other nationalities. (Gen. 38; Num. 12; Ruth 1-4; 1Sam. 17:12; Is. 11) [Moses' wife was Ethiopian. Read the book of Numbers chapter 12.]

The Nations that arose from the descendants of The Lost Ten Tribes of Israel, and the State of Israel did not happen overnight. (Is. 66:8) Neither did the national wealth and prosperity blessings of Ephraim and Manasseh come about in a single day. The State of Israel was in the making over the course of 31 years (1917 − 1948). [In God time that would be 31 yr ÷ 1000 yr × 24 hr/day = .744 hr] The entire House of Israel will be reunited at the return of Jesus Christ. (Ezek. 37:16-22) The flags of the United States, Great Britain, and Israel that are sewn together and burned by angry Arabs are a prelude to the fulfillment of that prophecy. (Ps. 83; Gen. 16:1-12)

The United States and Great Britain (Joseph) may succeed in their efforts to get Israel (Judah) to give up the West Bank, Gaza, divide East Jerusalem, and establish a Palestinian State. It was Judah's idea to not kill but sell Joseph to the Ishmaelite (Arab) traders. Arabs are the descendants of Ishmael. Most Persians (Iranians) are also the descendants of Abraham

Is Joseph about to sell out Judah? (Gen. 17:20, 25:1-6, 37:18-28; Is. 3:1-9; Zech. 12:1-6; Luke 21:22; Ezek. 16:53)

The 3.5 Times Prophecy

Daniel 7 is *The Four Beasts Prophecy* and the 3.5 times is found in Dan. 7:25. The entire chapter is an outline of world history from the Kingdom of Babylon to the return of Christ as King of Kings and the establishment of the Kingdom of God on Earth. This period began with the Babylonian Empire, and then comes to the present and the very near future. The four beasts represent the same world empires as the great image in King Nebuchadnezzar's dream. (Dan. 2) The four World Empires were the Babylonian (606-539 BC), Medo-Persian (539-333 BC), Grecian (333-168 BC) and the Roman (168 BC – 476 AD). Western Rome fell when the Gothic Vandals deposed Romulus Augustus as the emperor in 476 AD.

The three horns *plucked up by the roots* in Dan. 7:8 were the Vandals (429-476 AD), Heruli (476-493 AD), and the Ostrogoths (493-554 AD), which was the transition period to Papal rule or the *little horn* over the *western leg* of the Roman Empire. The first Pope appointed was Silverius, but he was imprisoned by Vigilius and died in 538 AD, then Vigilius reigned with the help of Theodora, the wife of Justinian I who ruled the *eastern leg* of the empire. Reigning wasn't the only help Vigilius got from Theodora.

Daniel 7:9-10 is the reign of Christ and the resurrections. Verse 11 is Daniel beholding the *little horn speaking great words* (Papal Ecclesiastical Dogma) and its future disposition. Verse 12 was the preceding three beasts passing away. Verses 13 and 14 describe the return of Christ and verses 15 and 16 set up the interpretation of the vision in verses 17-24. Verse 25 gives us a prophecy of what the little horn will do, that it will *think to change times and laws and the saints will be given into his hands.* The 3.5 times or 1260 years of Papal rule began in 538 AD and comes to 1798, which is the year General Berthier took Pope Pius VI captive, thus ending the church and state union of the Holy Roman Empire. Napoleon freed Europe from Papal domination but crowned himself as the King of Rome. This was the *deadly wound* in Rev. 13:3. The remaining seven horns transform into the seven heads, which the *scarlet woman* (false church) rides in Revelation 17, and is the same beast in Revelation

13 and 17. The seven remaining horns also represent the seven resurrections of the Roman Empire that follows:

(1) The Imperial Restoration by Justinian I in 554 AD.
(2) The Frankish Kingdom under Charlemagne in 774 AD.
(3) The German Head under Otto the Great – crowned in 962 AD.
(4) The Hapsburg dynasty under Charles V – crowned in 1530 AD.
(5) Napoleon's French Kingdom when he crowned himself King in 1798.
(6) Italy, Germany, & Japan Axis – Hitler, Mussolini & Hirohito (1936-1945).
(7) This will be the last and final resurrection of the Roman beast that will become a global *Church and State Union*, which is also represented by the *two legs joined at the hip* of the great image in Daniel 2. The ten toes of **iron mixed with miry clay** represent a global alliance of weak nations (The Ten Lost Tribes brought low by the Almighty) mingled with a strong nation (the nation the Lord chooses that brings them low). It will be broken in pieces and consumed at the return of Jesus Christ. (Dan. 2:31-45, 7:9-10,27-28; Rev. 16 & 20)

The 2300 Day Prophecy

This prophecy is the ram and goat vision in Daniel 8:1-14 and verses 15-22 gives the interpretation. Verses 23-25 are Herod's kingship over Judea and conclude with his attempt to kill Jesus and his own death. (Matt. 2:1-19) The two horns of the Ram were the kings of Media and

Persia. The goat was Alexander the Great who conquered the Medo-Persian Empire in 333 BC. When he died in 323 BC, his four generals divided the empire. The Seleucids ruled Syria and northern Palestine, and the Ptolemies ruled Egypt and southern Palestine. They were in constant conflict until the Roman conquest by Julius Caesar, who was the *little horn* in verse 9. This *little horn* defeated the third beast in Dan. 7:6, which gave rise to the fourth beast. It is not the same *little horn* in Dan. 7:8, but both are Roman.

There has been great confusion on the correct beginning of this prophecy. During the Adventist Movement of the early 1800's, the beginning point of the 2300 years was determined to be the same as the seventy weeks prophecy. With 457 BC as his beginning date, William

Miller (1782-1849) and his followers determined the seventy weeks prophecy was fulfilled in 34 AD. Then by adding the extra 1810 years to 34 AD, it was thought that Christ would return in 1844. It became known as *The Great Disappointment.* When the movement split, two major groups emerged. The Church of God Seventh Day disregarded Miller's interpretation and believes that Christ will return and reign on the earth for 1000 years after the first resurrection. The Seventh Day Adventists still insists the two prophecies began at the same time, but believes that an *investigative judgment* has been going on since 1844 in preparation for Christ's return, and the earth will be destroyed and lie dead for the 1000 years with Satan bound to it while Christ and the Saints prepare the books for the judgment in the second resurrection. [Sounds like only a desk job to me.] Both kept and still maintain the truth about the Seventh Day Sabbath and believe the *Great White Throne Judgment* follows the 1000 years. [Read Dan 7:9-10 and Rev. 20:4-15 carefully! Could Ellen White's vision of the earth lying in ruin with Satan bound to it wandering with no one to tempt have been the end of the first earth age? Surely it was!]

The confusion of the beginning date was due to not understanding Dan. 8:13. The translators added the words **concerning** and **sacrifice** to the word ***daily***, probably as an effort to simplify the passage. In order to gain an understanding of the passage, the key words and their definitions from the Hebrew Dictionary are as follows:

(1) daily – *tamiyd* – From an unused root meaning: to stretch, properly as a continuance. As an adjective: constant. As an adverb: constantly. A compound of: *tephillah* – a supplication, hymn, or prayer, and *qadad* – to bend the body or neck, to bow.]
(2) transgression – *peshu* – a revolt, rebellion, sin, transgression, or trespass. Derived from: *pasha* – (primary root) – to break away from just authority, to trespass, apostatize, quarrel, or offend.
(3) desolation – *shamen* – (primary root) – to stun. Intransitively to grow numb, to devastate. Figuratively to stupefy, to make amazed, be astonished, to bring desolate, be or make destitute.
(4) sanctuary – *godesh* – a sacred place or thing, consecrated, dedicated, hallowed, and made holy.
(5) host – *tsbaah* – a mass of persons organized as for worship, prayer, etc. Also, as for an army for war or rebellion.

From the definitions above, the question is better asked: *How long is the vision of constant rebellion, making the sacred place destitute and its worshipers to be trodden under foot (oppressed)?* The Jews began backsliding again after temple worship was restored under Ezra, and the Lord brought the sword upon them again. The answer was **2300 days; then (at a later time) shall the sanctuary (sacred place) be cleansed (delivered).** (Dan. 8:14) Adding 2300 years to 333 BC, which is the year Alexander the Great conquered Jerusalem, we come to 1967 AD. This was when the State of Israel won The Six-Day War repossessing East Jerusalem and the West Bank. The sacred place of worship, which is the Temple Mount, had been *delivered* back to the Jews.

Israel had been a sovereign state since 1948 and no longer oppressed, except for constantly having to defend their right to exist. They repossessed the old part of the city, but the *sacred place* still has one remaining problem, The Dome of the Rock. It was reported in the Haaretz that on June 7, 1967, a few hours after East Jerusalem fell into Israeli hands, that Rabbi Shlomo Goren told General Uzi Narkiss, "Now is the time to put 100 kilograms of high explosives into the Mosque of Omar so that we may rid ourselves of it once and for all." His request was denied and according to Goren's aide, Menahem Hacohen, he had not suggested blowing it up, but merely stated that, "if, during the course of the war, a bomb had fallen on the mosque and it would have – you know – disappeared – that would have been a good thing." [*To rid ourselves of;* ring any Iraq II bells?]

The Dome of the Rock issue should be resolved by Rev. 6:12. If not, then Zech. 14:4 and Rev. 19:11-14. The 2300 years of Daniel 8 and 2520 years of Leviticus 26 are sometimes considered as *the time of the gentiles.* Both relate to the city of Jerusalem and the land of Israel (Southern Kingdom of Judah). The 1967 date will prove to be the most important date in Daniel's timeline prophecies and is the pivotal point of the *last days* in prophecy. It will be verified in another prophecy!

The Seventy Weeks Prophecy

This prophecy is given in Daniel 9:24-27. Verse 25 gives the starting point of the prophecy, which is the *going forth of the commandment to restore and rebuild Jerusalem.* The proclamation was first given by King Cyrus I in 539 BC. (Ezra 1) There arose opposition to the city and Temple restoration, and it was stopped. (Ezra 4-5) King Darius I issued a decree to make a search of the house rolls, and the proclamation made by Cyrus was found. (Ezra 6) The final decree to finish the work was issued to Ezra in 458 BC by King Artaxerxes I (465-424 BC) in his seventh year. (Ezra 7) Verse 24 & 25 is the 69 weeks or 483 years from the date of the decree to the *anointing of Messiah the Prince*, which began in the mid-summer of 458 BC and came to the mid-summer of 25 AD. The fifth month of the sacred calendar is Ab (July - Aug.). Jesus was baptized in the mid-summer of 25 AD [25.5 AD], which was his anointing. (Luke 3:21-22 and Acts 10:37-38).

After Jesus' anointing and 40 days in the wilderness, he began his earthly ministry in early autumn [25.75 AD]. (Matt. 3:13 - 4:23) This began the last week or seven years of the prophecy. In *the mist of the week* (3.5 years) he caused *the sacrifice and the oblation to cease*. (Dan. 9:27) When Christ was crucified, *the veil of the temple was rent in twain* on Passover in the spring, Nisan 14, 29 AD [29.25 AD]. (Matt. 27:51)

Mathematically, the autumn of 25 AD is 25.75 and the spring of 29 AD is 29.25 [29.25 − 25.75 = 3.5]. The last half of the week or 3.5 years comes to the autumn of 32 AD. [29.25 + 3.5 = 32.75] That was when Stephen was killed, Saul (Paul) was converted, Peter had his vision, and the Gospel was delivered to the gentiles. (Acts 7-11) Most historians and theologians have Jesus born from 4 to 6 BC, and crucified from 30 to 32 AD. [I think that they may have skipped some math classes.] Luke 3:23 states he *began to be about thirty years* old. [30 − 25 AD = 5 BC] When reading Chapter IX, remember all the simple arithmetic in this paragraph.

The oddball part of this prophecy is verse 26, which is the 62 weeks or 434 years. Subtracting 434 years from 458 BC would be 24 BC. In verse 26, *after 62 weeks* modifies the phrase, *the street shall be built again, and the wall, even in troublous times* in verse 25. Herod the Great conquered Jerusalem in 37 BC after being made King over Judaea by Rome in 40 BC. During the next 13 years, he rebuilt the city streets, wall, and remodeled the temple during some very *troublous times,* which brings us to 24 BC. [37 − 13 = 24]

A different prophetic thought begins at *Messiah* in verse 26. Utilizing the definitions from Strong's Concordance and rephrasing: *Messiah will become cut off, not because of the people of the prince (Rome's) who will come to destroy the city and sanctuary afterwards. With an overflowing of endless wars, desolation is determined!* Rome destroyed Jerusalem in 70 AD. The rest has continued to this day!

The consummation (completion), and that determined (to point sharply or wound) shall be poured on the desolate (astonished) from Daniel 9:27 are the judgments of the seven seals and trumpets in the book of Revelation. When this is combined with ***everlasting righteousness*** in verse 24, which would be <u>after</u> Christ's return, a second fulfillment would be required. Since there are two advents of Christ, and Jacob fulfilled two weeks of years for Rachel, after being tricked by his uncle after the first seven, we need to find a second fulfillment for the 490 years.

During the beginning of the Ottoman Empire (1517-1917 AD), Suleyman I gave an order to rebuild the wall and restore the old section of Jerusalem in 1522. The 70 weeks or 490 years from that order will bring us to the year **2012**. The 69 weeks or 483 years in verse 25 was 2005. As far as I can recall, the only significant events that took place that year was hurricane Katrina and the second Bush's Afghanistan and Iraq II situation beginning to look like another Vietnam. The 62 weeks or 434 years was 1956. The only thing other than my second birthday that I can find in history is when Israel attacked Egyptian bases on the Sinai Peninsula advancing to within 10 miles of the Suez Canal.

The Second Advent of Christ pertains more to verses 24 & 27 than verses 25 & 26, and 1956 & 2005 are past. The seven seals in Revelation will be a seven-year period of testing and tribulation that parallels the week of years Jacob fulfilled. [2012 + 7 = **2019**] It will be the ***time of Jacob's trouble***. (Jer. 30:7) Everyone left alive (not behind) will experience it.

THERE WILL BE NO PRETRIBULATION RAPTURE!
(Zechariah. 13:8-9)

[Revision 2020/2021: In 2008 I neglected to consider both of the two weeks of years Jacob served for Rachel. (Genesis 29:9-30) The second week of seven years served by Jacob were more troublesome than the first week of years. (Genesis 29:31-30:26) The time leading up to the return of the Lord is also called "…the time of Jacob's trouble…" in Jeremiah 30:4-9. See Appendix IV.]

The 3.5 Times Prophecy

This is the second 3.5 times prophecy of Daniel and different from the one found in chapter 7. Chapters 10 and 11 are an outline of history from King Cyrus of Persia to 745-750 AD. Chapter 12 leaps forward to the last days or *time of trouble* and the two resurrections. (Dan. 12:1-2; Rev. 20) The question asked is: *How long shall it be to the end of these wonders?* The reply is 3.5 times, but *when he shall have accomplished to scatter the power (border) of the holy people* is the key. (Dan. 12:6-7) The Jews are still considered God's people, although they rejected Christ and remain in denial of his divinity to this very day (Zechariah 13:6).

When the Roman Empire was divided, the western leg had its capital in Rome and the eastern leg in Constantinople. The eastern division became known as the Byzantine Empire (395-1453 AD) but did not control Palestine all that time. The Eastern Empire had grown weak when the Muslims came along in the sixth century AD. They controlled Palestine and Jerusalem from 638 AD until the Ottoman Turks in 1517, except briefly during the Crusades (1095 - 1303).

The beginning of the 3.5 times or 1260 years was 515 BC. *Those days* and Daniel's *mourning three full weeks* was prior to and during *the third year of Cyrus.* (Dan. 10:1-2) Dan. 10:4-21 begins the time when the Lord strengthened Daniel before he began to show him the truth that begins at Dan. 11:1. The Lord told Daniel that He (the Lord) would confirm and strengthen (future tense) Darius. [The word *Also* at the beginning of Daniel 11:1 was added by the translators and not in the Hebrew text, as *also* is in most cases throughout the Old Testament. The verb *stood* is from the Hebrew term *amad* meaning: to *stand* as in: to appoint - ordain - raise up - repair - set up - make to. A better rendering would be *will stand* as the Lord was speaking to Daniel in the third year of Cyrus.] The confirming and strengthening of King Darius was to get the stalled work in Jerusalem going again. (Ezra 6)

Those days and the *three full weeks* are a prophetical literal 21 years that Daniel mourned and prayed for his people and the rebuilding of the Temple and the City. (Ezekiel 14:14-20) Dan. 10:2 parallels with and is a prophetical reciprocal to the *21 days (years)* in Dan. 10:13. Michael dealt with the Persian princes causing problems in Jerusalem while the Lord remained with the Persian kings. Cyrus reined 539-521 BC, and *a thing was revealed to Daniel* in his third year. [539 − 3 − 21 = 515] Darius reigned from 521-486 BC and the Temple was rebuilt in his sixth year or 515 BC. (Ezra 6:15) Using the mathematical ratio in 2 Peter 3:8, the 21 years would be *about the space of half an hour* in God time. (Rev. 8:1) Remember the following math when in Chapter VII's seventh seal's opening: 21 yr ÷ 1000 yr × 24 hr/day = .504 hr.

Daniel 11:31 happened when General Titus destroyed the Temple and erected a statue of the Roman god Jupiter in 70 AD. That was the **ABOMINATION OF DESOLATION** in Matt. 24:15. Dan. 11:32-39 is the western leg of the Roman Empire after 70 AD. Dan. 11:40-43 was the Muslim conquest of Syria, Palestine, and Egypt. In 632, the Saracens (Arabs) *pushed at* Constantinople with a 180,000-man army and a fleet of 2,500 ships but repelled by Leo III and the Bulgars. Leo regained most of Asia Minor by 741. Dan. 11:44 was the Abbasid family (Persian descendants of Mohammed's Uncle Abbas) that began their conquest to oust the ruling Umayyad family (also spelled Omayyad as in Omar, but of Arab descent – Ishmael) for control over Islam 745-750 AD. Mohammed outlived his sons. These two families (Arabs and Iranians) of Abraham are still at it today! (Gen. 17:20, 25:1-6) Both of these families want to destroy Abraham's first family – Israel, which is both The House of Judah and the House of Israel

The 1260 years added to 515 BC comes to the year 745 AD. The seas (plural) and glorious mountain in Daniel 11:45 are the Caspian Sea, Persian Gulf, and Jerusalem, which forms a triangle. In 750

AD, the Abbasid family moved the capital of Islam from Damascus to Baghdad, which is right in the middle of the triangle. The two feuding families became the two major sects of Islam known as the Sunnis and Shiites. [Did President Bush have any idea what he was getting the United States and Great Britain (Manasseh and Ephraim – the House of Joseph) into when they invaded Iraq? The Sunni and Shiite sects are still fighting each other over who will be rightful caliphate governing a *Theocratic State of Islam.*]

The land of Israel, also called Palestine, and the city of Jerusalem (mostly ruins) was conquered in 638 AD during the Muslim conquest. By 745 AD, the Muslims controlled the entire Middle East, Egypt, North Africa, Iraq, Persia, Syria, Lebanon, and Spain. The strict codes of Omar would not let the Jews own property, worship publicly, build houses higher than any Muslim's, and a host of other oppressive laws. Most Jews and Christians had left the Holy Land. The Jews had scattered all over the world. This was ***when He shall have accomplished to scatter the power (border) of the holy people.*** (Dan. 12:7)

The 1290 Days Prophecy

This prophecy is found in Dan. 12:11. Like the verses in Dan. 8:13 and 11:31, the translators added the word ***sacrifice***, but the word ***daily*** is the same. This is the third time that the ***daily*** was ***taken away.*** (Prov. 30:21) It is the second time ***the (an) abomination that maketh desolate*** was placed or set up. [The same Hebrew word (*nathan*) is translated ***set up*** and ***shall place***.] The abomination in Dan. 12:11 was something that was erected after the destruction of the city and temple in 70 AD. (Dan. 11:31; Matt. 24:15) In order to find the correct starting point we'll need to return to the period of time when the 1260 years period was ending in Dan. 11:41-45.

Mu'awiya I, Caliphate from 661 to 680 AD, moved the Islamic government from Medina to Damascus in 677, but the religious head was placed in Jerusalem and a shrine to Allah was erected on the Temple Mount. The Dome of the Rock was built in 691 AD. Part of its decorations is an inscription from the Koran: *God has no companion (spouse).* (Maryam 16:34-37) [It is taught to mean that Christ is not the son of God, which is antichrist as in 1 Jn. 2:18, 22 and 4:3.] The 1290 years added to 677 brings us to 1967. [2nd fulfillment for 1967]

Up to 677 AD there were a few poor Jews and Christians that remained in the area, and it was their custom to worship and pray at the temple site, although it lay in ruins since 70 AD. It would have been like the praying at the Wailing Wall today when they *bend and bow chanting hymnal prayers* and stretch out their hands to place prayers written on paper in the wall. Mu'awiya I hated the Jews with a passion, and refused them access to the holy sites, which was the third taking away of the ***daily***, or their *continual worship*.

The missing link in understanding the 1260 and 1290-day prophecies was the separate histories of the two divisions (legs) of the Roman Empire and the major role the Muslim conquest played in the eastern leg's history. A third confirmation to these two prophecies is both biblical and mathematical. When added together, they total 2550 years. The last group of Jews taken captive to Babylon was in the 23rd year of King Nebuchadnezzar. (Jer. 52:30) Note the following arithmetic: [606 BC − 23 yr = 583 BC] [583 BC + 1260 yr = 677 AD] [677 AD + 1290 yr = 1967 AD] [2550 yr + 583 BC = 1967 AD]. The missing link in the two timelines of Dan. 12:7 & 11 is 677 AD, and 1967 is crucial to the understanding the last timeline prophecy.

The 1335 Days Prophecy

This is the seventh timeline prophecy. From Daniel 12:12 the following key words are defined from the Hebrew Dictionary:

(1) blessed – *esher* – happiness. From: ashar – (primary root) – to be straight, level, right, happy. Figuratively, to go forward, be honest, prosper, as in to guide, lead. Also, to be relieved.
(2) waiteth – *chakah* – to adhere to, to tarry or continue.
(3) cometh – *naga* – to touch, to lay hands upon, as with a woman. Figuratively, to reach, acquire, or to arrive at.

The implication is that those who adhere to and continue in truth arriving to the 1335 days will be blessed. The faithful in the last days who understand truth will understand the meaning of Revelation's seven seals. They will know the return of the Lord is nearby. The ***tried*** in verse 10 are those who have adhered to truth throughout the ages and those of the last days who are wise to understand that the false Christ (Satan) will come first. The difference between 1335 and 1290 years is 45 years and when added to 1967, we get **2012**. [2nd fulfillment]

2012 is not the end of the world! Neither can it be the year of Christ's return, because it is less than seven years from now. We haven't seen the sixth seal signs yet! The sixth seal in Rev. 6:12 is the sign that Christ is about to return. The seventh seal is the seven trumpets that will come immediately after the signs in the sun, moon, and heavens. The seven seals is a seven-year period. Adding the seven-year seal judgments to 2012 brings us to **2019**. The Lord tells his followers that they can know the season, but not the day or hour in the parable of the fig tree. My fig tree buds out in the spring, and its figs ripen from mid-summer to early fall. Christ's return may be some hour on some day during the late summer or early autumn of 2019? [***Shorten*** or *eroded* 2020 cubits.] (Matt. 24:22-36) But if we have not yet seen the signs in the heavens with the opening of the sixth seal, at the least something global will happen in late 2019 or early 2020 beginning the time of sorrows. (Matt. 24:4-8, Rev. 6:1-17)

Both the 1798 and 2012 years have been *twice* derived. (Ps. 62:11; Num. 20:11; Job 33:14) The 1967 date has been *thrice* derived. (Matt. 12:40, 18:16; Acts 10:16: Eccl. 4:9-12; 1Jn. 5:7-8; Is. 17:6; Luke 22:61-62) The prophetic fulfillments of the three years 1798, 1967, and 2012 come to a total of seven. (2 + 3 + 2 = 7)

The additional seven seals years in the Book of Revelation could be considered an eight timeline, which is actually the 1000 year reign in Rev. 20:4-10. In scripture, eight represents a new beginning. This world will witness a new beginning when Jesus Christ returns to set up the Kingdom of God for all eternity. The new heavens and earth prophecy in Rev. 21 is the eternal continuation of God's Kingdom that is established by Christ. Unlike the promises of presidential candidates, it will truly be a time of **CHANGE!**

[Revision 2020/2021: In 2008 I neglected to consider both of the two weeks of years Jacob served for Rachel. (Genesis 29:9-30) The second week of seven years served by Jacob were more troublesome than the first week of years. (Genesis 29:31-30:26) The time leading up to the return of the Lord is also called "…the time of Jacob's trouble…" in Jeremiah 30:4-9. See Appendix IV.]

The Beasts of Revelation

The beast with seven heads and ten horns in Rev. 13 and 17 is the same beast as in Daniel 7, but Rev. 17 is more descriptive of the harlot that rides it. The seven remaining horns in Dan. 7:8 reciprocates to the seven heads in Revelation but have the *names of blasphemy* written on them. This *scarlet colored beast* has a woman (church) riding it. The *seven heads and ten horns* in Revelation represent a different Rome.

The Revelation beast began its reign during the transition period to Papal rule over the Western Roman Empire and was the *Church and State Union* that reigned over most of Europe during the Dark and Middle Ages. The *ten horns and upon his horns ten crowns* represents ten power divisions (horns) and sub-kingdoms (crowns) within the empire after the fall of Romulus Augustus in 476 AD. (Lombards, Huns, Heruli, Franks,

Burgundians, Saxons, Ostrogoths, Visigoths, Suevi, and Vandals) These *Ten Barbarian Tribes* were a mingling of descendants from the Assyrians, Lost Ten Tribes of Israel, and descendants from the Tower of Babel. The name *Saxons* is derived from *Isaac's sons*. (Gen. 21:12) [Ten is the link.]

The beast received a deadly wound to one of its heads. (Rev. 13:3) This was when the Pope was imprisoned in 1798 and all the Papal properties confiscated. Pope Pius XI and Mussolini healed the deadly wound in 1929 with the signing of the Lateran Treaty that returned most Papal property and established Vatican City as a sovereign City State. It is now a member of the United Nations. The Pope is Head of Church and State and claims the Catholic Church as the only true Church.

After the End of World War II, the Catholic Church regained most of her lost respect. Most Protestants now respect the Pope and the *Mother of Churches*. Vatican Council II (1962-65) resolved many differences between the Eastern and Western Orthodox. The goal of the council was *the unity of all Christian faiths under the Roman Catholic Church*. Today, the Pope is viewed as a great spiritual leader. The Church's recovery has been a world wonder. Who is able or willing to make war (fight, battle, rebel, or argue) against the ecclesiastical dictates of the *infallible* Papacy? (Rev. 13:3-4)

The 42 months in Rev. 13:5 is sometimes considered as the 1260 years of Papal rule, but prophetic time (year to a day) isn't given in months because the number of days can vary from month to month. The 1260 years of Roman Papal rule (538 - 1798 AD) are in Dan. 7:25 and Rev. 12:6 & 12:14 as the wilderness church fleeing the Papacy, and Rev. 11:3 as the Old and New Testaments (olive trees verse 4). The 1260 years in Rev. 11:3 reciprocates to a literal 42 months or 3.5 years that the two witnesses (candlesticks verse 4) give their testimony, which is a prophetic time yet to come and coincides with the 42 months in Rev 11:2 & 13:5 (false prophet). They are a literal time period of 3.5 years. The prophetic 1260 days (years) in Rev. 11:3 is the Bible's Old and New Testaments that survived in **sackcloth** through the dark and middle ages when the Roman Church strictly forbid the common people to possess or have access to the scriptures. The 42 month or 3.5 year period of the Holy City being trodden under foot, the two witnesses' testimony with power, and the false prophet's blasphemy with miracles occur during the last half of the seven seal years.

The Dark Ages of the Holy Roman Empire were bloody indeed. Kings and Princes fulfilled the will of Popes and were often replaced or killed for their disobedience. Countless Jews, Moslems, and defiant Christians who defied the Papacy's authority were detained, tortured, and then usually murdered. [Waterboarding is foreplay compared to their techniques.] The history of the protestant reformation is packed with the whimsical tyranny of Popes. Past events may be repeated, as history often repeats itself. There was an announcement on CBN July 13, 2007 (Friday) that the Pope had made a statement about the Catholic Church being the only true church and only Catholics would enter heaven. It was a lower official, but the Pope authorized the release. Will we reenter the Dark Ages again before Christ's return?

Revelation 13:11-18 is a fifth and a latter day beast in Bible prophecy. Daniel's four beasts came up from the sea, but this beast comes up out of the earth. This aspect with that of the earth opening to help the woman in Rev. 12:16 seems to resemble the United States. Some suggest the two horns are the two law making bodies of congress. If that were so, wouldn't the two bodies be the same size with equal power? Horns represent power in scripture. The two horns of this lamb-like beast are described in Deut. 33:13-17.

The **glory of Joseph** is described as like **the horns of unicorns** and **the firstling of his bullock**. Unicorns and bullocks are translated from words meaning *male lamb* with the unicorn being a *larger conspicuous wild bull*. The **House of Joseph** will **push (war against) people, together (united) with their horns (power) to the ends (uttermost parts) of the earth.** Sound like the United States and Great Britain? Ephraim's numbers are greater than Manasseh's because the United Kingdom's population also includes the commonwealth nations. Manasseh was born first as *firstling of his (Joseph's) bullock* and the *larger conspicuous wild bull*. [United States]

Since 1798, Great Britain and the United States have imposed its ideology around the world through economic sanctions, bribery, and militarily with war. They have been at the forefront of the many Bible Societies that have translated the Bible into hundreds of languages. The missionary work of Protestantism has been like that of Catholicism, although not as historically forceful as that by Spain and Portugal. The United States and Great Britain are the *political image* of Rome in its quest to democratize the world. Protestantism is the *religious image* of Catholicism by spreading her (Rome's) doctrines and traditions of men. Have democracy and religion ever fornicated?

The Church of England is the church established by English law after its break from the Roman Catholic Church when Pope Clement VII refused to annul the marriage of Henry VIII to Catherine of Aragon. In 1543, Parliament passed an act making Henry head of the church, thus cutting ties with Rome. The British sovereign is the church's supreme head. The Church of England maintained most Catholic doctrines and traditions and is also the head of the Anglican Communion. A more protestant-oriented split became known as The Anglican Church, but in the United States, The Episcopal Church. During the Methodist movement in 1738, a more zealous group formed calling themselves Evangelicals, which is a common term today. They form the foundation of the [not so] *religious right.*

In the image of Rome, the Church of England caused many dissenters from her authority to be put to death. Throughout the protestant reformation, groups that separated from the authority of both oppressive churches didn't dispose of the main doctrines and traditions of Rome. Even today, the old dictates of Rome are adhered to by most protestant denominations. The coming out of Babylon is not yet complete. Most Christians remain in the dogmatic captivity of the harlot's doctrines and tradition. (Rev. 18:4, 13:10)

Constantine made Sunday the official day of rest and worship a civil law in 321 AD. When the Church of England split from Rome becoming England's official church by law, she maintained Rome's Sunday tradition, thus becoming a daughter in the image of Rome. In the United States, we are guaranteed freedom of religious practice. The First Amendment states, "Congress shall make no law respecting an establishment of religion…" There have been some Sabbatarians that have thought Congress would pass a **Sunday Law** at some point in time. Although it would be a direct violation of the First Amendment, it is not necessary that Congress pass such a law. The main body of our Constitution already respects Sunday as the **official day of rest:** "…if any bill shall not be returned by the President within ten days (Sundays excepted) after it shall have been presented to him…" (U.S. Constitution, Article I, Section 7.) This clause respects Sunday as the **official non-workday** of the week. Does the U.S. Postal Service deliver mail on Sunday? Why are most of the Federal Government's buildings of Roman Architecture? Could these things be considered as *an image to the beast (Rome)*?

Some have supposed Idumea as being the United States. Idumea, or Edom, are the Edomites, the descendants of Esau. Their land was the Sinai Peninsula, southern Jordan, and the upper Red Sea shores of Saudi Arabia. Today, the Edomites are among the populations of Syria, Jordan, Saudi Arabia, Egypt and Lebanon. If Israel gives up the West Bank and East Jerusalem, Is. 3:1-5 will be fulfilled. The United States may be so bogged down in Afghanistan, Iraq, and possibly Iran, that Britain may need to supply the bulk of the troops for Israel's security. Efforts by the United States and Great Britain to establish a Palestinian State will not bring peace to the Middle East. Esau sold his birthright (land of Israel) to Jacob. With unforgotten jealousy, the descendants of Esau united with those of Ishmael's want it back. (Gen. 25:21-34; Is. 34-35; Ezek. 35-36)

Revelation 17 describes the woman (church) that rides the beast. Kings have fornicated with her and people have been deceived by her doctrines. Can you think of any church head or leader who is ***arrayed in purple and scarlet colour and decked (gilded) with gold and precious stones and pearls, having a golden cup in her (its) hand? MYSTERY BABYLON THE GREAT*** is the false church, and as ***THE MOTHER OF HARLOTS*** has many daughters. Churches that hold to her doctrines and traditions, which are the ***ABOMINATIONS OF THE EARTH***, are also harlots. [Like mother, like daughter.] The sheep that are led astray by their false doctrines are her victims.

Where is the seat of authority for this harlot? Rev. 17:9 reveals that she sits on seven mountains. Vatican City is in Rome, which is called *The City of Seven Hills*. When John recorded his visions, *five Kings had fallen, and* **one is...** (Rev. 17:10) the five fallen were Caesar Augustus (27 BC - 14 AD), Tiberius (14-37 AD), Caligula (37-41 AD), Claudius I (41-54 AD), and Nero (54-68 AD). The one in power at the time of his writing was Vespasian (69-79 AD). Most professional scholars and theologians agree that John wrote the Book of Revelation sometime between 70 and 80 AD. There were many rulers over Rome between 79 AD and its fall in 476 AD. The ***other (different one or type) is not yet come*** is that with the harlot riding it, which was the Papal and Church's control over the Holy Roman Empire. Will she ride the last and final resurrection of Rome?

The *hocus-pocus* of the beast in Rev. 17:8 & 11 is the dragon (Satan), which gave power to the beast (Rome – Papacy). To worship the beast or harlot is to worship the dragon by proxy. (Rev. 13:4) The ***bottomless pit*** in Rev. 17:8 is the same as in Rev. 20:3. The word *perdition* in Rev. 17:8 & 11 is from the Greek: *apoleia* – ruin or loss. From: *apollumi* – to destroy fully. When Christ returns, the beast and the false prophet will be cast into the lake of fire (Rev. 19:20), but Satan is bound for 1000 years. (Rev. 20:2) After the 1000 years are expired, he will be loosed. (Rev. 20:7) The *was and is not; and shall ascend out of the bottomless pit, and go into perdition* in Rev. 17:8 is the *bottomless pit* Satan goes in and out of in Rev. 20:3 & 7. *Into perdition (total ruin)* in Rev. 17:8 & 11 is also the *tormented (vexed)* in Rev. 20:10. The *book of life* in Rev. 17:8 is the same *book of life* in Rev. 20:12. The *even he is the eighth, and is of the seven* in Rev. 17:11 is the dragon behind the beast and false prophet that are *cast* into the lake of fire in Rev. 19:20. After the 1000 year reign of Christ and the Saints, *the devil (Satan's eighth)* and *death and hell (grave)* are cast into it. (Rev. 20:10,14; Is. 14:15-17; Ezek. 28:18-19)

The ten horns in Rev. 17:12-14 represent ten kings, kingdoms, or nations in the latter days that were raised up from the descendants of The Lost Ten Tribes of Israel. They will agree to give their power and strength (military and economy) to the beast (global banking, finance, regulatory, and government systems) when there is a total collapse of the current global economy. What would happen if those holding the security bonds of our mushrooming national debt were to demand payment in full? Can a nation declare bankruptcy and place its citizen taxpayers under the jurisdiction of a global receivership? The ten kingdoms will have power *one hour (first instant – at the beginning)* with the beast. **They will be making a deal with the devil!**

There was a very important lesson to be learned in Iraq. You do not put an unemployed army on the streets without a paycheck! If the United States government goes bankrupt, who will underwrite the budget for the DOD? In the event of a nuclear attack, numerous nationwide natural disasters, pandemic, and/or an economic collapse, there are executive orders in place to be utilized during a national emergency declaration that suspends the Constitution and places the nation under centralized martial law. If suspended, will the military oath to uphold it become null and void? Will loyalty be economical? Will they make war with its own citizens? Will they make war with the Lamb? (Amos 5:6, 6:6; Rev. 17:14, 19:19, 16:12-14)

The *ten horns* in Rev. 17:16-18 also represent ten protestant daughters of the harlot mother. There are ten prominent protestant denominations throughout the entire World: Lutheran, Episcopalian, Methodist, Baptist, Presbyterian, Unitarian, Mennonites, Jehovah's Witnesses, Mormon, and Pentecostal. The first seven came to the United

States from Europe to exercise religious freedom. They were trying to come out of Babylon but carried much of their mother's baggage with them like the children of Israel when coming out of Egypt. (Ezek. 20) The last three were established in the United States but have adopted most of the whore's doctrines and traditions. Today, there are granddaughters and great granddaughters. They all keep the main doctrines and traditions of the harlot church but will come to hate the whore because of her deceptions. God will put it in their minds to strip her naked and burn her with fire. God will judge her through the very ones that she has deceived. (Rev. 17:15-18)

The ***great tribulation*** of the near future is supposed to be the greatest time of trouble the world has ever seen or will ever see. (Matt. 24:21; Is. 22:5; Jer. 30:7; Ezek. 7:7; Dan. 12:1; Zeph. 1:14-16) The prophecy in Jeremiah 30 and 31 are for both Houses of Israel and Judah, and pertain to the last days we're in now. Jeremiah began his work in the days of Josiah, King of Judah (640-609 BC). (Jer. 1:2) The Northern Kingdom of Israel was already taken away captive in 722 BC. The Lord has given his people **The Scripture of Truth** in the books of the Holy Bible. It states that Satan can transform himself into an angel (messenger – human or divine) of light. (2Cor. 11:13-15) The scriptures also warn us there are wolves in sheep's clothing. (Matt. 7:15-23, 10:16; Luke 10:3; Jn. 10:11-13; Acts 20:29-31)

Most ministries and their pastors today are just hirelings in the occupational field of corporate sheep herding. The sheep are feed the doctrines and traditions passed down by its Board of Directors and/or CEO's. When the sheep decide that the food isn't to their liking, they reinvest into a different stock. Church attendance fluctuates with the market. The everchanging diets of the sheep just keeps them roaming, roaming, roaming; however, just keep those sheep a Roman - **Yo Ho**!

Chapter VII
The Divine Prime of Seven

The number seven represents **Divine Perfection** in the Holy Bible. (Gen. 2:2-3, Ps. 12:6) It is the *divine prime number*. Four represents completion. Ten represents government and law, and sometimes completion. The Ten Commandments are the complete spiritual laws for the entire universe. Is it only a coincidence that the first ten amendments to our Constitution is The Bill of Rights? There are also ten planks to the Communist Manifesto. [See Appendix I.]

There are four basic sevens in the book of Revelation. The seven messages to the churches, seven seals, seven trumpets, and seven last plagues are the complete divine revelation. The seven messages to the seven churches are warnings for correction and prophecy. The seven seals outline God's divine plan, history, and future for mankind. The seven trumpets are divine judgments announcing Christ's return as King of Kings and Lord of Lords. The seventh trumpet is the seven last plagues. The seven days of recreation week, seven timeline prophecies, seven messages, seven churches, seven seals, seven trumpets, and the seven last plagues, are seven sevens. [$7 \times 7 = 49$] Pentecost is the counting of seven Sabbaths and adding one. Fifty is also the number for jubilee. (Lev. 23:15-16, 25:8-10) [$7^2 + 1 = 50$] There will be **JUBILEE** when Christ returns as **King of kings!** [At least for those prepared!]

The seven messages addressed to the seven churches were for edification. They had both good and bad aspects about them, and the church at Pergamos had two things against it. Those who held the doctrines of Ba'laam and the Nicolaitanes had infiltrated them. The *falling away* from the true gospel (The Gospel of the Kingdom of God) was predicted to happen before the return of Christ, and the Nicolaitanes are signaled out. (Rev. 2:12-17; 2Th. 2:3-12, Act 6:9)

The doctrine of Ba'laam taught by Ba'lac was like that of Baalim as taught by the priests of Baal in the Old Testament. Baal (a Semitic word meaning lord, master, or husband) was the Canaanite deity or sun god. Shemesh was the Babylonian *god of the spring sun*. [The Hebrew word *shemesh* is translated *sun* throughout the Old Testament.] Ishtar (consort to Shemesh) was the Babylonian *goddess of fertility* (spring renewal and birth) and also known as Ashtaroth (Judges 2:13, 10:6; 1 Sam. 7:3-4, 12:10, 31:10), Ashtoreth (1 King 11:5; 2 King 23:13), and The Queen of Heaven (Jer. 44:18). The *Babylonian Mystery Religion* had its Greek and Roman parallels, but their mythologies had numerous variations. Most pagan religions had a sun or fire god. The Hebrew word for Lucifer is: *Helyel* – the bright and morning star. The sun of fire was his star, and Satan is the fallen Lucifer. The children of Israel constantly turned away from the true God and went whoring after the false god(s) of sun and/or fire.

The Nicolaitanes were a major sect of the Babylonian Mystery Religion and the seed of the apostate church that became more popular among the gentiles. The Greek word for Nicolaitanes is: *Nikolaties* – an adherent to Nicolaus, a teacher. From: *Nikolaos* – victorious over the people, a heretic named Nicolaus or Nicolas, a compound of: *nikos* (conquest, victory over) and *loas* (people in general). This sect became the harlot in Revelation 17. The Apostle Paul had warned of a *falling away* in his second letter to the Thessalonians. The Greek definitions for the key words are:

(1) falling – *aspostello* – to set apart. By implication, to send out on a mission. From: *stello* – to repress.
(2) away – *apostasia* – defection from the truth, or apostasy.
(3) Apostle – *Apostolos* – a delegate, an ambassador of the Gospel as commissioned by Christ.

The above definitions themselves prove there were false Apostles proclaiming an apostasy about Christ while the true Apostles as taught by Christ were proclaiming the true Gospel. (Rev. 2:2; 2Cor. 11:13-15; Matt. 24:5, 15:9, 7:15-23; 1Ti. 4:1-10) Jude 24 also warned of this *falling*. (*aptaistos* – not stumbling; fig. without sin – infallible)

The gentile converts were a very religious people within their pagan traditions. The Greeks were always ready to hear a new thing and well adept at mingling their philosophies. (Acts 17:16-23) Paul warned the Colossians not to be seduced by philosophy and men's traditions. (Col. 2:8) A different wisdom was forming. The Hebrew word for *WISDOM* in Proverbs 9:1 is a feminine form of the prime word *chakmowth*. It is used only three other times. (Prov. 1:20, 24:7 and Ps. 49:3) In Proverb 9, she's the *fallen wisdom* (Satan) that mingles truth with error (1-3). She speaks her mingled truths (4-12) then the first (alpha) *true wisdom* (Christ) rebukes her (13-18). She is the harlot that sits on seven pillars or mountains. (Ezek. 28:12-13; Prov. 8:22; Rev. 17:3, 18:7; Zech. 5:56:8) [The land of Shinar became the northwestern part of Babylon, which was also called Assyria. (Gen. 2:14) The city of Antioch located in the Roman providence of Asia (former Shinar) was the headquarters of early Christendom. (Acts 11:26-27) It is Antakya, Turkey today. Christian headquarters is now located in Vatican City, according to the claims of the Roman church.]

Fornication in scripture also means *to mingle or proselytize* with other beliefs. There is a scriptural clue as to whom the Nicolaitanes were. In Acts 6 we find **Nicolas a proselyte of Antioch** in verse 5 and **Libertines** in verse 9. You don't have to be a Sherlock Holmes to combine Nicolas and Libertines to get Nicolaitanes. The **certain of the synagogue** are the gentile converts who **suborned men (caused to commit perjury)** to the council of Jews about the things Stephen was saying concerning Moses and the temple. They became jealous of the **great wonders and miracles** that Stephen performed, which they were unable to do because **they <u>were not able to resist</u> (did not exercise by self-restraint – opposed) the wisdom and spirit by which he spake**. It was the people that chose the seven men, and then the twelve laid their hands upon them, but that does not mean that the other six had the spirit like Stephen. **At least four were the conspirators!**

*******MESSAGES*******

The seven messages to the seven churches also represent seven prophetic ages of the *wilderness church*. Their history would be difficult to follow because the church had to flee into the wilderness to escape persecution. (Rev. 12:6 & 14) I have read several good historical tracks by different authors. The one that seems to follow the path of this prophetic church best was given by Herbert Armstrong in his book, Mystery of the Ages. Utilizing secular history, various essays, books like Lost Christianities, and especially scripture, I offer the following as a brief history of the wilderness church.

*Ephesus (Rev. 2:1-7) This era was the early church that Christ began building through his Apostles. The message warned of false apostles who were found to be liars. (1Jn. 2:3-7) Their *first works* was proclaiming the *Gospel of the Kingdom of God*. (Luke 4:43; Mk. 4:11; Acts 28:21-31) The Apostates began preaching a gospel about Christ. (Matt. 24:4-5) Their adaptation of the popular pagan customs gained them more followers and money. (Jn. 10:12-13; Acts 16:16-21) The true Gospel and faith in and of Christ was being turned into mysticism and ritualistic pagan practice, and true salvation (by grace alone) through repentance (a reversal from sin) turned into license to sin. (Gal. 4:8-11; Jude 4; Mk. 7:6-23; 1Jn. 3:4, 5:2-3; Eph. 2:4-9; Jas. 2:10-20) The faithful followers of this era grew weary and became slack in their *first love,* but did despise the Nicolaitanes' deeds, which thing the Lord also hated. This first church era has very few historical records and is commonly known as the *dark period*.

*Smyrna (Rev. 2:8-11) Church history emerges after the dark period with two distinct types of Christianity with each having a variety of sects. The majority apostates had forsaken the Lord's Sabbath and worshipped on Sunday, the vernal day of the sun. In 321 AD, Constantine acknowledged Christianity as an official state religion and made Sunday rest (excluding agriculture) a civil law. The apostate church had gained state recognition and used their newfound authority to persecute the apostolic church. After Constantine's death in 337, the Catholic Council of Laodicea (364 AD) wrote their most famous cannon: *"Christians shall not Judaize and be idle on Saturday, but shall work on that day; but the Lord's Day (Sunday), they shall especially honor, and, as being Christians, shall, if possible, do no work on that day. If, however, they are found Judaizing, let them be shut out from Christ."* (The History of the councils of the Church, Vol. II, pg. 316) This proves Christians were keeping the Sabbath! Can a council of men shut out from Christ those keeping his Holy Commandment? (Rom. 8:35) Just who do you think this council was working for by changing God's fourth Commandment? (Dan. 7:25) It surely was not Jesus Christ! It must have been that other angel of light. (2Cor. 11:14)

Shemesh was the Babylonian *Lord of Sunday*, *vernal day of the sun*. The sun was restored on the first day of recreation week. Satan is the fallen Lucifer who was the bright and morning star (sun). God made the Seventh Day Sabbath by resting from his work. Should we rest and worship God on his first workday? *Thou shalt have no other gods before me* is the first commandment. The fourth is remembering and keeping the Sabbath.

LINK the two commandments together, and thus saith the Lord: *Thou shalt have no other rest and worship day before, after, or any other than MINE!* Can men change God's mind and his commandments? (Heb. 13:8; Mal. 3:6; Prov. 24:21)

*Pergamos (Rev. 2:12-17) This era began with the reign of the Papacy in 538 AD. Those few who kept the true faith had fled to the wilderness. (Rev. 12:6 & 14) They suffered great persecution and martyrdom. The Harlot was in control of the Holy Roman Empire and anyone that did not obey and honor her dictates was excommunicated, tortured, or murdered, but usually all three. The true flock was drastically reduced in size but carried the truth through the *Dark Ages* under constant persecution. The Roman Church had introduced image worship at their seventh general council, the second of Nicaea in 787 AD. Rev. 12:13 states that the Lord knows the location of Satan's seat. ***Antipas*** in Greek means *anti-father*, and in Latin *anti-pope*. (Matt. 23:8-12, 20:25-28; Luke 20:45-47; Rev. 17:1-6) [Rev. 12:13 is the only place the word, term, or name (authority) "Antipas" is used in Scripture and is futuristic.]

*Thyatira (Rev. 2:18-29) This era approximates the 12th through 15th centuries. During the late 12th century, Peter Waldo led a small group of followers called the Waldenses. Living in the Alpine Valleys of Southern France and Northern Italy, most were observing the Seventh Day Sabbath. They worked hard at hand producing copies of the Gospels and other single books of Scripture. The printing press was not invented until 1451, and complete copies of the Bible were rare and precious. The Roman Church had forbidden the common people to have Bibles and caused them to worship as the Papacy dictated. The Waldenses suffered great persecution by the Papal Inquisitors, and Pope Innocent VIII issued a Papal Bull to totally exterminate them in 1487. The Sabbatarian Christians were **super de-sized!** (Dan. 7:21,25; Rev. 13:7, 17:6) Their Bibles and other scriptural manuscripts were burned. [Isn't Innocent a rather unusual name for a murderer? This beast riding, ruthless whore's past can be found in most books of Inquisition history.] ***Jezebel*** in the Greek is used as a synonym of a termagant or false teacher.

*Sardis (Rev. 3:1-6) This era describes a few that have not defiled their garments. A small remnant of the Waldenses fled from the persecution by the Roman and Spanish Inquisitors and began to migrate toward Normandy and the British Isles. They quietly keep the Seventh Day Sabbath in the seclusion of their poverty, but a different type of persecution was beginning to emerge.

During the late 15th and early 16th century, there was an uprising within the Roman Church. Many began to doubt her authority, and this was the first call for those professing the name of Christ to come out of her. The protestant reformation had caused many religious wars, but a few Sabbatarian Christians had already found their way to Northwestern Europe and Great Britain. In 1650, a small group of Sabbatarians established a church calling themselves **Seventh Day Baptists** in England, but English Puritanism holding fast to most of the Roman Church's doctrines and traditions soon engulfed them.

Protestants and Catholics persecuted each other during their religious wars, which were known as *The Thirty Years War* (1618-1648). Both persecuted the Sabbatarians! During the 16th and 17th centuries, the reformers' greatest impediments were the Church of England as well as the Roman Church, but as prophesied in Rev. 12:16, the new world had opened its doors to religious freedom as well as a land of new opportunity. Vast numbers of Protestants crossed the Atlantic in pursuit of freedom and liberty to practice their faiths. The Sabbatarians had also found their prophesied eagle wings. *Freedom of religion* was a second calling for Christians to come out of Babylon. (Rev. 18:4; Job 33:14; Jude 11-12)

Although the Protestants began their exodus to freedom, they carried the Harlot's *baggage* with them like the children of Israel when coming out of Egypt. (Ezek. 20) Many protestant denominations were born during the reformation, but soon after their early founding fathers died, they established their individual creeds and maintained many essential doctrines and traditions of the mother church. **THE MOTHER OF HARLOTS** had given birth to many daughters.

The first American Sabbath keeping church was founded in the colony of Rhode Island in 1672. In 1636, a settlement was founded and established at Providence, RI by Roger Williams, who was a Baptist separatist fleeing persecution by the Massachusetts Puritans. The Puritans wanted to maintain a connection with the Church of England, but Williams insisted on the separation from the central authority of men and *independent religious thought*. He established the first Baptist church in America in 1639, but he later changed his views and recognized no one true church. In 1644 Williams secured a charter for the new colony of

Rhode Island that *guaranteed its independence and secured its boundaries against encroachments by its orthodox neighbors, Massachusetts and Connecticut*. Today, the Puritans are known as the Anglican Church of America.

Rhode Island became the first colony in America to be founded on the principles of *freedom of religious expression* and *separation of church and state*. Stephen Mumford, a Seventh Day Baptist, came to Rhode Island from England in 1664. Finding no one that kept the Seventh Day Sabbath, he began fellowshipping with the local First Baptist congregation on Sundays, but kept the Sabbath privately. Several members noticed and began keeping the Sabbath with him. They established the first Seventh Day Baptist Church in America. Their historical record exists in the museum at Newport. A second congregation was later established at Hopkinton, but persecution by First Baptist's and other Sunday churches forced them westward.

During the Advent Movement of the early 1800's, the year of Christ's second coming was predicted through the teachings of William Miller. After the Great Disappointment of 1844, many of his followers departed. The movement yielded two other Sabbatarian groups. The Church of God Seventh Day believes Christ will return and reign for 1000 years over a *live* earth. The Seventh Day Adventists believe the earth will lie *dead* during that period. (Rev. 20:3-7) They both retained the doctrine of God's true Sabbath.

Philadelphia** (Rev. 3:7-13) The ***open door (intense portal) for this era was the beginning of radio and television. Out of the Church of God Seventh Day, the Radio Church of God was started under the leadership of Herbert Armstrong (1892-1986) and later became the Worldwide Church of God during the early television age. Many scriptural truths lost throughout the centuries were recovered. The **Gospel of the Kingdom of God** was broadcast worldwide on *The World Tomorrow* program, and many free booklets were offered for the asking. The church grew into the world's largest Sabbath keeping congregation following World War II, but something caused the church to split apart and scatter into many splinter groups after Armstrong died.

In 1988 I began taking some Bible courses offered by the Worldwide COG Ambassador College. I later requested the number and address of a local minister, but for some reason I delayed until 1992. When I did call,

I received a cursing out, and what sounded like chaotic screaming of demons in the background. That scared me so much, I did little Bible study during the next seven years and did not really care for any kind of a church. In 1999 and after my conscience meltdown following 5 days on a civil jury, I found an advertisement about a Pentecost Feast service being held in a town about an hour and a half drive. It turned out to be a small splinter group from the Worldwide Church of God. It did not take long to get their account of what happened just prior to and after Armstrong's death.

After the long drive became difficult, I began alternating between them and a closer Seventh Day Adventist group on Sabbaths. I soon learned about the history of the Miller movement in the 1800's. I found some teachings of Ellen G. White to be biblically erroneous, and any other understanding was forbidden. Then the other group turned my re-baptism into a party. I felt disappointment by both and have remained to myself in independent study. I still believed that the Lord had something for me to do, but all I could see at the time was that which is written in scripture, **Satan, which deceiveth the whole world.** (Rev. 12:9) I began to dissect the Bible utilizing the Strong's Concordance. (Acts 17:11; Zech. 11:15-16) Hungry for scriptural truth, I started my own Comprehensive Scripture Investigation or **CSI**.

*Laodiceans (Rev. 3:14-22) We are in this last and final era now. The events stated in verses 15-17 happened to the Worldwide Church of God. There are also separatists within the Seventh Day Adventists. David Koresh and his followers in Waco, Texas were one such group. Today, some are hot, some cold, but the majority are the thousands of lukewarm groups scattered around the world. Some still preach and teach the Gospel of the Kingdom of God, but where is the latter days' message for God's people to come out of Babylon? The *gold tried in the fire* in Rev. 3:18 is *as gold is tried* in Zech. 13:9. The Lord will soon return! Those held captive by the harlot are in a state of delusion. She must be stripped, exposed, her mark identified, and the truth widely published. The true shepherds have become lazy while false shepherds are eating the fat of the flocks. (Zech. 11-14; Ezek. 33-34; Jer. 50-51; Is. 13 & 56)

[The missing link in following the path of the wilderness church's history was following the Sabbatarian's trail.]

*******SEALS*******

Revelation 6 reveals the book with seven seals and only the Lamb of God is found worthy to open them. The first four seals opened are commonly called **The Four Horsemen of the Apocalypse**. The four faces of the middle Pyramid at Giza (present Adam) are symbolic to the four horses and Satan is at the pinnacle of their control. Man is the rider of each horse, and the four corners are the foundation of his fall with three aspects per face. [Think of it as like a merry-go-round with the four slopes as the rein for each horse.] The format for their description will be: (horse number) – color – (color representation) – three historical aspects of man's fall:

(1) white (pestilence) - innocence - disobedience - curse
(2) red (war) - violence -murder - rebellion
(3) black (famine) - natural disasters - food control - starvation
(4) pale (death) - curse - disobedience - innocence (original loss)

Envy, lust, and desire lead to man's fall from the beginning of his original innocence, and by his disobedience through free moral agency (freedom of choice) he brought on himself the curse of death. (Gen. 3) The tree with the knowledge of good and evil looked good for food (envy), was pleasant to the eyes (lust), and desired (coveted). Choosing to disobey God caused the loss of their innocence and access to the tree of life or immortality. Later, Cain became jealous of Abel and spilled the first blood. (Gen. 4:1-10) The rest is like a merry-go-round of human history. As the end time draws nearer, the merry-go-round will begin to spin out of control. (Dan. 12:1) [See Appendix IV.]

The fifth seal in Rev. 6:9-11 was opened during Christ's crucifixion. (Matt. 27:50-53) The Old Testament Saints arose from their graves and appeared unto many. When Christ resurrected three eves later, he gave them white robes and told them that *they should rest (return to sleep – to repose) yet for a little season (time)*, until their fellow servants should be killed. Christ is the pinnacle of the Great Pyramid. He is building its foundation for His Kingdom by calling out the elect who will join the *reposed* fifth seal saints when he returns to set up the Kingdom (Government) of God on Earth.

We now await the sixth seal, which are the signs in the heavens pointing to the coming of Christ. (Rev. 6:12-17; Luke 21:10-11; Jer. 10:2) This comes immediately after great tribulation because the Lord said so! (Matt. 24:29) The *great earthquake* will most likely destroy the Dome of the Rock, unless some zealous Jews or Christians haven't blown it up by then. If this earthquake doesn't get it, then the last one surely will. (Rev. 16:18; Zech. 14:4) It will be like the time that Daniel spoke about, but many will be happy to see it destroyed.

There will be an attempt to explain away these signs, but those who know the truth won't buy it. The explanation will probably be a *polarity shift* of the earth's magnetic poles that many scientists believe will happen and is past due. The color spectrum's electromagnetic frequencies passing through a reversed magnetic field would cause greater atmospheric visual effects than that of the Aurora Borealis. A magnetic shift in the poles would most surely cause all the magnetic material in the earth's crust to *shake* when re-polarized. It would also cause a communication blackout because all our planet's communication systems work on electromagnetic pulse. It would require some time (about 21 days) to re-polarize all the planet's communication equipment. (Is. 24:1, 10, 23)

The seventh seal in Rev. 8:1 **immediately** follows the sixth seal and *was (holding) silence in the heavens (sky)*. That which is done in heaven is cast upon the earth. (Rev. 8:3-5/6:12-17) Utilizing prophetic math, 1000 man-years to one God-day, and 48 half-hours in a 24-hour day: [$1000 \div 48 = 20.8$] The reciprocal of the *year to the day* principle is *a day to the year*. The 20.8 years are 21 days (3 weeks) a global communication blackout takes place between the sixth and seventh seals. Recall the math in Chapter VI? This is the *prophetic mathematical reciprocal*. It will be a period of mourning and silence. (1Sam. 2:9-10; Is. 41:1, 47:5; Hab. 2:20; Zech. 2:13; Prov. 1:20-33)

The seventh seal is the seven trumpets preparing to sound, which will be a full year of judgments that will come to pass over the entire world. (Rev. 8:1-6) It is called **The Great Day of the Lord!** (Zeph. 1:14; Mal. 4:5; Jer. 30:7; Rev. 6:17)

Recreation week was 7 days
******* Judgment week (seven seals) will be 7 years *******
It is the "Time of Jacob's Trouble"

*******TRUMPETS AND PLAGUES*******

The seven trumpets are the seventh seal. The first six trumpets are sounded in Rev. 8:6 through 9:21, and the seventh in chapter 16. There have been many interpretations for these events in both the literal and figurative senses. **It does not matter how you interpret the method of causes in each trumpet event because the result will be the same!** The locusts in the fifth trumpet are not Apache helicopters; however, the sixth trumpet does sound like nuclear weapons. When man *created* the first elements that did not naturally exist, the first thing he made was a weapon of mass destruction. Would it be divine justice if God told the sixth angel to utilize man's own creation?

The ***great burning mountain*** in Rev. 8:8 is best defined as a **volcano**. It ***was cast (thrust up) into the sea.*** The Greek for *cast* is: *ballo* – to throw, arise, cast out, and thrust up. Comparable with: *rhipto* – to fling (through the idea of sudden motion). A third of the world's shipping moves on the Atlantic Ocean, which has earth's deepest volcanic depths.
Will we see some evidence of The Lost City of Atlantis?

Revelation 10-15 is an *intermission* between the sixth and seventh trumpets giving more detail of the overall prophecy. The seventh trumpet is the seven last plagues that will be poured out on man's systems of government and religion, and those with the mark of the beast. (Rev. 16) When ***It is done!*** Christ will return, stand on the Mount of Olives, destroy the armies fighting against Jerusalem, and subdue **all** the nations. (Rev. 19:11-20:6; Zech. 14; Is. 24-35)

When reading Revelation 16 very carefully, you will notice that no humans are killed by the seven plagues, unless they *live in the sea.* **How can people blaspheme God if they are dead?** The fourth plague is not global warming but may be directly related to the fourth commandment. The armies that gather to fight the Lord will be killed. The remaining third of man ***brought through the fire*** will come under the reign of Christ and his Saints. (Zech. 13:9; Matt. 24:22; Rev. 20:4-6) The first order of business will be the gathering of Israel's remnant, then the burying of the dead for seven months (Is. 10:20-23, 11:11-12; Jer. 23:3-6; Ezek. 39:11-14). The New City and Temple will be built, the land divided, and a pure system of worship established. Then, and only then, will there be peace on earth! (Ezek. 40-48; Is. 2:4)

All the trumpets have fire, burning, falling stars and/or the sun's scorching heat in common. Connect these links: anointed cherub – fallen Lucifer – Satan – bright and morning star – sun – fire – false sun gods – lord of the vernal day of the sun – Sunday. God separated light from darkness on the first day of recreation week (Sunday), made man on the sixth day (Friday), and the Sabbath by resting from his work on the seventh day (Saturday) while giving Adam the commandments, then *freedom of choice* beginning **day one – week two**.

There has been much debate about establishing world democracy, and the theocratic rule of any religion not being compatible with democracy. The coming Kingdom of God will be a **Theocratic Monarchy** and mortal humans will not have any ruling authority. Jesus Christ will be KING OF KINGS AND LORD OF LORDS! There will be no ifs, ands, or buts about it. What the Lord has said he will do, **HE WILL DO.** There will be no elections! There will be no petitions of grievousness and no protests!

Today, people elect politicians who can raise the most money, sell the best platform, make the most promises, and really talk the talk. The 2008 *Damnocritical Particularism Primatology* was the most ridiculous display of childishness, schoolyard bullying, and religious teasing I've ever seen. The general election wasn't a grand display of civil campaigning either. [I now have to take that back. 2020's is about one slur from an abomination!] If Jesus Christ were to run for president, which party would he run under? **He's not going to run for a damn thing!** He is going to return and subdue all nations and THANK GOD NO MORE ELECTIONS! (Rev. 11:15, 19:11-16)

The system of government our forefathers founded was the best system (republic) that man could possibly design. It is a shame we have made a **demockery** of it. We were guaranteed freedom of religious practice (this is where freedom of choice is implied) speech, press, and peaceful assembly. The ACLU forbids the other option of man's existence being taught in public schools. Christian adoption information and views of life are not allowed in public abortion clinics as an alternative option. Is that pro-choice? Do denied options support freedom of choice in any matter or issue?

I think that options in all things should be available, but that does not mean that we can pervert the sacredness of such long held institutions as marriage and the Ten Commandments. God will be the judge of man's choices! I strongly support the separation of church and state in man's governments and religions, but I do not support the church being thrown out of the state when the issues are based on freedom of choice. We are all endowed with that right by our creator!

The real choice is between good and evil, but the reasoning of man has turned that choice into the lesser of two evils. I hope and pray all people will choose to trust Jesus Christ as Savior, Lord, and King. **The third that is brought through the fire most surely will!** (Zech. 13:9; Is. 66:23; Jer. 23:5; Rev. 12:5, 19:15, 20:4; Prov. 22:15) See Appendix IV.

[Revision Addition 2020 Revised 2021]

President Trump may have made America great again, but prophecy warns the House of Israel that their fall will be great prior to the captivity in the last days. (Is. 5:7-25) Trump took office in 2017 and economic conditions did change for the better along with other things. China (Land of the Dragon) owns about 1.08 trillion of the national debt or 15% of the 6.8 trillion held by other countries. They presently own Smithfield Foods. Your pork chop may be made in America, but China owns it! Most everything in Walmart is made in China, and it did not shut down. After Jacob served two weeks of years for his wives, he served another six for his cattle and goats (wealth). When Jacob departed from his Uncle Laban after 20 years, the Laban clan was left bankrupt. (Gen. 30:25 - 31:42) The last attack on our country was 2001. [2001 + 20 yrs = 2021] and [2020 - 20 yrs = 2000] Two contested elections - one with hanging chads, the other a plugged in cable and/or misplaced envelopes with signatures.

It doesn't make any difference who is President. The Nation will go bankrupt! Who will be the receivership? The real question is, will the United States see a fair election in 2022 and 2024? Ever since and prior to the election of Ronald Reagan, my vote has been independently conservative for the lesser of two evils. [Didn't vote for John McCain. Voted for Sarah Palin.] Election 2020 was no different. Biden may be a friend to China and hand the U.S. over on a silver platter. Trump would have been tough in standing up to China, but he holds a nuclear football. Which is more evil, economic slavery under communism or nuclear war? Slavery is a word that has made a comeback and evolved into a critical theory these days! I voted this year and will continue to do so as long as there are elections. Next time, I will write in Jesus Christ, King of Kings and Lord of Lords!! Ladies of the View, can yawl say, **"King Jesus"**?

Chapter VIII
Prime Numbers 1, 2, 3, and 5

One is the loneliest number you will ever find. Two can be as lonely as one, but the number one is the loneliest. I can recall a song that utilized those two sentences from my High School years in the late 60's to early 70's, but I'm not sure of all the lyrics. However, they can greatly assist in understanding an important principle. Throughout scripture, **one** represents unity, and **two** represents both division and unity. [$1 \div 1 = 1$ and $1 \times 1 = 1$, but $1 + 1 = 2$ and $1 - 1 = 0$] These four simple mathematical functions utilizing the first two prime numbers (1 & 2) can explain many things. **Two** is the **only even prime number** and represents **unified duality** found throughout scripture.

In the beginning was **The Energy.** Being lonely, He transformed a portion of Himself into the express image called **The Light** and gave Him the selfsame wisdom and truth He possessed. Energy now has a son and creating partner, and the two were of one mind and purpose; however, there was still loneliness. Together, they developed a plan to build many mansions (galaxies) in infinite space and proposed to fill it with children, but first they had to create the **matter** necessary to accomplish the task. With the supreme trimorphic intellect of understanding, knowledge, and wisdom both possessed, it was by the will of the Energy that the Light said, **"Let $M = E \div C^2$."** **[The Big Bang]** (Heb. 1:3; Jn. 1:1, 14:2; Gen. 1:1; Job 38:7) The perpetually of all creation had begun.

Billions of years later after the earth had come to pass into an *indistinguishable ruin*; God remade it in six days, and on the sixth day said, *"Let us make man in our image, after our likeness"*. The Lord God saw that man did not have a companion and was lonely, so he took a portion of the man (a chromosome) and made (genetically designed) a woman, and together they are two in marriage, yet one as in the image and likeness of God. (Gen. 1:26-27, 2:7,21-23) Since man is in the *image* and *likeness* of God, God is an *image* and *likeness* of man. God creates, man procreates, which is the *likeness*. The human male needed a female helper to procreate as the Father needed a helper to create all that exists. God is a unity of two as man is a unity of two, which is the *image* of God. God's purpose is to bring many children to glory. (Rom. 8, Gen. 2:23-24, 5:1-2) The Eternals' procreation is through the transformation of Their energy/light into little lower intelligent matter mankind (Adam – male/female). (Ps. 8:4-6) [*Angels (mal'ak)* in verse 5 is the only place translated from *Elohiym,* the Hebrew word for *God(s).*]

Two, which represents unity as well as division, is the foundation of the duality of understanding. In the biology of human reproduction, only one single sperm enters a single egg, then cell divisions begin to create a new life. There are rare examples of identical twins, which is a single conception that self-divides into separate but physically identical individuals. Maternal twins are two separate conceptions. Most multiple births today are the result of successful fertility farming.

The most important prime of two is the Godhead (God-mind), and the Bible is quite clear about it. *And God said; Let us make man in our image, after our likeness.* (Gen. 1:26) *In the beginning was the Logos, and the Logos was with Theos, and the Logos was Theos.* (Jn. 1:1) Logos and Theos are two, yet they are one in spirit (mind-character), and the Logos is the creative partner to Theos. (Gen. 1:1; Jn. 1:2-3) Man and Woman are two, yet one in marriage. (Gen. 2:23-24) The female is the creative partner to the male, although she does the gestatory work like Logos in which *all things consist (to set together, introduce, exhibit).* (Col. 1:17) *Labor* or *pain* is a better translation for *sorrow* in Gen. 3:16.

The definition of *Holy Spirit* is *sacred breath, sacred character,* or *sacred intellect*, i.e. the very mind of God. Wisdom is given a feminine personage in Proverbs, but she is not part of the Godhead. The best way to explain the Godhead is with the pure language of mathematics. [$1 + 1 = 2$ **not 3**] Any other suggestion is mathematical error! However, the two are one. [$1 \times 1 = 1$ & $1 \div 1 = 1$] Without one or the other, there is nothing. [$1 - 1 = 0$] That is the simplicity of arithmetic! It is also the simplicity that is in **Christ**[2]. [**Truth × Light**]

The *Spirit of Truth* is the **Word of God**. (Jn. 1:1, 15:26, 16:13, 17:17; Jas. 1:18) The Father and Son are two spirit entities, but one creating unity, which is the Godhead or God-mind. [Revision Addition 2020: **The Holy Spirit is streamed from the Father thru the Son!** (Rev. 19:10) The Holy Spirit is the **Power (Watts)** of the Father's **energy (Voltage)** expressed through the Son who is the **light (Current)** of mankind. (Power = Voltage × Current) Man is like a resistor. (Power = Current^2 × Resistance) When man rejects Christ[2] (current[2]) there is no connection to the power of the Father. Man does have the freedom of choice to connect by being either **on with OR off from** Christ. I am a certified Journeyman Electrician by the Dept. of Navy, U.S. Dept. of Labor, and IBEW. Those three certificates and my High School Diploma are the only four certificates I can hang on a wall.] The Holy Spirit is the supreme intellect of Elohiym (Theos/Logos) and in the divine prime of seven constitutes the seven spirits of the Lord: fear, counsel, might, knowledge, understanding, wisdom, and truth. (Is. 11:2; Jn. 15:26)

The spirit in man is the human spirit. *Spirit* is literally defined as *breath* or *air*, and figuratively as *intellect* or *mind* in both the Hebrew and Greek. Air contains oxygen necessary for life. Life is in the blood. The blood supplies oxygen to the brain, which works by electro-magnetic impulse. It is where the intellect resides. Spiritual conception is when the electro-magnetism of man's mind (human spirit) is begotten by the electro-magnetism of God's mind (Holy Spirit) that a new creature is formed, then begins to grow in the body of Christ, but you're not yet ***born again***. (2Cor. 5:17; 1Pet. 1:23) The word *born* in 1Pet. 1:23 is translated from *anagennao* – to beget. It is translated ***begotten*** in 1Pet. 1:3. The word ***born*** in Jn. 3:3-8 is translated from: *gennao* – to procreate, procreation (lit) and to regenerate, regeneration (fig). **Wisdom** is the **womb** in which the newly begotten creature grows. (Rev. 12:1-2; Eph. 3:9-11; 1Cor. 2:7; Luke 7:35, 11:49; Matt. 11:19, Prov. 1-8) The rebirth or *regeneration* of the saints to an immortal body will take place at the last (seventh) trump. This is the first resurrection. (1Cor. 15:47-55; Rev. 20:4-6) The birth pains of the new birth in being **born again** is at either of the two resurrections after the first death. The second death does not have power in the first resurrection. But in the second resurrection, the second death does have power! (Rev. 20:11-15)

In the United States and other countries, fetuses are willfully aborted daily by free choice. Spiritual abortion is when a converted person begotten by the Holy Spirit continues to willfully sin. (Ezek. 18; Is. 55:69) It is incorrect to say, *"I'm born again"*, but it is correct to say, *"I'm begotten again"*. Read carefully what Jesus said in John 3. If you are indeed ***born again***, I would like to see you disappear then reappear, or change form and walk through solid matter. (Luke 24:36-37; Mk. 16:12; Jn. 20:26; Acts 26:13; 1Jn. 3:9; 1Cor. 14:44)

What more love could the creators have for their creation than for the Father to **willingly** sacrifice his only begotten Son who **willingly** laid down his life honoring his Father in redeeming their creation? (Jn. 3:16, 10:17-18) If Christ had failed in his mission on earth while in the flesh, the entire universe would have imploded, leaving the Father (energy) without the son (light). Take light out of the equation $M = E \div C^2$ and what do you have? The entire universe would have become a black hole, a gravitational field of energy absent of light with no possible way for life to exist, regenerate, or continue. All matter would have just vanished. Jesus Christ's sacrifice was much more than just the redemption of man. It was for the restitution, salvation, and stability of the entire creation. That is the true **PASSION OF CHRIST!** The evidence is hidden in the **Shroud of Turin**.

It was necessary from the foundation of creation that the creator should become as the created. The squaring of light's velocity was critical to the equation $E = mc^2$. Christ's first sacrifice was the sharing of himself in the process of creation. His second sacrifice was for the reconciliation of man (matter) to the Father (energy). To redeem man's fallen state, Christ became a flesh born man (matter) in order to bring man back into unity with and under the Father. Christ became flesh by the equation's fourth transposition. **Christ^2** is the root (power) of **creation × salvation**. (Is. 11:10-11; Job 19:23-28; Rom. 11:16-36; Col. 2:6-10; Ezek. 41:21; 2Ti. 2:15; Rev. 21:22, 22:13,16) Christ in the flesh was to be of the root of Jesse father of David. That is why Jesus also called himself **son of man.**

$$c = \sqrt{E/m} \quad \text{or} \quad \text{Christ in the flesh} = \sqrt{\text{Father}/\text{man}}$$

There are two books of life in the Bible, and they are the two resurrections. *The Lambs Book of Life* is found in Rev. 21:27 and Rev. 13:8, and the *Book of Life* is found in Rev 20:12 and 17:8. In the Old Testament, the two are stated *the book* with no distinction between the two, but are actually both since the word can also be plural. (Dan. 12:1-2) The two books have two different purposes, but the names found written in them have eternal life in common. The *Lamb's Book of Life* is the first resurrection describing those in Rev. 20:4-6, and the first *some* in Dan. 12:2. The second death has no power over the first resurrection. The *many* in Dan. 12:2 is from: *rab* – abundant (in quantity, size, age, rank, and quality) A contrast from: *rabab* – (primary root) – *to cast together*. The indication is that all who have ever lived will be raised, each in their **order**, which is better translated *series* or *succession*. (1Cor. 15:22-23) [This is the only place *tagma* is translated **order**. It is a derivative from: *tasso* (primary verb) – to arrange in an orderly manner, i.e. to assign or dispose. The word *tagma* is also translated: **addicted** in 1Cor. 16:15; **determined** in Acts 15:2; **appointed** in Matt. 28:16 and Acts 22:10; **ordained** in Acts 13:48 and Rom. 13:1] Everyone born of the flesh is *assigned* to a resurrection.

The Almighty Holy Father in heaven is the only person who writes names in the Lamb's Book of Life, and these names are the Saints. (Jn. 6:39,44, 17:1-26; Luke 10:20; Zech. 14:5) The custom of the Catholic Church is to submit names, and then vote on who is elevated to Sainthood. The word **draw** used in John 6:44 is translated from: *heiko* – to drag (lit. or fig.) and akin to: *haireounia* – to take for oneself, also comparative to: *helisso* – to coil or wrap. The Father takes for Himself those whom He chooses and if necessary, drags them through His written word to coil and wrap them in His truth, which is His son Jesus Christ, the truth and the light. (Jn. 1:1-4, 17:17, 3:21) He doesn't necessarily send them to philosophical schools of theology!

In Rev. 14:12 the *faith of (in) Jesus* is conjunction to *they that keep the commandments of God.* The *faith of (in) Jesus* is: He stepped down from His eternal existence to become earthly flesh, was anointed King of Kings, won the battle of Satan's temptation, then delivered the Gospel of the Kingdom of God, taught His disciples while healing the sick and lame, suffered trial and persecution, then nailed to a cross spilling His blood dying for the sins of all mankind, and resurrected from the dead so that all mankind may have an opportunity to eternal life. (Jn. 3:16) The Disciples of Christ who *keep God's commandments* and have the *testimony of Jesus Christ* will have the faith necessary to **STAND** in the face of the beast because they *loved not their lives unto the death*. (Rev. 12:11)

The second resurrection is found in Rev. 20:11-15 and the second *some* in Dan. 12:2. This is the *book of life*, which is known as **The Great White Throne Judgment** and takes place after the 1000-year reign of Jesus Christ and the Saints. In this resurrection the second death has power! It is the **Last Great Day** as foreshadowed in God's festival found in Lev. 23:33-36. All God's holy festivals found in Leviticus 23 are important to Him and foreshadow the entire plan of redemption and the reconciliation of man to God. The eighth day following the seven feast days is the seventh annual Sabbath of the year and represents the divine perfection of God's new beginning for mankind. The eighth day is the beginning of a new millennial workweek, as the 1000-year reign of Christ is the earth's millennial **Sabbath Rest** from Satan's influence during the last six millennial workdays (6000 years). Since the fall of Adam, this old world has seen 6000 years of rebellion, bloodshed, war, famine, disease, hunger, pain, misery, oppression, lies, and all kinds of deception. But when Christ as King of Kings comes to establish the Kingdom of God, planet earth will have her Sabbath Rest. Mankind will live in a unified world of peace, harmony, and love for God and each other. Jesus Christ, Kings of Kings will rule with a rod of iron! (Rev. 2:27, 12:5, 19:15; Psalm 2:9)

The penalty for sin is death, and all of mankind has sinned and suffer death. Those in the second resurrection will be raised up in the flesh. (Ezek. 37:1-14) This is the judgment in which the second death has power. The *shame and (or) everlasting contempt* in Dan. 12:2 is the verdict according to the works found in the other books. (Rev. 20:12-13) The Hebrew words used in Dan. 12:2 are as follows:

(1) shame – *cherpah* – disgrace, rebuke, reproach, contumely; derived from: *charaph* – (primary root) to pull off, expose (as by stripping) specifically to betroth (as if a surrender).
(2) contempt – *dera'own* – to repulse, an object of aversion, abhorring.

Considering *order* or *succession* with the definitions above, the second resurrection may take some time. (Rev. 14:17-20, 20:11-15) The word *space* refers to time. That is why the last great day is the beginning of a new millennial workweek. That is the time when things will be made clear for all those who have died in deception or have never heard the truth. Some teach the second resurrection is for the wicked, and all of them will be cast into the lake of fire. If that is true, then why is there a book of life opened? That teaching doesn't paint a pretty picture of God's intelligence or mercy. Why would he resurrect the dead just to destroy them? There are some that say that there is not a second chance and today is the only day of salvation. That teaching limits God's mercy, and I do not dare place limits on God's love, mercy, or power. If we are prejudged in this life and bound for all eternity in either a blissful heaven or a burning hell at the time of death, why are the resurrections and a final judgment necessary? There is no great degree of wisdom in understanding all this; however, it does require some degree of common sense, unless you're a Vulcan with simple logic – 101.

Those who are found with shame will receive healing (Rev. 21:4), but those who are found with contempt will be cast into the lake of fire. (Rev. 20:14-15) This is the second death, which is eternal death. It is not everlasting life in hellfire! It is everlasting nonexistence, eternal nothingness, and to be totally forgotten. (Ex. 32:33; Rev. 21:8; Dan. 4:35) It will be like district court where it is best for everyone to plead guilty, but the blood of the lamb will have already paid the price. All things will be exposed. *Some* will acknowledge their *shame* and God will strip off their disgrace and heal them. *Some* will want to argue with the Judge about the doctrines and traditions they have known and always believed. They may be found in *contempt* of court and cast into the lake of fire. There may be others that will think themselves above judgment. Those will surely be cast into the lake of fire! Like the Borg say on Star Trek, **resistance is futile**. It is not a second or any other number of chances. It will be the only chance because it is the final judgement! (Is. 9; Matt. 18:21-35; Jn. 3:17-21)

When Satan was bound to his tree in the Garden of Eden, he could have said, *"ssssssssh, stay away, you do not want this fruit, for you will become like me, and it will bring upon you – death. Listen to and obey your Lord and maker."* Would God have forgiven him and gave him a second chance? When Satan is released after the 1000 years, does he have to go out to deceive the nations? Will this not be a last chance for him to repent? We know what happened in the garden. The Scriptures state what will happen at the end of the 1000 years. Satan's mind is so twisted, warped, chaotic, and just plain screwed up, all he wants to do is **destroy, destroy, destroy**! Satan is so far gone; he is like the Derelict in the BBC series, Doctor Who. As in baseball – strike three, you're out!

The innocent sheep that are led astray by false shepherds and the doctrines and traditions of men will bare their shame and guilt more easily than the false shepherds who misled them. The false shepherds will be judged to a higher standard, especially those who profited, and their supervising shepherds to a much higher standard. There will be no B.A.'s, M.A.'s, Ph.D.'s, or any other type of manmade degree in philosophy, theology, sociology, psychology, or religion admitted as evidence in this court of judgment. The truth in scripture cannot be found in the theological schools of man, but only in the Holy Word of God with the assistance of the spirit of prophecy and truth. The prophecies against these shepherds are found in Isaiah 56, Jeremiah 23, Ezekiel 34, and Zechariah 11.

Throughout the New Testament, there are two phrases used in the hope for eternal life. The **Kingdom of God** and the **Kingdom of Heaven** are the same as they relate to eternal life, but the Kingdom of God is the first resurrection, and the Kingdom of Heaven is the *new heavens and earth* that follows the Great White Throne Judgment. Jesus taught to seek first the Kingdom of God. (Matt. 6:33-34) Many are called, but few are chosen to rule in the Kingdom of God; however, the ones not chosen to rule may find themselves as subjects in the Kingdom of Heaven. (Matt. 20:1-16 and chapters 5-7) Our Father in heaven chooses the saints who will rule with Christ. (John 6:44, 17:1-26; Matt. 22:1-14; Rev. 20:4-6) The birth pains of the new birth (being born again) in the first resurrection is the first death! (1Cor. 15:50-58)

The knowledge of Christ and the redeeming power of his blood are the only things that any person can carry to the grave for their future benefit. The false shepherds will answer for their leading the sheep astray in doctrine. The message for these last days is to come out of the Babylonian mess we're in, and it is for both shepherds and sheep. What resurrection or book of life will I be in? That is totally up to my Father in heaven, and it doesn't really make any difference to me, for either book of life will be a reward of eternal life. Those who like to consider their own selves great and already written in the Lamb's Book of Life may be fooling themselves. (Matt. 18:1-7, 23:1-12; Lk. 14:7-14, 18:9-14, 22:24-30; John 10:25-30)

The number three is often associated with God's mighty power. Many things came by threes, such as the number of days Jesus' body was in the grave (Matt. 12:40), months Moses' mother hid him (Ex. 2:2), Noah's sons (Gen. 6:10), Job's daughters (Job 42:13-14), righteous men who could save their own souls (Eze. 14:14), Saul's days without sight (Acts 9:9), gates on each side of the holy city (Rev. 21:13), and the three temples. Two were destroyed. The first was in 587 BC and the second in 70 AD. The third will begin construction in 0001 ACR (After Christ Returns). **It will stand forever!**

The only *trinity* or *trilogy* you will find in the Bible is the trimorphic intellect of understanding, knowledge, and wisdom. The three parallel with the three major vesicles of the human brain, which are the forebrain (prosencephalon – *pro-sense*), midbrain (mesencephalon – *me-sence*), and hindbrain (rhombencephalon – *om-bense*). It is not three brains in one mind or three minds in one brain, but one brain with three major parts that constitute one trimorphic mind in a single person. As previously stated, the Holy Spirit is not a person, but the very mind or intellect of God. [There are no gender pronouns in the Greek. The particle *autos* can be translated **he, she, him, her,** or ***it.***] The following definitions are from the Greek Dictionary:

(1) knowledge – *gnosis* – the act of knowing, knowledge, science.
(2) understanding – *suniemi* or *sunesis* – to put together, to comprehend, or to mentally discern. Also: *nous* – the intellect i.e. the mind (human or divine). [The word **intellect** is not used in the New Testament. *Nous* is translated **understanding** in Lk. 24:45; 1Cor. 14:14, 15, 19; Phil. 4:7, and Rev. 13:18. It is also translated ***mind*** in Rev. 17:9; 1Cor. 1:10, 2:16; Rom. 1:28, 7:23,25, 11:34, 12:2, 14:5; Eph. 4:17, 23]
(3) wisdom – *sophia* – the act of being wise – wisdom (whether higher, lower, worldly, or spiritual). From: *sophos* – wise, akin to: saphes – clear, to make clear.

There are three angelic messages found in Rev. 14:6-12. (Since the number of verses total to seven, they can be considered a supreme divine message for all mankind.) The first two angels are not numbered first or second but described only as **another**. These two and the ***third angel*** follow the description of the 144,000 in the proceeding verses, but don't necessarily sequentially follow the event; neither do they follow each other in the order written. The message in verse 6 is the preaching of the ***everlasting gospel*** that some believe was accomplished during the Philadelphia era of the church. That can't be true because verse 7 states: ***for the hour (times/season) of his judgment is come***. It is also preached before and during the seven years of judgments. (Rev. 7:18, 8:13)

Since the Lord has ***spewed*** out of his mouth his lazy church, the 144,000 sealed during the sixth and seventh seal's opening and 21 days of silence may be the ones who bring this message during the Great and terrible day (year) of the Lord. They are a special group because ***they are virgins...and in their mouths was found no guile; for they are without fault before the throne of God.*** The word ***guile*** is translated from: *dolos*

– from an obsolete prime *dello* (to decoy) – a trick (bait) i.e. (fig.) wile – craft, deceit, guile, subtlety (nicety). Their message will be direct and forward without regard to the sensitivity of hearing and the doctrines and traditions of men. They are redeemed from mankind and don't necessarily have to be all males. A virgin (maiden) retains their purity for marriage, whether male or female. That might be hard to find among today's youth, but there is a special group of people that might fit the calling. A caring society often calls them *special*, but a careless society calls them *retards*. Now that is something to think about! They are the Lamb's chorus that sings the song that no man can learn and the Lamb's entourage that follows him everywhere He goes. (Rev. 14:1-4)

The third angel message in Rev. 14:9-12 is the warning about the mark, the receiving of the mark, and the worship of the beast and his image. Verse 10 states that they will receive punishment and have no rest from it. Review the fifth trumpet and the seven last plagues. It is the smoke of their torment that ascends forever as an everlasting testimony, not the torment itself. That message is for today! It is for God's people to come out of the Babylonian harlot and her daughters, or they will receive her plagues. (Lev. 26; Is. 13:11, 24:21, 26:21; Jer. 9:25, 25:29, 30:11, 46:28, 49:12; Rev. 8, 9, 16)

The angel in Rev. 14:8 that announces, **Babylon is fallen, is fallen** is the same angel in Rev. 18, but is giving more detail of Babylon's fall. In Rev. 18:4, the other voice is the third angel in Rev. 14:9-11. The Apostle John did not necessarily write the book of Revelation in the sequence in which the revelation was given him, nor did the visions come in time sequence during their revealing. That is why the book has always been such a mystery. People like things handed to them on a silver platter. God doesn't work that way. You must study God's Word with a sincere desire for understanding and thirst for knowledge; then wisdom will manifest itself *precept upon precept, line upon line, here a little, there a little.* (Is. 28:9-15)

A comprehensive understanding of Daniel and Revelation would be withheld until the last days because God doesn't want his people to soon forget. Look at the way things are happening today. Yesterday's news is forgotten within a week or two. If you were to ask people that watch the news how many brave young soldiers have died in Iraq and Afghanistan for their commander in chief, most couldn't tell you; but, if you were to ask them about Paris Hilton or Michael Jackson, you couldn't shut them up. I can remember seeing Paris strutting down the streets of LA with a Bible under her arms on the news.

There are **three woes** stated in Revelation 8:13. The first woe is the fifth trumpet and does not appear to kill anyone, but the second woe is the sixth trumpet and kills the third part of men. (Rev. 9:13-18) The two witnesses in Rev. 11 are finally killed after 3.5 years of giving their testimony with power, left in the street to rot, and then are raised 3.5 days later at the close of the sixth trumpet and sounding of the seventh. That will take place about late fall or early winter, which is about Christmas time. *And they that dwell upon the earth shall rejoice over them, and make merry, and shall send gifts one to another*, then the last of the three woes, which is the seventh trumpet that is the seven last plagues.

[WOE-WOE-WOE!!! This will be the last HO-HO-HO-!!!]

The two witnesses begin prophesizing between the fourth and fifth seal *with power*. They will ascend to heaven as the seventh (last) trumpet is being sounded. Revelation 16 describes the plagues, but only affects those who have the mark of the beast, while 17-18 describes the harlot (false church), and her judgments. Zec. 14, Is. 66, and Rev. 19 thru 20 are Christ's return to rule and reign over the third brought through the fire.

Five is an important prime number in scripture. There were five wise and five foolish virgins. (Matt. 25:1-12.) Elisabeth hid herself five months after conceiving John the Baptist. (Lk. 1:24) The fifth trumpet is five months of torment. (Rev. 9:5) Five is often associated with grace as with the five loaves in Matt. 14:15-21, but there were seven loaves in Matt. 15:34-38. Five and multiples of five are mostly associated with the dimensions of the tabernacle, Solomon's temple, as well as the new temple, city, and dwelling place of the Lord in Ezekiel. (Ex. 26-27; 1Kings 6; Ezekiel 40 thru 48)

In Numbers 7, the peace offering made by each of the twelve tribes was 2 oxen, 5 rams, 5 he goats, and 5 lambs. A pyramid has four faces and three sides per face. [$3 \times 4 = 12$ tribes] In the Giza group, the pinnacles of the largest two are in a NE alignment, and there are three sets of five corners.

The first five prime numbers have great biblical significance. Could the missing link in Biblical understanding be basic Math? The *fiveness* was noted in the pyramids. The four prime numbers (1, 2, 3, & 5) in our system of numbers (1-10) are associated with the pyramid as well as the human being. One pyramid (soul) has an interior and exterior (1 mind in 1 body), but the two are one thing or one being with a trimorphic intellect. (3-point side view) There are five corners as we have five fingers and toes on each hand or foot. The pinnacle is the fifth corner and represents the freedom of mind (free moral agency – freedom of choice) to make one of only two choices. There is no and will not be a third option!

Christ and eternal life ◀ OR ▶ Satan and eternal death

[2020/2021 Revision Addition]

Everyone has Freedom of choice! You were endowed by your creator with it! I can only pray that all will exercise that right with some wisdom. Revelations 20:11-15 describes the Great White Throne Judgment. One of the books opened in the first part of verse 12 is considered a book of remembrance as well as The Book(s) of Truth and the other - The Book of Life. The Eternal is the Judge and Jury. There will be no defense lawyers! The Blood of the Lamb of God is the only witness that can enter a plea for mercy. I personally will not judge any individual in this issue; however, the Spirit of Truth has placed it in my heart to ask two questions that should be very carefully considered before a choice is made. Although it would be considered unusual, would it be fair and just if the very smallest of the dead (those denied the chance to the breath of life by their mothers by only a choice made because of "inconvenience") be risen and stand as witness against those who denied them the chance to that very breath? The Lord can forgive and is full of mercy, but would the little ones have mercy over the shame or would the claim to free choice be held in everlasting contempt? (Daniel 12:2)

Chapter IX
Doctrines and Traditions of Men

How many doctrines can a Christian man learn, and how many traditions can he observe? The answer my friend is set forth by the councils of men, and there are many blowing in the wind. In Bob Dylan's song, "**Blowing in the Wind**", the answers to all the world's problems stated in its lyrics were blowing in the wind.

In these latter days, there are many believers in Christendom who fly in the winds of doctrine. They may be searching for truth, intrigue, or simply enjoy church hopping. The numerous denominational, non-denominational, freewill ministerial, philosophically hybridized, theologically engineered, and humanistic doctrines to choose from is like an open buffet with all you can eat for a simple price. Searching for truth in the vast sea of confusion and deception is like searching Wal-Mart for something not made in China or made in the USA.

Since the beginning of Christianity, many false doctrines and traditions have crept into Christendom. Most have been in practice for over a thousand years. The early Apostles warned the followers of Christ that there would be a *falling away* prior to his return. (2Th. 2:1-12) The Apostle Peter warned of false teachers making merchandise of the sheep. (2 Pet. 2:1-3) Jesus Christ prophesied that there would be many coming in his name preaching about him and saying that he was indeed the Christ but deceiving many. How? Most teach their own ideological doctrines. (Matt. 24:4-5, 15:8-9, 7:21-23; Is. 29:13)

The Jews that became followers of Jesus Christ had a better understanding of God's ways than the Gentiles because of the former knowledge given them. The only thing that the Jews were lacking was a true spiritual understanding of the knowledge they possessed prior to the teachings of Christ. They were well adept in the letter of the law but had many shortcomings in the spirit of the law.

Many gentiles believed the Gospel (good news) of the Kingdom of God when it was delivered to them, but had to discard their pagan customs and be instructed in God's commandments and ways. The biggest problem in the early church was some of the converted Pharisees zealousness in getting their hands on the converted Gentile's penises to cut off their foreskins. (Acts 15:5) The Apostle Paul had a difficult time convincing them that it was circumcision of the heart and not the flesh that was more important. (Deut. 10:16; Jer. 4:4, 9:25; Jn. 7:21-24) The legalistic issue in John 7:21-24 was the performing of circumcision (custom/law of Moses) on the Sabbath (commandment) *versus* the healing of a man on the Sabbath. They condemned the Lord for healing a man and making him whole on the Sabbath, yet they considered it lawful to whack off the foreskin of a male child's penis. Should the lawful custom of men supersede the doing of a good deed on the Lord's holy day?

The Gentiles were accustomed to paying tribute to their false gods and keeping the pagan customs of the time. They worshipped the Greek and Roman deities and/or the deities that had been worshipped during Old Testament times. The *Babylonian Mystery Religion* was widely practiced, and one of its priests was even converted and baptized, but he erred when trying to buy the power of the Holy Spirit. (Acts 8:9-24) That Simon, a Samaritan sorcerer, had the same name as the Apostle Peter who rebuked him, and I do not think that he (sorcerer Simon Peter) walked away without the intension to adapt this new religion to his old one. The *falling away* that the Apostle Paul wrote about was already in progress during those early years of Christianity. (Col. 2:8; Gal. 2:4; 2 Th. 2; Jude 4) Even some of the popular converts can be found flip-flopping and disserting the faith to return to the world. (2Tim. 4:10)

Barnabas was Paul's first traveling companion. (Acts 9:26-28) After they returned from Jerusalem, they went to Antioch. (Acts 12:25-13:1) In Acts 13:2, the Holy Spirit said, **separate me Barnabas and Saul for the work whereunto I have called them.** In the Greek, the word *"autos"* is the reflexive pronoun for self or selves: *she, her, he, him, them, their, they,* and *it*. The conjunction **and** is translated from the primary particle *kai,* having a cumulative and/or copulative force: *and, also, even, so, then, too, which,* etc. The word **separate** is from the Greek *aplorizo* meaning: to set off, limit, exclude, or sever as well as appoint, and a compound of the primary particle *apo* (from, off, or away as in separation) and *horizo* (bound, mark out, decree, specify). The prime particle *gar* translated *for* is often used with other particles to assign reason. Acts 13:2 should be translated: *As they gave praise unto the Lord and fasted, the Holy Spirit brought word that it would separate itself from Barnabas so Saul therefore (without doubt) can work wherever I (the Lord) call him (Saul).*

Shortly after the Jerusalem Council, Paul and Barnabas got into a disagreement about Mark, and then they separated with much strife between them. (Acts 15:36-41) In Paul's letter to the Galatians, he recounts his experience while in Jerusalem. In Gal. 2:13 we find Barnabas carried away with the Jews ***dissimulation (hypocrisy).*** When comparing Acts 15:1-7 with Gal. 2:1-13, Barnabas had flip-flopped on his position about the circumcision issue. Paul's Epistle to the Galatians indicates some degree of frustration. (Gal. 3:1, 6:17) Acts 15:39 is the last time scripture has Barnabas associated with the work. He is mentioned in 1 Cor. 9:6 in connection with the privilege of receiving compensation for the work, which thing Paul did not do. (1Cor. 9:15-18) The only other time he is mentioned is in Col. 4:10. The Greek word *dechomai* (middle of a primary verb) translated ***receive*** has a sense of *keeping in suspense* when tracing it back to the primary verbs *haireomai* and *airo*. The verb *dechomai* translated ***receive*** in Col. 4:10 is also translated ***take*** in Lk. 16:6, 7 (dishonestly) and Eph. 6:17 (precaution), and again ***accepted*** in 2Cor. 8:17 and 11:4.]

In Paul's second letter to Timothy, his last epistle, he indicates that some of the converts and his close friends have fallen away and returned to the ways of the world. (2Tim. 4:6-11) When reading the passage correctly, Crescens and Titus have also forsaken (deserted) Paul and departed. All three people in this statement had deserted Paul but went three different directions. The second Epistle written to Timothy was when Paul was imprisoned in Rome. (2Tim. 1:15-17) Paul wrote the Epistle to Titus, who he had left in Crete, while he (Paul) was still free to travel. (Titus 1:5, 3:12)

[Revision 2020 addition]

Is it highly possible that this young Titus (early 20's) latter became emperor of Rome? Paul was beheaded by Nero in 67 AD. Titus (Roman emperor) was born 40 AD and became emperor in 79. Nero died in 68, then Galba 68-69, Otho Jan. - April 69, Vitellius July - Dec. 69, Vespasian (Titus' father) 69 - 79, Titus 79 - 81 (**3 yrs.**), then Domitian (Titus' younger brother) 81 - 96. Vespasian's family home was Dalmatia! In 70 AD, the then General Titus (**the Prince**) destroyed Jerusalem while crushing the Jewish (not Christian) rebellion. Could he have simply found the last living Apostle, John, and only placed him in (on) the isle of Patmos or someplace in Asia Minor around the territory of the seven churches as a relocation for protective custody? (Rev. 1:9 & **Dan. 9:26**) Domitian was the despot that persecuted Christians. The letters that became the Book of Revelation were written while John was on Patmos. Christians were killed if they didn't kneel and worship Domitian as King. Who supplied John with the materials and seclusion to receive and write the Revelation? Titus was considered as the most just and gentle emperor during the first century. (Christian kindness and charity?) At some point in time prior to or right at the beginning of the reign of Domitian, John was placed on Patmos. Do the Math!

****

There are two books from the **Lost Scriptures** that didn't make it into the New Testament called *The Letter of Barnabas* and *Pseudo-Titus*. The Barnabas Letter promotes everything non-Jewish, even worship on Sunday. Barnabas was a Levite! (Acts 4:36) It seems that Barnabas was like many politicians or ministers today that flip-flop on the issues or principles and will say most anything to get a vote or convert. (Gal. 3:1; Eph. 4:14; Rom. 16:17-18) The Pseudo-Titus Letter promotes strict celibacy, even within marriage. That teaching probably pissed many fiancés and husbands off. It was contrary to the teachings of Paul. (1Cor. 7:1-17; Col. 3:18; Eph. 5:22)

Most Church historians will acknowledge that the Church went through a dark period with little recorded history at the close of the first century AD. History reveals Christianity again at the end of the second and beginning of the third century after Constantine had acknowledged Christianity as the official religion of the empire, but there were two very distinct groups. Some were Sabbath keeping Christians, but the majority was keeping Sunday and many other pagan traditions. The Apostle Paul's letter to the Galatians (4:8-12) is evidence of that. The **weak and beggarly elements** that they were returning to was their former pagan traditions, **not** Jewish traditions. The Galatians were a religious people, and their pagan deities had numerous festivals and customs. It was those they were returning to! I suppose there were some false apostles who discovered the best way to sell a new religion was to repackage the old one by altering its manufactures' instructions and sell it as new and improved.

During the second century of Christianity, Rome persecuted all Christians. Theological discrimination was not a problem! All Christians had the equal right to be tossed into the lion's pit, burned at the stake, beheaded, or nailed to a pole. Be assured, that no matter what, those who fearlessly profess the name of Jesus Christ in the face of death are worthy of the Lamb. (Rev. 12:11) There were numerous sects with various doctrines within both main groups. Some were outright pagan but called themselves Christian. Religion is much the same now as then. Today, it is big business!

Major Corporations have a CEO and a Board of Directors. The Board meets to establish corporate policy and the CEO administers it. The Board may sometimes give the CEO *infallible* control of running the company. The current Universal Church (Catholic) is like a corporation. Its Board of Directors is the Council of Cardinals, the CEO is the Papacy, and the Pope is a mortal man that gets voted into the position. Its Board meetings are Ecclesiastical Councils that determine canon law for the church. From 325 AD to 1962 there have been 21 Catholic Councils. The first four approved doctrines that are a direct violation of the first four commandments. (Dan. 7:25)

Council of Nicaea (325 AD) This was the first council and was convened by Constantine. The time and day for keeping the Passover was changed. The idea and philosophy of the trinity doctrine was introduced, although not widely accepted. Constantine had made Sunday the official day of rest a civil law in 321 AD.

Council of Laodicea (364 AD) This council issued the famous decree that Christians should not *Judaize* by keeping the Seventh Day Sabbath, which is the fourth commandment. If Christians were found *Judaizing*, they were to be excommunicated and cut off from Christ. [How can men cut off from Christ those who are keeping his holy commandments? In their minds, by killing them! (Dan. 7:24, 11:32-35; 2Th. 2:3-12; Rev. 3:16-19, 12:11-17, 14:12, 16:8-9; Matt. 24:9-13, 15:7-9, 22:37-40; Jn. 14:14-15; Ex. 20:1-17; Is. 58:13-14, 66:23)]

Council of Constantinople (381 AD) This council adopted the final formula for the trinity doctrine that was later incorporated into the

Athanasian Creed. From the time that the concept was first introduced there had been much controversy over the godhead and the nature of Christ. The Holy Spirit was given a separate entity status (personage) in order to make the *God in Three Persons* formula plausible. [The triad godhead in the Babylonian Mystery Religion was Ishtar, Sin, and Shemesh. Ishtar, the Goddess of fertility and rebirth could not be replaced with *Mary Mother of God* because it would have been too obvious. To whom are we to pray? (Mt. 6:5-13; Lk. 1:28,42-43)]

Council of Nicaea (787 AD) This council was called by the Empress Irene, which ordered the restoration of **images** in the church, but declared that they should only be venerated, not worshipped. [Look up the definitions in the English dictionary for venerate, veneration, and worship. Is there any difference? There is a possibly that just a little bit more difference exists between George I and George II than those words!]

These four councils established doctrines by majority vote that violates the first four commandments that Jesus Christ summed up into one when asked the trick question: *Which is the great commandment in the law?* (Matt. 22:33-40) The lust for power, authority, and the murder that ensued while enforcing the council's dictates violates all of God's Ten Commandments, not just the first four. The history of the eastern and western orthodox churches, the ecclesiastical councils, and some of the philosophical theology in support of the doctrines and traditions approved can be found in most any Encyclopedia.

Constantine the Great became sole ruler of the entire Roman Empire in 324 AD after Licinius, ruler over the eastern division, was murdered. His father, Constantius I, had ruled jointly with Galerius and Maximianus, and was killed in battle in 306. Afterwards, the army proclaimed Constantine as Caesar, and Galerius was then forced to recognize the title. Constantine's position was further strengthened by his marriage to Fausta, who was the daughter of Maximianus. In 310, Maximianus tried to oust the young emperor and was murdered.

Maxentius, son of Maximianus, sought revenge and was killed in battle in 312 AD. It was just prior to that battle that Constantine was supposed to have seen in the sky a flaming cross bearing the legend *"in hoc signo vinces"* or "in this sign conquer". [Can anyone believe that this was a sign from God? Does it remind you of anything else sinister?] The legend purportedly led to Constantine's Christianity. He is considered one of the ablest rulers of the Roman Empire, although his reign was beset by much political and religious intrigue. His many reprehensible murders included his wife, Fausta, and his own son, Crispus. He did protect the empire's new religion, which was the officially recognized form of Christianity by empowering the Catholic Church, but he did not officially become a Christian until his deathbed conversion in 337 AD.

Due to the theological conflicts within Christendom, Constantine ordered and directed the first Council of Nicaea in 325 AD. The eastern churches in Asia and western churches in Greece, Italy and Spain had already adapted Sunday as the Christian day of worship and rest. [Sunday was revered as **the day of the sun** in Sun god worship. (Gen. 1:3-5; Eze. 8:16)] After Constantine had recognized Christianity as the empire's official religion and made Sunday the official day of rest (excluding agriculture) a civil law, the official church could legally persecute Christians keeping the Lord's Sabbath.

Any Christian sect that did not adhere to the Roman Church's newly established authority was declared heretic. The true flock began fleeing to the wilderness. (Rev. 12) When the poor Sabbath keeping Waldenses emerged during the 12th to 15th centuries with their copies of scriptures from the Bible, the papal bull to exterminate them was issued by Pope Innocent VIII in 1487. [Ironic name for such a supposedly holy, but murderous man.] Their copies of individual books of scripture and even their complete Bibles were burned, and then they were killed in a variety of tortuous ways. The Gutenberg printing press wasn't invented until 1440.

The councils of men that have been held throughout the centuries set the church's doctrines, traditions, regulations, and canon law by majority vote. In the Council of Trent, third session 1562-63, Papal supremacy was recognized, and the church was purified (forgiven) of her past abuses (sins) by the council's reforms. Vatican Council I (1869-1870) passed the Pope's **infallibility** in matters of faith and morals. [Thus, saith the Pope: "Thou shalt..."] Can a man or a church forgive its own sins? What height has the Papacy elevated itself? (Rev. 18:7; Dan 11:32-39) The Council of Cardinals and Papacy are in the image of the Roman Beast (Senate and Emperor).

There are several pagan traditions that were transformed into Christian traditions. One is Easter, which was a celebration to the Babylonian goddess of fertility – Ashtar. The English spelling is derived from Eostra, the Teutonic goddess of spring. [The three are pronounced the same.] The pagan festival was close to the day of Passover following the new moon nearest to the spring equinox, which was adopted at the Council of Nicaea in 325 AD. The early Eastern Church celebrated Passover on Nisan 14, the sacred calendar's first month that began on the first new moon nearest the spring equinox, but the Western Church the Babylonian weekend festival of Ashtar. Any encyclopedia has the history!

The pagan tradition goes back to the Old Testament days. The Israelites often turned to the goddess of fertility, or Queen of Heaven, and this was an abomination to God. (Jer. 44:17-28) Easter morning's sunrise service can be found in Eze. 8:16 and the baking of hot cross buns in Jer. 7:18. The only place in the entire Bible you will find the word **Easter** in the Authorized King James Version is Acts 12:4. The word is translated from the Greek word *pascha*, which is translated **Passover** in every other place in the whole New Testament. I don't know why the translators used Easter in this single verse. Maybe the answer is in 2 Th. 2:3-11.

Jesus Christ is our Passover. The Passover Feast is the time we should keep the remembrance of his sacrifice. (1Cor. 5:7-8, 11:20-29) **Unworthily** is translated from *anaxios,* which means *irreverently.* Is it reverent to substitute the time and tradition of Passover with a pagan one? The precious blood Christ shed for the redemption of sin should not be polluted with a fertility celebration with rabbits and colored eggs. I've raised both rabbits and chickens, but I've never seen a rabbit lay an egg. The Easter tradition also states that Jesus was crucified on *Good Friday* and resurrected Sunday morning. If my math is correct, that totals to 1.5 days (36 hours). Jesus said he would be in the grave **three days *and* three nights** (72 hours). (Matt. 12:39-40) Doesn't that tradition call Jesus a lair? Ever wonder why there are **three woes** in the book of Revelation?

Jesus Christ was not crucified on a Friday! Days were reckoned from sunset to sunset. Passover is the 14th of Nisan and it is eaten at sunset beginning the 14th. The day that follows the 14th is the 15th and at sunset begins the seven-day Feast of Unleavened Bread. The 15th of Nisan is also the first annual holy convocation (high day) or annual Sabbath. (Jn. 19:31; Lev. 23) Both weekly and annual Sabbaths were commonly called **Sabbath.** Christ's body was taken and placed in the tomb just prior to sunset on the 14th. When the sun was set, the annual Sabbath (high day) began, which also began the 15th. (Lk. 23:52-56) The Sabbath that the women rested on the day after Passover was the annual Sabbath, not the weekly Seventh Day Sabbath. Passover week is eight days, Passover Day plus The Seven Days of Unleavened Bread. (Nisan 14 thru 21)

It was early, just before sunrise on the first day of the week (Sunday) that the tomb was first found empty. Christ was already risen! Let's back up ***three days and three nights*** and trust what our Lord tells us in his written word. Passover began at sunset on what we call Tuesday evening, which biblically begins the week's fourth day – Wednesday. That night was what is called the Lord's Supper. After Christ instituted the wine and bread as a memorial and washed the disciples' feet, they went to the garden where Jesus was betrayed. It was our Tuesday midnight to Wednesday afternoon that Christ was ridiculed, mocked, beaten, interrogated, tortured, and then crucified. He was placed in the tomb just prior to sunset Wednesday evening, which began the annual Sabbath on Nisan 15. COUNT: Wednesday sunset to Thursday sunset (day one), Thursday sunset to Friday sunset (day two), and Friday sunset to Saturday sunset (day three). Christ rose from the grave late Saturday afternoon or early evening. Why was the tomb found empty early Sunday morning? **He had already risen!**

Passover can fall on any day of the week from year to year. The term *sabbath day* in Lk. 23:56 is plural. There was the annual Sabbath on Thursday and weekly Sabbath on Saturday. The women could not do the customary service to Jesus' body on Thursday because it was the High Day, plus the fact there was no admittance allowed. The Jews had the Romans post guards. (Matt. 27:62-66) That is how those high priests and ruling Pharisees kept their annual (High Day) Sabbath.

Christmas is another pagan tradition that Christianity has adopted. You can read its complete history in any encyclopedia. The shepherds tending their flocks by night would have been in the spring/summertime. Winter rains in the region is what brings about green grass in the spring. By the end of summer and early autumn, the grass is dry and if tall enough usually cut as hay for winter forage. During the winter months, sheep and goats were kept in lower rooms, barns, or caves. Although a Christmas tree is found in Jer. 10:1-4, man has philosophized with various doctrines a humanistic defense of the Christmas tradition, but none are scriptural. It is difficult for man to change generations of tradition. **But the King of Kings and Lord of Lords surely will!** (Is. 66:23)

If Christ really wanted us to celebrate his birthday, the scriptures would give us a clear clue as to when he was born. The most accepted year is 5 BC. What was the month and date? Have you ever searched for something while it was right under your nose the entire time? Luke begins his first letter with the parents of John the Baptist. (1:5-25) Elisabeth conceived and hid herself five months; then, Luke directs his narrative to Mary.

Verse 26 begins with the angel Gabriel going to Nazareth in the *sixth month*. This is a sacred calendar month, **not** the sixth month of Elisabeth's pregnancy, which is a fact stated in verse 36. Elisabeth's sixth month of pregnancy ironically happened to be in the sixth month of the sacred calendar when Gabriel visited Mary! Carefully read the first chapter of Luke. He wrote to a friend who was a high official of Rome and would not have duplicated the same fact in such a confusing matter as most preachers preach. (Lk. 1:1-4)

The sixth month of the sacred calendar is Elud (Aug. – Sept.) When Mary had come to full term nine months later, Jesus was born in the third month of Sivan (May – June) the following year. (Lk. 2:5-7) On the eighth day, after purification of separation, he was brought to the local Levitical priest, circumcised and named. (Lk. 2:21-23; Lev. 12:2-7) The festival of Pentecost (Firstfruits or Weeks) is in the month of Sivan. (Lev. 23:10-22) Was Jesus was born on Pentecost? Christ is the firstfruit of salvation! (1 Cor. 15:20-23) Most likely, Jesus was born seven days prior to Pentecost just as he ascended to heaven seven days prior to Pentecost. Was he circumcised on the annual Sabbath of Pentecost? (Jn. 7:21-23) Let's do the math in Lev. 23:15-18, Lk. 24:46-53, Acts 1:3-5 and 2:1. Pentecost counts seven Sabbaths after Passover and adds one day. [7 x 7 + 1 = 50] Christ was crucified on a Wednesday late afternoon, in the grave three whole days, and then resurrected on a Saturday (Sabbath) late afternoon. He ascended to heaven after spending forty days with the disciples. Pentecost was *not many days hence.* The counting of seven Sabbaths following Christ's crucifixion on a Wednesday (Passover) began three days later – Saturday, which was the day he arose and the first Sabbath following Passover. [3 + 40 + 7 = 50]

Sivan (May – June) is about the middle of our solar year because the summer solstice is June 21. Jesus was born sometime in the late spring 5 BC. Mathematically, his birth date would be between 5.25 BC and 5.5 BC. Recall the math in Chapter VI in the Seventy Weeks Prophecy? Nisan is the first and Sivan the third month on the sacred calendar, a lunar type, which can vary as much as 28 days with today's solar calendar.

Jesus was crucified one to two months short of his 34th birthday. [30 (years old when He was baptized) + 3.5 (years of ministry) = 33.5]

John the Baptist was born late Chislev (Nov – Dec). Should we start celebrating his birthday on the 25th of December? [If so, say *Merry John-the-baptist-mas*] You could research the year 5 BC, cross reference the Jewish lunar to the Julian solar, correct it by the Gregorian and find Jesus' birthday on today's calendar. Should we bake him a cake and sing happy birthday?

In Revelation 18, merchants will weep and mourn over Babylon's fall because no one will buy ***their merchandise anymore***. If we were to not keep Christmas, Easter, New Year's Day, Valentine's Day, and Halloween, nor buy any of their associated merchandise, plus not buy the other relics, trinkets, statues, candles, rosaries, pictures, incense, crucifixes, and other graven images we like to display, what would their manufacturers and retailers do? It is better to have God **IN** our hearts and minds instead of **ON** our walls and bodies. After Christ returned to the right hand of God, he has been putting up with man's crap for almost two of His days. [2008 – 29 AD = 1979 years] The Lord has three woes ready for man's almost two millennial days (1,979 and counting years) of denials and/or contradictions. (Mk. 14:30; Job 33:14; Num. 20:11; Ex. 34:23; Acts 10:16; Jude 12)

I would like to introduce a new and different doctrine. I call it **Comprehensive Scriptural Investigation – Doctrine of Definitions** or **CSI – DOD**. The only thing this doctrine teaches is a method of studying the Word of God. You will need to acquire the King James Version of the Bible, The Strong's Concordance of the Bible, and a Standard English Dictionary (international edition) as your weapons of mass learning. [Do not worry about the DOE, FBI, ATF, and/or the state police. They shouldn't invade your study, burn you down, or take your children if someone from the Vatican calls Homeland Security on you, and the CIA has little or no interest in truth.] Look up the Greek and Hebrew definitions of key verbs and nouns as you study. Dissect entire passages with definitions if they seem confusing. Study all the passages related to words such as soul, spirit, body, salvation, grace, Sabbath, and any other word as a subject of interest. With sincere study and prayer, God will reveal his mystery. (Rev. 10:7)

Coming out of Babylon will be the most difficult thing that God's children will ever have to do. If we truly love the Lord, we will do as he tells us and keep his commandments. (Jn. 14:15, 15:10, Ex. 20) We know the fourth commandment is to remember and keep the Sabbath. If the commandments were nailed to the cross, as some do teach, can we commit murder, adultery, theft, or covet? People say, "It doesn't make any difference which day we keep." That isn't what Jesus said! Jesus is Lord of the Sabbath. (Mk. 2:27-28) Who made the first day of the week (Sunday) a worship day? Not being sure, which day would you bet on? How difficult would it be to just switch days? (1Jn. 5:3) People say, *"Thank God it's Friday!"* Why? Saturday is indeed the Sabbath Day of rest. Are they ready to rest? Maybe, but I am reasonably sure that most are only ready to just party – party – party. At least they're too hung-over to sun worship!

Most Christian doctrines teach that if you don't get saved in this life, you will die and spend eternal life in everlasting hell fire. The Bible does not teach that! It makes God out to be a tyrant, and God has more mercy than that. Others teach a heaven and hell with a purgatory halfway house with some method of working through purgatory to get out of hell, then into heaven. It is all crap! Every human being that has ever lived and died is dead (sleeping – REST IN PEACE) but will be resurrected. The first resurrection is of the elect to eternal life because the second death has no power, but the second resurrection is to judgment, and the second death will have power. (Rev. 20) If you are not found written in its book of life, you will surely die the second death. It will not be painless! There will be the gnashing of teeth. (Matt. 13:37-43) Eternal life should be the most important thing for man to consider, and not just something easily tossed to the wind.

[2020/2021 Revision Addition]

Just in case you may be interested in the day when Jesus Christ was born in the flesh in 5 BC, you will have to trust in some things the Lord said in John 7:21-23 and elsewhere in the Bible. This is the only place in the Gospels that circumcision was used in defense of some of the things He did on the sabbath day He was Lord of. The *Religious Right* of today are not any different from those of yesteryears. Jesus rebuked them for their hypocrisy, doctrines, and traditions on many things throughout the Gospels; however, in this case I believe He used a very personal experience of Biblical proportions.

Jesus was born in the mid to late spring of the year. Jesus said that He was Lord, even of the sabbath day. (Mark 2:28) Wouldn't it be logical that He would be born on the same day of the week as His Ascension Day? He picked up His life again (resurrected) on a weekly sabbath day. It was his custom to preach on the sabbath days. (Luke 4:16,31, 6:1-10) If John the Baptist's custom was to preach and baptize on the sabbath days also, then Jesus would have been baptized on a sabbath day too! It was also the custom of the Apostles to preach the good news on the sabbath days as well. (Acts 13:14,27,42,44, 16:13, 17:2, 18:4)

According to the Biblical Circumcision Law (Leviticus 12:1-4), Jesus would have been born seven days prior to His circumcision. The sabbath can be either the weekly or one of the annual seven. If Jesus would have returned to the Father on the same sabbath day as He was born, the only Sabbath that His circumcision could consistently be on from year to year is Pentecost, the third annual sabbath of the year and always on the first day of the week – Sunday. Weekly and the seven annual sabbaths were all normally called sabbaths, even the High Day - first annual sabbath of the new sacred calendar year which began in the spring.

Jesus' birthday would be the weekly Sabbath Day seven days prior to His circumcision. He ascended back to His Father seven days prior to Pentecost. Therefore, His birthday would consistently be seven days prior to Pentecost from year to year. This year, Pentecost is May 31, 2020. Carefully read Lev. 23:5-6 and 15-16. This year Jesus' birthday would be May 23rd and it will fall on the sixth weekly sabbath day after Passover which is seven days before Pentecost (the one and only annual Sabbath always on a Sunday) every year for all eternity. Read Lev. 12:1-4, Luke 2:21-24 and Acts 1:1-5 and do the Math! [7 + 33 = 40] Forty is a significate number in scripture! I hear Christians say that Christmas should be every day! I think and believe we should keep the Lord's birthday every week! It is His weekly sabbath and commandment! Just something else to think about. If you truly love the Lord, prove it! (John 14:15,21, 15:10; Matt 5:19, 19:17; Rev. 12:17, 14:12, 22:14; 1John 5:2-3; 2John 6)

In 2020, Jesus' earthly birthday in the flesh was sabbath day May 23rd. In 2021, it was May 15th. In 2022, it will be the sixth weekly sabbath after Passover. **NOT EASTER!**

Chapter X
Delusions and Illusions

A state of delusion is believing in an erroneous concept, idea, doctrine, or a supposed fact that is deceptive. Thousands have died and billions have been spent on the deceptive fact that Iraq had weapons of mass destruction. The entire nation was in a state of delusion on that issue. We are told that the economy is fine, and that its fundamentals are strong. The prophets of Wall Street are never wrong. If you believe that, then you are most definitely delusional.

One of the greatest delusions today is that of home and property ownership. Do you own your own home or property? Are you making payments while it is the collateral security of the usury loan? If your answer to both questions is yes, then you are in a state of delusion. My property is free and clear, and I possess the deed, but every year I must pay the county tax collector for the right to own it. I suppose that makes me somewhat delusional, but I prefer the term *ripped off*.

I am the third generation to possess it. My grandfather paid "Valuable assets and Ten - - - - - dollars" for it in 1957. The county's current assessed value is 58,761 dollars. Property taxes are based on the assessed market value of the property and reassessed every four years. Will its reassessed value in 2010 honestly reflect the current falling market prices? A 3.45% increase in the sales tax for the county was voted down in the 2008 election, and the county commissioners promised to increase the property tax rate if voters rejected it. They kept that promise with a 12% increase! Within one year, the State raised the sales tax. Who got screwed? Politicians are addicted to tax and spend. Voter intervention seems useless. Although property tax is supposed to be based on *fair market value*, I seriously doubt anyone will ever see a tax decrease when market values plummet.

My delusion of property ownership is not as severe as the one still in usury servitude to mortgage bankers. That state of delusion will manifest itself as properties devaluate and foreclosures increase. Even if people can renegotiate their mortgages, will they continue to make payments on a principal balance that may be 20% to 30% less than the value of the property? If the debt of servitude becomes greater than the value of the thing for which the servant is indebted, does the slave to usury have the liberty to abandon the thing and forsake the debt? [Shattered Dreams] Will the day of justice ever come for greedy bankers? (Is. 3:15, 5:9; Prov. 22:26-27, 28:8; Matt. 18:22-34) I assure you that it will!

There are several religious beliefs that are also delusions. We have been led into a Babylonian captivity by the doctrines and traditions of men. (2 Th. 2:10-12; Is. 66:4) These two passages are the only places the word *delusion(s)* is used in the entire Bible. The Hebrew word for *delusions* is *taaluwal* – caprice or any fanciful idea(s). The Greek word for *delusion* is *plane* – fraud, deceit, fraudulence, or error. Why would God *choose* or *send* us delusions? The Greek word for *send* is: *pempo* – to dispatch (in the subjective sense). The Hebrew word for *choose* is: *bachar* – to try, by implication to select, and is synonymous with: *bachan* – to test. Both passages pertain to the last days. The doctrines and traditions of men are the delusions (fanciful ideas, error, deceit, fraud) to which men have been subjected to throughout the centuries. Their delusions will be *selectively tried and tested,* and the Lord **will bring their fears upon them** because they **received not the love of the truth.**

Most Christians believe that the Lord will first come to secretly rapture his church (fly away) and they will escape the *Great Tribulation*. Those left behind will have to face the *Antichrist* and suffer persecution unless they accept the mark of the beast. Moslems believe Christ will come back to fight the *Antichrist*, and Jews are waiting for the Messiah to come the first time. The pre-tribulation rapture doctrine has been made very popular by the fictional series, "Left Behind". Millions of dollars have been made on the books and movie rights. It does make some good science fiction. **But it is still fiction!**

The whole concept is based on *The Antichrist* rising and deceiving those left behind after the rapture. The term **antichrist** is used in 1John 2:18 & 22, 4:3 and 2John 7, and is found nowhere else. To deny that Christ came in the flesh, died, and resurrected is to be antichrist. John said there were many already in the world. To deny the divinity of Jesus Christ as the only begotten Son of God is also to be antichrist. Technically speaking, Jews, Muslims, Hindus, Buddhists, and any person who denies Jesus Christ or his divinity are antichrist. Atheists are just anti-any-ole-god!

Anti- means: to oppose, antagonize, contradict, or counteract. Antichrist is anyone or anything that is in opposition to, contradicts, or counteracts anything that Christ did or taught, which is antagonistic towards Christ.

The truth about tribulation can be found in the following scriptures: Deut. 4:30-31; Judges 10:14; 1 Sam. 26:24; Matt. 13:21, 24:21-31; Mk. 13:24; Jn. 16:33; Acts 14:22; Rom. 2:8-13, 5:1-5, 8:35, 12:12; 2Cor. 1:4, 7:4; 1Th. 3:4-5; 2Th. 1:4-8; Rev. 1:9, 2:9-11, 2:21-23, 7:14-17. Tribulation is something to expect and will come upon all human beings. It is something in which God's people can find faith, patience, and even comfort and joy. During the last days, those who have the faith of Jesus and keep the commandments of God will have patience in it, even to the death. (Rev. 14:12, 12:11) It is not something that we are going to escape by being beamed up to heaven by an angel named Scotty on the Good Ship Lollypop. Revelation 7:14 states, **they which came out of (through) great tribulation** are made white. You cannot get hamburger unless you first run the meat through a grinder. (Zec. 13:9; Is. 48:10; Amos 9:9; Ps. 7:6, 66:10; Dan. 12:10; 1Pet. 1:17; Rev. 3:17-22)

The secret rapture theory did not appear in the churches until after 1830 AD. It was unknown to all the early church fathers. Justin, Irenaeus, and Terullian were convinced that the Christian Church would go through great tribulation at the hands of many antichrists before the Lord returned. The 18th century protestant reformers Huss, Knox, Wycliffe, Luther, Calvin, Cranmer, and Wesley never taught the *Rapture Theory* that many theologians do today. It covertly crept into the church and must have had a strategic purpose for its introduction. Most assuredly, Satan had his hand in it. He has it in everything else man has screwed up!

During the period of the reformation, the first Protestants believed and taught that the Papacy was antichrist, and the Roman Church was the harlot system of Revelation 17. Certain Romish theologians had thought it necessary to take the pressure off the Pope, so a new interpretation of prophecy was invented. The Jesuit priest Ribera (1537-1591) was first to teach that the prophetic events of Daniel and Revelation would not be fulfilled until the last 3.5 years at the end of the age when a global dictator or *The Antichrist* arose. The Roman Church was and still is the fulfillment! Like a CIA cover story, the Roman Church had to establish a cover story to conceal the truth. What else have they covered up?

Despite the efforts of Ribera and those of Cardinal Bellarmine later, it wasn't until the early 19th century that this new futurist doctrine began to gain acceptance by Evangelical Christians. In 1830 Margaret

McDonald, a young member of Edward Irving's so-called *Catholic Apostolic Church*, prophesied that there would be a secret coming of the Lord to rapture those who awaited his return. [If this girl was a true Prophetess, then let's all live off happy meals and wait for Captain Ronald McDonald of the Good Ship Lollypop.] (Eze. 13:17-23) Irving devoted his talent as an artful preacher to spreading the secret rapture theory until he died in 1834.

It has long been pointed out that *pre-tribulationism* is a relatively new doctrine. The present-day apocalyptic action-packed version has been the best-selling doctrine in all of Christendom. Not all Christians buy into the theory, but those who do are in a state of delusion. They think they will escape tribulation. (Is. 60:8-9; Eze. 13; 1Th. 5:1-3) This state of delusion I call, **THE GREAT FALSE HOPE**.

During the time of trouble, the Christians who believe they will fly away and escape the tribulation will fall into the *pit* of false hope. (Is. 24:16-18) The *snare* will be a new lie to explain away the first lie that got them into the pit in the first place. Those who believed they would not go through the tribulation will wonder what went wrong. Shortly before the 21 days of silence (global communication breakdown), the false prophet will come forth with an answer. He will probably be someone highly decorated with man-made theological degrees.

It is time for sleepy headed Christians to wake up! The time of trouble is at hand. The Great Depression, World War I & II, Korea, Vietnam, Afghanistan, and Iraq I & II have all taken place in just the last 95 years (1914-2008). [$95/1000 \times 24 = 2.28$ hrs in God time] These are only the beginning of sorrows. (Matt. 24:4-8) The Greek word for **rumors** is: *akoe* – hearing, audience, something preached or reported. From: *akono* (primary verb) – to hear, to give audience, to report. Daily, World War II was reported on radio and Vietnam on TV. The beginning of the Iraq I & II and Afghanistan was seen live on CNN. Today, some preach an Iran War. Where are we at in prophecy? What is about to come and why? Read the Bible! Keep in mind that Britain and the United States are Joseph's horns of the House of Israel, and the State of Israel is the House of Judah. Ammon is Syria, Moab is Jordan, Iran is Persia, Iraq is Babylon, Arabia is Ishmael, and Edom is among them. Assyria is Germany, Gog and Magog are China and Russia. **Prophecy will be fulfilled!**

The Holy Bible is the complete history of God's people of promise, and the future for all mankind. It is like a 7000-year drama, mankind the actors, and Act 7 is the 1000-year millennial reign of Christ. The new heaven (universe) and new earth of Revelation 21 will be a new eternal drama called **EVERLASTING**. King Jesus Christ and his Saints will do more in 1000 years than man has ever dreamed possible. Man has achieved much while under the influence of Satan, but imagine the resources and wealth that can be peacefully utilized when Christ returns and forces mankind to *beat (recycle) their swords (implements of war) into plowshares (implements of agriculture)*. He'll establish truth, justice, and equality with no more elections, bribery, greedy corporations, and manmade judiciary. **There will be truth and justice for all!**

Will politicians forsake earmarks, special interests, kickbacks, or bribery, and do what is right for the working taxpayers? Capital gain and corporate taxes on money making more money for the wealthy are reduced, and investment income is tax exempt. Oh, that provides jobs! Are the jobs for Americans? The tax burden is increased on those who buy bread and pay utility bills by the sweat of their brow. Who will end up paying the new carbon tax?

The financial institutions tell us a weak dollar is good, and the credit markets are fine. Have you been watching the news lately? I have seen economists with bags under their eyes because make-up artists can't hide their despair. Paper is traded for paper, which is backed by more paper, and that paper is used to back more paper that was traded for the first paper, which is then backed by more paper. If there isn't enough paper to keep everybody's indebted butts cleared, then the Fed just prints more paper to pile on the mountain of crappie paper that is decomposing the economy. Maybe we can use the paper compost to organically grow corn to make environmentally friendly green fuel for our cars while we all starve to reduce *fart emissions*.

Major Banks, Investment Firms, and Mortgage Companies are beginning to fail. The politicians that gave them the deregulatory tools to dig their hole are now being asked to fill it back up. They have dug a hole so deep that all the taxpaying surfs on the planet won't be able to rescue them. Real estate values are taking a nosedive. Freddie Mack and Fanny Mae are in trouble. It may come a time you can't even get a *Mc-Mae Happy Loan* for $1/10^{th}$ the value of your home. Property was meant to be a possession and an inheritance, not leverage for credit, investment, and taxation. Since money and houses are made from trees, maybe we are seeing a metaphoric first trumpet burning of a third of them. (Rev. 8:7) Trees make paper that becomes money, which buys food, then after digestion – more paper wipes butt. God help us, we need more paper. God, save the trees!

The stock markets go totally nuts over the slightest bit of news. We've seen insurance companies fail after major disasters. [Blessed insurance for my house so fine, if a storm comes and it is torn down – will blessed insurance restore what is mine?] What would happen if there were major earthquakes on the west coast, floods, drought, and severe tornadoes throughout middle America, major hurricanes on the gulf and eastern seaboards, major fires and pandemic all across America, and a major terrorist attack of a nuclear type, all in the same year that the stock market crashes and banks lock their doors? Is there enough FEMA to go around? Will the American Idols come to our rescue? If our government was to go bankrupt, who would write the paychecks for our military? You cannot place an unpaid armed army on the streets. It was tried in Iraq! Remember what followed? [18 years later, we're still there!]

We could wake up one morning and find the entire global economy collapsed. Remember the old game *paper-scissors-rock*? Paper is the global economy, and scissors is the greedy beast that cuts the paper. It will be a time of trouble such as the world has never seen. The only people that disappear will be the bank and corporate CEO's responsible for it. They will retire to luxurious secret places with their electronic trillions, then set the snare for those in the pit. The rock that crushes scissors is Jesus Christ, King of Kings – Lord of Lords, then everyone will say:

"IN GOD WE TRUST!"
(Daniel 2:34-35 and 44-45)

WHAT DO YOU TRUST? WHO DO YOU TRUST?

[2020 Revision Addition]

The next five pages were not in the 2008 publication. Originally written in 1999, it is now added to show that there were signs to look for in these last days (years). The COVID-19 outbreak is only the *beginning of sorrows.* A Constitutional Crises will put the United States in a state of **Great Tribulation.** With the short time that this world age has left I think it be best to dig out your Bible instead of the U.S. Constitution.

CAN MONEY TALK?

As we draw closer to the last days, God will give us warning signs. We are to be watchful of the world around us. The prophecies of the Bible will be fulfilled! Just as the prophecies fall on death ears so will the warning signs. (Ps. 74:4-10) Those who bring them to light will be dismissed as fools with wild imaginations or insensitive doomsday alarmists. Some signs will be dismissed as only illusions seen by delusional fools. Can we not discern the signs of the times?

Following the S&L scandal and the government's bailout of those criminals in 1989, it was <u>ten</u> years later during President Clinton's acquittal on articles of impeachment for perjury that the new design of our present 20-dollar bill was put into circulation. In early 1999, when they first appeared in Onslow County, I wrote an article to the editor of our local paper, which was published in March of 1999. In the weeks that followed, several people wrote in response to my letter claiming that I was only seeing things and delusional with my illusions. I made a photocopy of the new and old bills preserving the remembrance of the old design. The following four items are various things I initially saw in the new design and refer to the photocopy:

(1) The old seal has 31 points around its circumference, which represented USC-31 the Banking Code. Many banking and lending regulations were relaxed during the Reagan and Clinton Administrations. Both Republican and Democratic Congresses are responsible for years of consistent de-regulation.

(2) We now have a **Federal Reserve System**. The seal of the system is used in the center, but the 31 points are missing. Congress surrendered its Constitutional authority over money in the Federal Reserve Act of 1913 and Monetary and Banking Acts of 1933 and 1934, which took the U.S. domestic economy off the gold standard. [Read the U.S. Constitution Art. I Sect. VII and X.]

(3) In the old design, **In God We Trust** was placed in a banner, and the flag with its staff was <u>under</u> God. This was symbolic of one nation under God – indivisible.

(4) In the new design, **In God We Trust** is taken out of its banner and the flag placed <u>above</u> God! The flagstaff now divides and separates **In God** from **We Trust.**

The design was accepted in 1996. It took about two years to engrave the new plates, approve them, and verify the work before the new bills could be put into circulation. The first series was printed late 1998 and went into circulation early 1999. You will not find any of the old bills in circulation today. The following are three more things in the prime of seven as in the Revelation Countdown:

(1) 1996 (new design) – 1989 (S & L scandal) = 7 years
(2) 1996 + 7 years = 2003 (Iraq invasion based on false information)
(3) 2003 + 7 years = 2010 (the year American securities sold to European banks come due.)

In 21 years, the S&L scandal will come full circle. We are still paying for that bailout! [1989 + 21 yrs = 2010] Remember the number 21? (Dan. 10:3, 13) [1999 + 21 = 2020] From the time the S&L Scandal went before a Congressional hearing in 1989 to 1999 when President Clinton was acquitted on perjury about his adulterous affair was a span of ten years. [1999 + 10 = 2009] What will happen in 2009? (Hillary got a SOS job after losing the primary in 2008) Since 1989, the ACLU has relentlessly opposed and destroyed the public displaying of the Ten Commandments, school prayer, carrying a Bible on government property, and the right of Christians to practice and live by their convictions.

In the S&L scandal and Clinton affair, there were at least four of the Ten Commandments (coveting, theft, adultery, and bearing false witness) violated by government and banking officials while giving testimony **under oath**. The sign on the back of the new twenty is: *the nation has stripped God of honor and raised its flag above him.* On national television, **finger-pointing perjury** was witnessed by the entire nation. **Remember that!** Today, the Nation is seriously divided!

The taking of God out of his banner and placing the flag above God symbolizes a violation of the first commandment; *Thou shalt have no other Gods before (above) me.* In hindsight, take a new 20-dollar bill, turn Jackson upside down, fold in half length-wise top to bottom, fold right half down at a 45° angle, fold left half down at 45° angle, hold the point of the fold between thumb and index finger, and then turn right side up. What do you see? Is it an illusion? I am no delusional fool!

During the *Month of September 2001*, Islamic terrorists destroyed the two towers of the World Trade Center. The Pentagon that is the icon of our military strength was also attacked. Thousands of souls unexpectedly died that day. Could our government have foreseen such an evil event? Is the sign in the design only an illusion? From the time the twenty's new design was approved (1996) to its first printing (1998) was two years. From 1998 to 2001 was three years. It also took three folds to see the hidden sign in the design. Two towers fell five years after the new design was approved. [2 +3 + 2 = 7] ALSO [1963 (Last year <u>silver</u> used in coins) + 7^2 years = **2012**] (See Appendix IV.)

The two towers symbolize the Global Economy and have already fallen. Seven years later, the Global Economy goes into a downward spiral. In the *Month of September 2008,* the Stock Market fell 777.7 points. Presently, **Main Street** is at the mercy of **Wall Street.** What will be the third tower of the Global Economy to fall? (Is. 30:25, 33:18-19, 32:12-15) The government continues to feed the economic beast of greed by sacrificing the poor and the future children of the nation on the altars of taxation. (Is. 3:13-15, 5:9-16, 10:1-4, 25:1-7, 26:4-6, 29:18-21, 32:7-15, 66:1-2; Eze. 22:23-29; Zec. 7:9-10, 11:4-17) And the shepherds have also led their flocks astray in the doctrines and traditions of men. (Is. 56; Jer. 25:27-38; Eze. 34; Jn. 10:7-18; Rev. 3:14-22)

Once the events on 9-11 were understood and before government officials could get a grip on the situation, Flight 93 went down by the courageous act of forty unselfish souls who sacrificed themselves so that others may be spared. A film with forty memorials was made in their honor. The number 40 has great significance in the Bible. It rained for forty days and nights in the flood. (Gen. 7:12) The children of Israel wondered in the wilderness for forty years. (Ex. 16:35) Moses was on the mount for forty days and nights. (Ex. 24:18) Jesus fasted in the wilderness for forty days and nights. (Matt. 4:2) After Christ resurrected, he spent forty days with his disciples. (Acts 1:3) Both Martin Luther King and Bobby Kennedy were killed in 1968. Forty years later (2008), America elects its first black president. In another four years is the year **2012.**

Numbers and arithmetic are very useful in the understanding of prophecy. Most people will say that I am just seeing illusions in all these sevens and other significant biblical numbers. Some may accuse me of delusional math, but recent events in our nation and the global economic mess the world is presently facing is adding up. Is simple arithmetic the missing link in the understanding of prophecy?

Missing links

We are presently seeing the old five-dollar bills being replaced by a new design approved in 2005. (2nd fulfillment of the 69 weeks – Chapter VI) Both of Jacob's weeks of years are seven-year periods. (2005 + 7 yrs = **2012** and 2012 + 7 yrs = **2019**) Look at the back of a new five. Although there is no flag on the Lincoln Memorial, **In God We Trust** is taken out of its banner encircling a memorial that represents a reunited nation once divided. Does the new shading <u>behind</u> the memorial look like a mushroom cloud? If money really talks, is anyone listening?

[2021 Revision Addition]

Photo of pre-2005 five dollar Bill found on internet.

Chapter XI

Badges

The definition for **badge** in the Standard English Dictionary is as follows: 1. A token, mark, decoration, or insignia of office, rank, or membership. 2. Any distinguishing mark.

Within the book of Revelation there are two types of badges, which are the ***mark of the beast*** or the ***seal of God***. Those with the seal of God will not be hurt by the 5th and 7th trumpets, but those with the mark of the beast will suffer them. (Rev. 9:4, 16:1-21) All Christians understand that fact, but most do not understand what the *seal* and the *mark* represent.

The number 666 is the total numerical value of ***the mark, or the name of the beast, or the number of his name.*** (Rev. 13:16-18) The Greek word for ***name*** is: *onoma* – a name (lit. or fig.) – authority. With all the imaginable conceptions this number has among people, you could make it into a comedy series called **Funny – Funny – Funny**. **"F"** is the sixth letter of the alphabet. Have you ever seen people at check-out lines that will get something else if their total bill is all sixes? On the news recently, a phone district was assigned the area code 666. The people petitioned and got a new one. [Ring...Hello...Is Lucifer home? I can remember laughing, but not the city's name. To make an international call you first dial 011, the country's code (Italy – 39), then the city's code (Rome – 6 and Vatican City – all 3 major points – 6). Could the Papacy's global hot line be 011-39-666-pope?

What does the mark of the beast and the seal of God represent? There is a conflict of authority between the two. Both directly involve the forehead or memory. Although the hand is only mentioned with the mark, it is also related to the seal. Note the following definitions:

(1) mark – *charagma* – a scratch, or an etching, i.e. stamp (as a badge of servitude) – mark. From: *charax* – to sharpen to a point (through the idea of scratching) a stake, i.e. (by implication) a palisade or rampart – trench. Akin to the primary verb: *grapho* – to engrave, especially to write, figuratively to describe. [The English definition for rampart is widespread and unchecked, as in an erroneous belief or superstition.]

(2) seal – *sphragis* – a signet (as fencing in or by the protecting from misappropriation) by implication the stamp impressed (as a mark or badge of privacy or genuineness) – seal.

The two definitions have *stamp* and *badge* in common. A badge is an insignia of office or rank, and the same thing as a signet. God's servants are sealed with the genuine protection of God's signet in their foreheads. (Rev. 7:2-3; Ex. 20:8-11) The **mark of the beast** is the signet of a man or manmade authority, and something that is in direct conflict with the genuineness of God's signet. Both are in the forehead, which in the figurative sense has to do with remembering something and servitude or service to it. (Dan. 7:25; Rev. 13:16-17)

When Moses spoke to the children of Israel in Exodus 31:12-18, he is speaking of the ***perpetual covenant*** which is an ***everlasting sign***. The Hebrew word for ***sign*** is: *owth* – in the sense of appearing; a signal (lit. or fig.) as a flag, beacon, monument, omen, prodigy, evidence; mark, sign, token, or signet. The perpetual covenant of God is his Holy Sabbath, which he made by resting on the seventh day of recreation week. The Elohiym (Theos/Logos) that speaks in Genesis 1 is the Word that became flesh in John 1. The Lord made the Sabbath by resting from his work. This covenant was not only transgressed but changed by Rome. (Gen. 2:13; Dan. 7:25, 11:32-39; Hos. 8:1-3; Heb. 13:20; Ps. 25:10, 103:8-18, 105:5-10, 111:4-10, 132:12)

Jesus said ***the Sabbath was made for man, and not man for the Sabbath.*** (Mk. 2:27) All Jews are men, but are all men Jews? His beef with the Scribes and Pharisees was their hypocrisy in keeping it. They constantly accused Jesus of violating the Sabbath while doing a good deed.

When Jesus said, **"I'm Lord even of the Sabbath day"**, it despiteously pissed them off. They wanted to destroy him. (Matt. 12:1-14) On Passover, Nisan 14, 29 AD, they did! They also fulfilled the prophecy in Isaiah 53.

The fourth commandment is: ***remember the Sabbath, to KEEP IT HOLY.*** Memory is a brain function, which is in your forehead. The Sabbath is for rest and communion because the Lord put his presence in it. The Hebrew words for work ($m^e lakah$) and rest (*shabath*) associated with the fourth commandment means: *to desist from any usual employment, business, occupation, or severe labor, and commune with (worship) the creator.* (Gen. 2:2-3; Ex. 20:8-11; Is. 56, 58:13-14; 66:23;

Ps. 92-101) What about emergencies, firemen, policemen, and medical emergency personnel? Read Luke 6:9. What are soldiers to do in war? To study (to be engaged in learning, practice and participation in) war no more, man has not yet learned!

The day (time) of rest and worship was changed by Rome. (Dan. 7:25) There are many passages of scripture that are misinterpreted in defending Sunday, and Col. 2:16 is the most misused passage. There is no Greek word for **of**. The Greek prime particle *e* is read **or** when disjunctive, or **either** when comparative. The Greek prime word *oun* is read **certainly** as an adverb, and **therefore** when a conjunction. The translators added *days*. The verse is better translated as: *Let no man certainly judge you in meat (eating), or in drink (drinking), either in respecting a holyday (feast), or the new moon, or the Sabbath.* (Lk. 7:31-35; Ps. 104:14-15) **BUT** avoid drunkenness! (Lk. 21:34)

The fourth commandment is the badge that God's people are sealed with; therefore, the badge of the beast must certainly be some other day by another authority. The Lord made and has not changed the Seventh Day Sabbath. (Gen. 2:2-3; Jer. 13:23; Mal. 3:6) A man or manmade authority made the change. Doesn't that constitutively place that man or manmade authority above God? Jesus Christ is head of the church; therefore, any other church head doing such an act would certainly be placing themselves above God. Daniel 7:25 was fulfilled by Rome (the beast), the Catholic Church (mother of harlots that rides the beast), and the Papacy (the false prophet of infallibility).

We have already reviewed the history of the changing of the Seventh Day Sabbath to Sunday, but let's get it right from the harlot's own mouth and other authorities. Seven reinforcements follow:

(1) *"The Sunday is a Catholic institution, and its claim for sacredness can be defended only on Catholic authority. In Holy Scripture, from the beginning to the end, we find not one single text which justifies the transfer of the weekly public worship service from the last to the first day of the week."* (Catholic Press, Sidney, 8-25-1900)

(2) *"We celebrate Sunday instead of Saturday, because the Catholic Church has transferred the sacredness from Saturday to Sunday at the council of Laodicea in the year 364 AD."* (The Converts Catechism of Catholic Doctrine from P. Geiermann, the work of Pope Pius X, on 1-25-1910)

(3) *"It pleased the church of God to transfer the celebration of the Sabbath to Sunday."* (Published Roman Catechism, p. 247, after the decision of the Council of Trent by order of Pope Pius V.)

(4) *"The Sabbath, the best-known day of the law, was changed into the Lord's day. These and others have not ceased because of instructions received from Christ, (because he himself says, I have not come to destroy the law, but to fulfill it), but because due to the authority of the church they have been changed..."* (Archbishop of Rheggio, Sermon 1-18-1562, Mansi 23, p. 526)

(5) *"The seventh-day Sabbath was kept by Christ and the apostles and was celebrated by the first Christians and acknowledged as such until it was abolished by the Laodicean Council. This council first settled the question about the Lord's Day and forbade the keeping of the seventh-day Sabbath under the issue of an Anathema (Curse)."* (William Prynne, from "Dissertation on Lord's Day", pg. 32)

(6) *"It was the holy Catholic Church who transferred the rest day from Saturday to Sunday, the first day of the week...Which Church does the whole civilized world obey? The Protestants...acknowledge great reverence towards the Bible, and yet by celebrating the Sunday they acknowledge the authority of the Catholic Church. The Bible says,*

'Remember the Sabbath day, to keep it holy', but the Catholic Church says, 'No, keep the first day of the week holy!' – and the entire world obeys her!" (Pater Enright on 12-15-1889)

(7) *"The celebration of Sunday has always been a man-made arrangement."* (Neanders Church History, Vol. 1, p. 399)

The Catholic Church openly admits there is **no authority from Christ**, but it was **for her own pleasure**. Sound like a harlot? Why do Protestants that claim the Holy Bible as the only authority of God continue to honor **her** authority by resting and worshipping on Sunday? Who is the head of this beast-riding whore, Christ or Satan? Why do God fearing, Bible believing Protestants accept the signet of **her** authority by wearing **her** badge? One would think that after the announcement made by the Catholic Church on July 13, 2007 (ironically on a Friday – CBN News) that only Catholics would enter into heaven, Protestants would literally trash every dogmatic doctrine that the Catholic councils have ever **etched out on paper with ink!**

Protestants used to teach that the Catholic Church and Papacy were the harlot beast system at the beginning of the reformation. What has happened over the past 500 years? Jesus said, *"...in vain do they worship me."* (Mk. 7:7; Is. 29:13; Prov. 28:9) The time is soon coming that lip service simply will not cut it anymore. You will wear either **the badge of the beast/harlot** or **the badge of God**. Any 1 out of 7 will not be acceptable!

The **name** *(onoma)* is a title or official position of authority. Since Vatican City is a sovereign independent state and a member of the United Nations (sitting membership only with no vote as of now) it must have a leader. The Papacy is **Head of Church and State**. The King of Vatican City wears a crown, as most kings do, and his is called a *Mitre*. It is a triple crown with a cross on top, and the following ETCHED across the front band: **VICARIUS FILII DEI**. In Latin it translates: **Representative of the Son of God**. The Bible tells us the Holy Spirit is representative. (Jn. 14:26, 16:12-15; Rom. 8:26, Is. 32:15) Can a man represent or only witness? There are hundreds of passages that proves the Holy Spirit of God deals with man directly, and not through any human agent. If the Pope is the Holy Spirit, can he be poured into his subjects? Can he go up high in the heavens and be poured upon us? The Pope is also to be properly addressed as **Most Holy Father**. Jesus tells us to *call no man your father upon the earth*. (Matt. 23:9) Our Holy Father is in Heaven! (Matt. 5:16, 45, 48; 6:1, 9; 7:11, 21; 18:10, 14, 19) He is not in Vatican City! (Rev. 2:13, 17:9) Can you now see the abomination? (Lk. 6:39 Matt. (15:14; Dan. 7:25; Is. 24:5,16-23) If not, would a Seeing Eye Dog help?

The Latin (Roman) alphabet has numerical values based on the Roman numeral system. The numerical value of **VICARIUS FILII DEI** follows: **V = 5, I = 1, C = 100, A = 0, R = 0, I = 1, U = 5, S = 0, F = 0, I = 1, L = 50, I = 1, I = 1, D = 500, E = 0, and I = 1.** (U and V have the same numerical value - **5**.) When you add or *count the number*, it totals to 666. According to Daniel Webster's Dictionary, the word *deity* (dei + ty) comes from the Latin *deus*, which means: (god + facere, to make) – the state of being a god – a god or goddess – the Deity God. The other Daniel tells us he will not regard the *desire of women*. (Dan. 11:37) I don't know about little boys or girls. The Harlot should be down to her panties and bra by now. Next act – adult books only! (Is. 47-48; Rev. 17) The word *causeth* in Rev. 13:16 is translated from the Greek word *poieo* meaning: (as an apparent prolonged form of an obsolete prime) to make, or cause to do (in a very wide application, more or less direct: agreement +

commitment + ordain, observe, perform + transgress the law) and comparable to: *prasso* – a primary verb meaning: to practice, i.e. to perform repeatedly or habitually. The **mark of the beast** is the **prolonged practice of transgressing the fourth commandment!** Presently, it is voluntary through the freedom of religious practice. Was there ever a time in history when the Roman Church accused Christians that kept the Seventh Day Sabbath of heresy, and then murdered them if they did not recant and return to her authority? How could this be enforced today?

Most people don't like to read a book. They prefer to wait until the movie comes out. Maybe some movie producer will come across and read this little book. If so, I would like to submit for the next Hollywood fiction thriller of *Apokalupsis* proportions the following story line and plot. Other writers can add the romantic subplots.

A Time of Trouble

The financial markets of the world are failing. All the capitalist nations and their government's bailouts are proving to be in vain. The world's major banks begin declaring bankruptcy. Trillions have disappeared. There is no credit. True unemployment is approaching 50%. Currencies throughout the world are becoming worthless. Inflation and deflation have become meaningless terms.

Millions of houses lie empty, but many are broken into and some used as overnight camps by unemployed homeless transits. People's electricity and water are shut off because they can't afford to pay their bills. Food pantries are empty and closed. The economy has ground to a halt, and finally the entire global economy collapses. People are stealing food from any place they can find it. The world begins to slip into a state of anarchy, and systems of government are in chaos.

The State of Israel has attacked Iran's nuclear facilities. Terrorists have succeeded at acquiring and using nuclear materials on the United States and Great Britain. The U.S. military forces have been bogged down in Iraq, Afghanistan, and other Middle East Countries for the past 21 years. UN and NATO forces are unable to handle the world's situation in a conventional manner, and the Superpowers have footballs with nukes. The planet is on the brink of nuclear war. It is the year 2022.

The Pope claims that Christ has come instructing him to declare a type of Biblical Jubilee (Lev. 25), then endorses a charismatic leader from some nation in whom the entire world has placed great hope but is barely holding the world together. A plan is devised that can quickly restart the global economy. All debt is forgiven. There will be a fresh start. Everyone will be issued a free electronic account of credits and benefits by receiving a personalized microchip ID implant on the back of their hand for scanning and preventing identity theft. It is like the soup lines of the Great Depression. Acceptance is to give allegiance to the Universal Church and all its infallible **G**lobal **O**rthodox **D**irectives. Many signs and miracles are being performed. Most people will accept the New World Order. Very few will resist! They will think Christ has returned, but it will be the false one.

After a short period of time and global conditions stabilize, the UGSW (United Global Space Watch) detects a large unusual elongated object enter the solar system that appears white and is not behaving like other comets. Suddenly, the sixth seal opens! The earth's magnetic poles shift polarity. The planet is magnetically turned upside down. There is a communications blackout. The entire world is silent and its people are terrified. After 21 days of silence, global communications are restored. The world is in a state of shock and confusion. Many disillusioned people will wonder why there was no rapture.

The space object detected before the days of silence is determined to be an alien invasion and its trajectory is the Middle East. The UGSW telescopes can see a name written on the vessel – **JCKKLL Galactica Supreme**. All the armies of the world gather to the trajectory area to prepare for **The Great Battle for Planet Earth.**

[2020 Revision Addition]

How can Christians, Catholic or Protestant, support the killing of unborn innocents and gay marriage, yet call themselves true Christians? How can the Episcopal and Anglican Church (Romish England's American Branches) have openly gay Bishops and support abortion, LBGT and gay marriage, then at the same time be addressed as *Most Reverend* without being a daughter of the harlot and an **ABOMINATION OF THE EARTH?**" (Rev. 17:5) Are Priests and Ministers still molesting children? An accused Archbishop from the U.S. is now liaison between the Vatican and China. Is this **New Age** the latter day **Dark Ages**?

Chapter XII
The Ultimate Reality

We are presently living in an inept world of inequality and confusion. The opposing dualisms of good or evil, morality or immorality, and righteousness or wickedness have become a blending of black and white causing a dense gray fog obscuring the light in which truth and justice resides. The global economic crisis is casting people into perilous times daily. The accumulated wealth of a greedy few is cultivating jealously and consuming the patience of many, even the working class and poor. The pinnacle of injustice may soon cause their fury to burst forth, thus setting the stage for the ultimate reality that will soon be revealed.

What is the ultimate reality? Just as we are born into this world bare-butt naked, helpless, and dependent on the parents that begot us, so shall we go out of it unless we cloth ourselves with faith in the hope that a loving heavenly Father can call us from the grave. There is no hope beyond the grave, unless one comes to understand that there is a purpose and plan for all mankind. The Holy Bible reveals that plan, the Supreme Architect of its design, and the Light by which we may see it. The Word of God contains the secret to the universal truth of everything. By today's increased knowledge, we can comprehend it.

The Truth of the Beginning of Everything
$E = mc^2$

In the beginning of the beginning, prior to the commencement of the sublime, exists the omnipotent omnipresence Energy, Supreme and Divine. The tri-morphic intellect of His first thought, understanding of knowledge did define, the brightness of His glory, the express image He called mine. For the Light was begotten by the womb of His wisdom, thus began the eternal continuum – we call space and time.

Light was in the Energy, and Energy was in the Light, thus together they co-existed in the vast darkness of the abysmal night. Comprehension,

comprehension, the darkness declared, by the Light of Energy's truth the darkness could not, sadness so great was its despair. Pity and mercy were in the heart of the Light, for He thought to share His trimorphic intellect with the darkness of the abysmal night. With the understanding of knowledge and the continuum of time, wisdom opened her doors and gave birth to the Universe, the eternal sublime.

Man is an intelligent form of matter, and all matter is the dividend of energy by light's expression. Likewise, energy and light must also be intelligent, and their supremacy is unquestionable since they can make and change inorganic matter into organic matter. I understood this when I found the mistranslation in Psalm 8:5. The Hebrew word translated *angels* is *Elohiym*, and the only place in the entire Bible. Elsewhere, it is translated **God**, and *angels* is translated from *mal'ak*.

*"Oh Lord our Lord, how excellent is thy name in all the earth, who hast set thy glory above the heavens! When I consider thy heavens, and the work of thy fingers, the moon and the stars, which thou hast ordained; what is man, that thou art mindful of him? And the son of man, that thou visitest him? For thou hast made him a little lower than **God**, and hast crowned him with glory and honor. Lord, what is man, that thou takest knowledge of him! Or the son of man, that thou makest account of him! Man is like to vanity: his days are as a shadow that passeth away. To every thing there is a season, and a time to every purpose under the heaven: A time to be born, and a time to die, a time to plant, and a time to pluck up that which is planted; A time to kill, and a time to heal; a time to break down, and a time to build up; A time to weep, and a time to laugh; a time to mourn, and a time to dance; A time to cast away stones, and a time to gather stones together; a time to embrace, and a time to refrain from embracing; A time to get, and a time to lose; a time to keep, and a time to cast away; A time to rend, and a time to sew; a time to keep silence, and a time to speak; A time to love, and a time to hate; a time to war, and a time of peace. HEAR, ye children, the instruction of THE FATHER, and attend to know understanding. For I give you good doctrine, forsake ye not my law."*
(Psalm 8:1, 3-6; 144:3-4; Eccl. 3:1-8; Proverbs 4:1-2)

When we let the spirit of truth and prophecy guide us through the Word of God; beautiful are all its revelations. I thank God for the knowledge He has opened to my understanding. I continue to pray for the wisdom to utilize it for His glory, and that the use of His gift of the trimorphic intellect in my mind may be found worthy in His eyes.

One night I asked the Lord for a job, and He led me to write this little book. After He led me to Ezekiel 33 and Zechariah 11:15-16, I almost played Jonah. I can only hope and pray that the alarm will be heard, received, and relayed to others. I do not possess great writing skill, but that is part of the task. These last pages are written in a form of parable like short stories in the hope that they may convey understanding.

The Comeback Mountain

For almost 2000 years, there have been deceptions upon deceptions, lies upon lies, here a little, there a little, until almost all mankind is blinded to the truth. About 500 years ago, brave men began tearing down that old mountain of deception, and suffered persecution and torturous death, but those that followed picked up many of the old pebbles and stones, and then built a new mountain. Behold! It looks much like the old one. The time is at hand, when the healed old mountain will require of the new mountain, "Become one mountain under me, for your pebbles are my pebbles, and your stones are my stones. Come back to me, keepers of my pebbles and stones, and repent of the damage done!" Then shall the creator of the heavens and earth, by whom both mountains stake their claim, place in the hearts of the new mountain: *Make the old mountain naked and desolate and burn it with fire.* Then, shall the hearts of both the mountains be brought through the fire by which all mountains shall burn. Those under its pebbles and stones will ask, "Why do we suffer?"

Sweet Pastures

The Scripture of Truth is like a beautiful pasture of plush green grass, and many sheep flocked to it to graze, but the taste was a little bitter. So, the sheep looked for shepherds who would sweeten the taste, and when the sheep grazed upon the flavored grass, the taste was not yet sweet enough. So, the shepherds sprayed the grass with a sweeter flavor, but the sheep were still not satisfied. Some other shepherds said to the sheep, "Try this other pasture, it is greener and sweeter." So, the sheep followed those shepherds, and began to graze in the other pasture, and it was very sweet grass. The sheep grazed and grazed until they became very fat and lazy, and the shepherds were also made fat by the gratitude of the sheep.

Then the Head Shepherd returned for his flock and found his true pasture almost empty. So, he asked the shepherds there, "Where are my sheep? There were once many, now there are so few." Then the shepherds of the true pasture said, "They have found a greener and sweeter pasture." Then the Head Shepherd asked, "Were you so lazy to not call out unto them and bring any of them back?"

So, the Head Shepherd went to the other pasture and asked those shepherds, "What is this thing that you have done to my sheep, for I left them in my holy pasture?" Then, those other shepherds, trying to defend themselves, said, "It was the sheep! They wanted the sweeter grass, so we only did that which the sheep had asked."

Then the Head Shepherd stood between the two pastures and shouted, "Woe to the idol shepherds that leave the flock! The sword shall be upon his arm, and upon his right eye: his arm shall be clean dried up, and his right eye shall be utterly darkened. Woe to the shepherds of the flocks that do feed themselves! Should not those shepherds have feed the flocks?"

Then the fat and lazy shepherds asked, "How were we to know you would come by the old pasture first?" Then the Head Shepherd replied, "Did I not send you watchmen sounding the alarm to return to my holy pasture and have patience in my testimony?"

Then all those shepherds cried, "Yes, but we thought he was just a crazy old fool blowing on an old Jewish horn!"

Which Day To Go Swimming

Many people go swimming in the sea of deception, faithfully trusting in the life raft of delusion. As the rip tide draws nigh, many will be upon it. Over-crowded by a false hope and sinking in disappointment, they cry for the lifeguard. Many shall swim through fiery waters and most will drown. But few are those that resist the warm waters in the sea of deception and ride the perpetual covenant on the life raft of truth, for the true lifeguard will know his own by the signet banner they hoist.

__Two Resurrections__

Men are like grapes, the fruit of the vine, growing ripe for the harvest time. Will their juice be sweet, or will it be sour, when the tester of wine brings it to the judgment hour? The elect grapes that ferment in the natural sweetness of truth will be the first to be served, but that which is quickened with yeast shall be put on reserve. Listen you husbandmen who kept the vine, for the Lord will again set the table and judge the taste of the wine.

Jesus Christ will soon return as **KING OF KINGS AND LORD OF LORDS**. The deceptions and delusions of man's doctrines and traditions will be corrected. **COME OUT OF BABYLON, HER JUDGMENT IS NEAR** Truth's ultimate reality will come to pass!

[2020 Revision Addition the 21st of August]

The beginning of this little book goes back to January of **1999** when I was selected to the jury in a civil lawsuit against Harry Brown, owner of National Dodge, Jacksonville, NC, and now retiring majority leader in the NC Senate. The trial took place while Clinton's impeachment was before the Senate. I was fearful of being accused of perjury due to circumstances during jury selection. I went against my better judgement of the facts and voted with the other jurors. I was the last holdout. After returning home, I had a conscientious meltdown. It took some time to reclaim my sanity. By spring I was back to my gardening business. It was later that spring while packing mustard greens for the local Piggly Wiggly, I heard Geese and went outside to see them. Five came from the north and as they were above me everything went into slow motion. I was elevated above the ground and my mind swelled as if receiving something. As they disappeared to the south two Dove came from the east, confirmed and disappeared to the west. I settled to the ground, then went back to work astounded. Then I heard the Geese again, went outside and as before was elevated. As they disappeared back to the north the two Dove flew from the west, confirmed and returned to the east. The spirit of the Lord moved me to an intense CSI-DOD during the next seven years. I began the little book in **2000**. The visitation is what I now call – the seven thunders. It has been **20** years since it all began. The Great Day (Year) of the Lord is soon upon us!

Bibliography

The Holy Bible – Authorized King James: translated 1611, Published by Thomas Nelson Inc.

AND

The New Strong's Exhaustive Concordance of the Bible: the work of James Strong (1822-1894) – Nelson Inc. – 1990

PLUS

- Introductory Applied Physics, 3rd edition, by Norman Harris and Edwin Hemmerling: McGraw-Hill Books – 1972
- Biology – The World of Lie, by Robert A. Wallace: Goodyear Publishing – 1975
- Technology of Industrial Materials, by H. C. Kazanas, Roy S. Klein, John R. Lindbeck: Chas Bennett Inc. – 1974
- Mystery of the Ages, y Herbert W. Armstrong: Worldwide Church of God – 1985
- Mystery of the Unknown – Mystic Places: Time Life Books Inc. – 1990
- The Great Controversy, by Ellen G. White (original copyright 1888): Pacific Press Publishing Assoc. – 1974
- Lost Christianities, by Bart D. Ehrman: Oxford University Press, Oxford, New York – 2003

- The United States and Great Britain in Prophecy, by Herbert W. Armstrong: Worldwide Church of God – 1980
- The Faith of Israel, by H. Rowley: SCM Press – 1956
- The Incredible Human Potential, by Herbert W. Armstrong: Worldwide Church of God – 1978
- The New York Public Library – Desk Reference: Stonesong Press Inc. 1989
- The American Peoples Encyclopedia: Excelsior Trading Corporation – 1976
- The New Standard Encyclopedia: Standard Education Corporation, Chicago – 1988
- Bible Almanac, Who's Who in the Bible, Fascinating Bible Facts (3 book combination): Publications International – 1999
- Educational programming on Science, History, Discovery, PBS, FSTV, and other channels
- Various websites on the worldwide internet since mid-July 2020.

Appendix I

Karl Marx and Friedrich Engels wrote the Communist Manifesto in 1847. The following are its ten basic platforms as generally applied to the most advanced countries. [American's implementation]

(1) Abolition of property in land and application of its <u>rents</u> to public purposes. [The property tax, HUD, and Public Housing]

(2) A progressive or graduated income tax. [IRS, State Revenue]

(3) Abolition of all rights of inheritance. [The inheritance tax]

(4) Confiscation of emigrant and rebel's property. [Delinquent tax foreclosures, deportations with property left behind]

(5) Centralization of credit in the hands of the State by means of a national bank with State capital and an exclusive monopoly. [The Federal Reserve System, government bail-out of banks]

(6) Centralization of the means of communication and transportation in the hands of the State. [FCC, DOT]

(7) Extension of factories and instruments of production owned by the State, the bringing into cultivation of wastelands, and the improvement of the soil generally in accordance with a common plan. [Dept. of Reclamation – damns, Army Corps of Engineers, Dept. of Agriculture – conservation, Dept. of Interior – grazing]

(8) Equal liability of all to labor, establishment of industrial armies, especially for agriculture. [SSN (Socialist Slave Number), Federal and State emigrant farm labor programs]

(9) Combination of agriculture with manufacturing industries, the gradual abolition of distinction between town and country by a more equitable distribution of population. [Federally subsidized corporate farms with processing facilities, zoning and land use laws – Federal, State, County, City annexations and ETJ]

(10) Free education for all children in public schools. [Dept. of Education – Federal, State, and Local Boards]

****

The Manifesto is a philosophy for establishing socialism on a democratic society, which is classless, humanistic, and embracingly godless. **Communism** is an economic form of Socialism by totalitarianism through a single party or dictator. **Capitalism** is an economic philosophy of property rights both real and monetary. It too is failing due to excessive greed, power, and lust for total control. Neither one is classless! Our Constitution established a Republic form of government with guaranteed rights. Our nation has evolved into a Socialist Democracy. Two **C's** failed to deliver its promises. Like the three pyramids in Giza, the largest, or the third **C,** is **Jesus Christ**. He will establish his kingdom forever! **It will never fail!**

[August 18, 2020 Revision Addition]

The collapse of the USSR (**Union** of Soviet **Socialist Republics**) began in mid to late 1980 during Ronald Reagan's presidency (1981 to 1989) and ended in 1991. On June 12, 1987, President Reagan in his famous Berlin Wall speech said, "Tear down this wall". The wall had separated Communist East Berlin from Democratic West Berlin since 1961. Germany was divided between Russia and the US/UK Allies after World War II and began its reunification after the collapse of the Soviet Union (USSR). The other Eastern bloc countries gained their independence and are now members of the EU. Today, their systems of Government can be classified as Democratic Socialism. Communism is one party Socialism. Two or more party Socialism is practiced by most Democracies. Democrat Bernie Sanders is a professed **Socialist** and is supported by most millennials and is now comrades with Biden. The United States is supposed to be a Constitutional **Republic**. Will the USA become the USSA (**United Socialist** States of America? Folks, this is a hell of a lot more than just word play. Read the History!

[2021 Revision Addition]

The history between 8/18/2020 and present has been all over the news, both mainstream and all other sources. The great global separation has begun. The convergence of latter day prophecy is upon us!

Appendix II

The Genesis Record			
Name	Year born (BC)	Year died (BC)	Age (years)
Adam & Eve	4131 (created)	3201	930
Seth	4001	3194	807
Enos	3896	2991	905
Cainan	3806	2896	910
Mahalaleel	3736	2841	895
Jared	3671	2709	962
Enoch	3509	3144	365
Methuselah	3444	2475	969 (Note 2)
Lamech	3257	2480	777
Noah	3075 (Note 1)	2125	950 (Note 4)
Japheth	2575 (Note 1)	?	?
Ham	2574 (Note 1)	?	?
Shem	2573 (Note 3)	1973	600
Arphax	2473	2035	438
Salah	2438	2005	433
Eber	2408	1944	464
Peleg	2374	2135	239 (Note 5)
Reu	2344	2105	239
Serug	2312	2082	230
Nahor	2282	2134	148
Terah	2253	2048	205
Abraham	2183	2008	175 (Note 4)
Isaac	2083	1903	180
Jacob	2023	1876	147

Notes

(1) Noah was 500 years old before he begat his three sons. (Gen. 5:32)
(2) The flood was 2475 BC. [3075 - 600 = 2475] Methuselah died in the flood. (Gen. 7:5-11)
(3) Shem was 100 years old 2 years after the flood. (Gen. 11:10-11)
(4) Noah lived 350 years after the flood. (Gen. 9:28) Abraham was 58 years old when Noah died and may have known him.
(5) The language was confounded at the tower of Babel during the years of Peleg between 2374 and 2135 BC. (Gen. 10:25, 11:1-9)
(6) The Exodus was 1446 BC. [1876 - 430 yrs. = 1446] (Ex. 12:40)
(7) The first Temple was built 966 BC. [1446 - 480 yrs. = 966] (1 Kings 6:1)

[2020 Revision Addition]

Joseph was sold into Egypt at age 17. (37:2) He was given charge over all Egypt during the 7 plenty & 7 famine years when 30. (41:46) He was expert at record keeping and knew the Egyptian Hieratic script (25 letter alphabet - 3000± BC). He was married to the Priest's daughter! (41:45) By 17, I'm sure Jacob taught him to read and write the family's native Mesopotamian **Semitic** Akkadian script (59 letter alphabet - 2350± BC) before being sold. Abraham, Isaac, and Jacob were wealthy and literate! Joseph merged the two into a *Semitic* upgrade of Hieratic script. Moses was educated while in Pharaoh's house some 400 years later. Hebrew has 24 constants and 10 vowel points (32). Recent evidence discovered in the Sinai and the Arabian Peninsulas are proof. Egotistical blind professionals say – not so! Too damn ashamed!

Joseph brought his entire family to Egypt in the second year of the famine. (45:6) Jacob lived in Egypt for 17 years until his death in 1876 BC. (47:28) Joseph was 56 when his father died. [30 + 7 +2 + 17 = 56] Joseph was born 1932 BC. [1876 + 56 = 1932] Joseph died 1821 BC. (50:26) [1932 - 110 = 1821] The Holy Bible is the most accurate History book on the planet! The Egyptian time period that Joseph and the children of Israel prospered in Goshen was the 12th Dynasty. Goshen was called the **land** of Rameses, Ramesses or Ramses in Genesis, which was a Hebrew blending of Sesostris I, II, III and Amenemhat II - Risamenses, Rimesses or Rimses. Over the course of time the Israelites were probably taxed by successive administrations into slavery. Sound like 1776 to 2020? Since 1913, 17 Administrations in 107 years have done the same!

Joseph was given a royal burial. (41:39-44) He acquired all the wealth of the Egyptian and surrounding people, both money and land, but only retained one fifth for the Priests, his family, then himself. The other $4/5^{ths}$ was Pharaoh's for famine recovery and building the 12th Dynasty! (47:1-27) When main street bailed out WALL STREET in 2008, main street suffered its $4/5^{ths}$. Now that main street is suffering and WALL STREET is booming (Aug. 18th) where the hell is main street's $4/5^{ths}$?]

Appendix III

A Lunar Sign

During the week of Passover, I saw a sign from heaven, but not in the heavens itself. It was in the current calendar that we use today which is the Gregorian. It is a solar-lunar type based upon the solar-lunar Julian calendar, which was corrected by Pope Gregory XIII in 1582 because Easter just kept **distancing** itself from the spring EQUINOX. The Jewish calendar is a lunar type that is corrected every 3 to 4 years (7 times in 19 years) by adding a 29-day month (VEDAR) between ADAR and NISAN. This was to keep the spring plowing in line with the spring equinox; unlike the one the ancient Babylonians kept. Today, the Jews use two kinds of calendars: The *Civil* for kings (government), childbirth and contracts, and the *Sacred* for which the Lord's festivals are computed. The civil begins with TISHRI (Sept-Oct) and the Sacred begins with NISAN (Mar-Apr). Our federal government's fiscal year ends on October 31st. In November they begin another year of more borrowing and throughout the year borrowing more again and again - ∞ (infinity). There is no debt ceiling now. The sky is the limit!

It just happened this past week, that Passover Week (April 8-15) fell within the same week as the Pagan celebration to Astar (pronounced Easter) the goddess of fertility, which is called the "queen of heaven" by the prophet Jeremiah. This happens from time to time throughout the years, but this year is the first time that I can recall that the resurrection of Christ took place on the pagan Easter Sunday; however, **IT WAS NOT IN THE MORNING!** Biblical days are reckoned from sunset to sunset because the evening and the morning were the first day. The only way that I can think of in finding this calendar thing out is to ask the computer that played Jeopardy.

You will also notice that there was a full moon the night of April 7th, the night before Passover Day - Nisan 14. When I was looking at the calendar the morning of the ninth and remembering that it was last night that the Lord was betrayed, the full moon symbol appeared as a large red dot, similar to the black dot symbol for the moon's conjunction. The Spirit of the Lord came upon me and instructed me to resurrect the little book I prematurely published in 2008 and begin editing and updating it for republication.

Also, when counting seven complete Weeks of Sabbaths following the Passover and High Day, there is a new moon (Conjunction) on the night of the 22nd of May, which begins the sixth Weekly Sabbath of counting. The Biblical New Moon is the first moon following the conjunction, which would be sunset the 23rd (Ascension Day) and Pentecost begins in 8 more days. Pentecost is always on the first day of the week. [7 × 7 = 49 + 1 = 50] (Lev. 23:15-16; Acts 2) The Roman Church just counts seven Sundays from Easter Sunday, which is only 49 days. That is just another one of their deceptions! **BUT!** Pentecost is May 31st this year!

I believe what Jesus said was the sign of his resurrection; that he would remain in the grave for **three days and three nights (72 hours).** Passover began at sunset on April 8th and it was that evening Jesus instituted the wine and bread after the Passover meal. [The **(this)** that they were doing was the **keeping of Passover** and as **often** as they did (keep Passover); they were to do so in remembrance of Him. It was throughout that night and the next morning that He was betrayed, tried and beaten. Just after the noon hour He was crucified and died during the ninth hour (4:00 PM). He was placed in the grave by sunset on the 9th, which also begins the High Day or first of the seven annual Sabbaths. It was not the day before the Weekly Sabbath! Three nights and three days later **(72 hours sunset to sunset)** He arose! Where did he go during the dark hours that began the evening of the fourth day? It was light on the opposite side of the planet. Ever wonder why many Native Americans call their God the GREAT WHITE SPIRIT?

This year most people had to stay home from their festival of Easter eggs and bunny rabbits which are symbolic to fertility. Some ministers have defied the stay at home order and vow to take it to the Supreme Court. I suppose their constitutional right to assemble is more important than their eternal possibility. I think that the best thing to do while we have all this time on our hands is to pick up a Bible and start studying, then, think about **social distancing** ourselves from the doctrines and traditions of men! It's amazing what some folks have invented while staying at home.

Since April 10th, I have gone back to the little book written on a Brothers II Word Processor and published with a POD Publisher in 2008.

In 2009 I had a Marine friend at Camp Lejeune reformat it for my sister's ex-Windows 1998. The text was saved, but the format had to be literally raked back together. In 2012 I transferred it to my Uncle's friend's old Windows XP Home Edition and left it mostly alone for the next 7 years. At the age of 65 it is now on an HP Desktop with Windows 10 and I have internet access for the first time in my life (5-20-20). It will be republished by the same publisher soon. I'm working for my Lord now, but I'm no computer Geek.

I have seen a lot on TV about the COVID-19 virus. It seems that everyone has a theory on it. Some are wondering if it is the time of the end. It is most definitely ***the beginning of sorrows*** and the white horse (the first of four) has begun its ride. (Matt. 24; Rev. 6:1-2) Others claim it to be a Chinese retaliation to the presidents' trade war. The United States and Great Britain are the birthright nations of the two sons of Joseph and along with the other eight lost tribes (Western Europe) they are the House of Israel in prophecy. Gog is China. (Ezek. 38:10-16)

It seems that the nations of the world have taken different approaches to battle this global pandemic. The one thing common among them, whether recommended, required, or outright enforced is **social distancing,** which is a type of scattering (*puwts – disperse –* put distance between). (Is. 24:1)

The birds are singing praises and the animals are dancing with joy, all unto their creator the Lord on High - King of Kings, because he has cleansed the air of their heavens and opened the streets of their former domains. They give praise unto their creator with song and dance, and it is a joy within their heart that they see not the likes of man. Hearken unto the Lord your God ye men of the earth, for the days of his postponement are few!

******* LORD COME, AMEN! *******

Appendix IV

Revelation Countdown

In the book of Revelation there is a countdown to the return of our Lord and Savior Jesus Christ as King of Kings and Lord of Lords to set up the government of God here on this earth. (Is. 9:6-7) There won't be any election campaigns nor will there be an election! During the countdown, things on this earth will get to the point of great tribulation. (Matt. 24:21-22, Zech. 13:7-9) It is something that no one is going to escape! The only people left behind (alive) are the third that is brought through the fire. Some flesh has to be saved for the sake of the Saints. Why? So that there will be some flesh to rule and reign over! (Rev. 20:4-6, 19:15) The countdown is a seven year (week of years) period represented by the seven seals in Revelation.

I've seen many things containing the number seven or multiples of seven over the years. During the month of September 2008, I saw many sevens associated with our economy's dilemma at that time. It has only grown worst! The debt balloon of today's economic system is about to burst. The following article was published Oct. 3, 2008 in the Daily News, Jacksonville, NC. (Back in my word processor days.):

To The Editor,   September 29, 2008

Remember the story about the boy who cried wolf? Why did Congress not pass the "bailout package" the 29th of September? When the President cried wolf about weapons of mass destruction in Iraq, Congress quickly gave him a green light and a blank check. After five years, 4,000 plus dead, and billions more of debt, they are still scratching their heads.

Remember the story about Chicken Little? When the President cried, "the economy is falling", the government began to bail out failed institutions of credit and finance. After a few hundred billion here and there, the government realized that it could not overcome by bribery the economic forces of greedavity (greed + gravity).

During the four weeks of September, the government has been trying to appease the "gods of economics" that can create something from nothing. They create capital from credit by re-circulating the same money and call the difference debt. Then, when their debt becomes unbearable, they ask the over indebted taxpayers to once again sacrifice themselves upon their altars of greed. Remember the Savings and Loan scandal?

I find the following seven facts interesting: It has been seven years since 9-11-01. Leviticus 26 has the "seven times" stated four times. (7777) Revelation has seven churches, seals, trumpets, and the seven last plagues, which are the seventh seal. (777.7) The President asked for a 700 billion sacrifice by the indebted taxpayers. After seven days passed, Congress, still scratching its head over the boy who cried wolf said "NO" to Chicken Little. The Feast of Trumpets (Rosh Hashanah) was September 30th this year. The stock market fell 777.7 points that day! (Proverbs 18:10-13, 22:21-27) Read Leviticus 25 and remember the month of September!

Phillip Yarbrough
Richlands, NC

There is an epochal period of time that happens every 19 years and we'll call it Epoch-19. [Woe Nelly, that's COVID's number!] The sacred calendar for keeping track of Gods holy festivals is a lunar type based on the moon phases. Each month begins on the new moon (crowning not conjunction) and the new moon nearest the spring equinox begins the new year with the month of Nisan (Mar. - Apr.). It is corrected 7 times every 19 years by adding a 13th month of 29 days. [5 x 3 + 2 x 2] Three other months alternate between 29 and 30 days. These corrections and alternations keeps the lunar calendar in line with the Spring Equinox. The Jewish Civil Calendar as used in the State of Israel (Kingdom of Judah) begins on God's fifth festival of Rosh Hashanah (Feast of Trumpets) - Tishri 1,2 (Sept. - Oct.). There are seven feasts with three in the spring and four in the fall. There are no annual feasts during summer and winter.

There are two different lunar events that occur every 19 years on our commonly used calendar (Gregorian) which is a solar type. One is called the "Blue Moon" where we have 2 full moons in the same month, and it happens every 2 - 3 years. This is because the moon orbits the earth every 29.5 days and our solar type calendar has 30 or 31 days, except February because it has only 28 days, but 29 on leap year every 4th year as in presidential elections. There is never a "Blue Moon" in February; however, once every 19 years it has no full moon at all, which last occurred in 2018. Every 19 years the first two full moons following the Autumn equinox occurs in the month of October. I called it "Blue Moon October" this past year - 2020. There was also a planetary conjunction of Jupiter and Saturn on the winter solstice December 21, 2020 which happens once every 800 years. (20 yrs. (Gen. 31:41) × 40 yrs. (Ex. 16:35) = 800 years)

* **2008 + 19 = 2027** > 2008 Letter to the editor + Epoch-19

* **2020 cubit/years + 7 seals/years = 2027** > The Great Pyramid Chapter V

* **2012 + 7 + 7 = 2026 (6th seal)** > then 2027 the 7th seal/year > Chapter VI, Daniel's last timeline prophecy, page 96.

"And God said, Let there be **lights** in the firmament of the heaven to divide the day from the night; and let them be for **signs**, and for seasons, and for days, and **years**:" (Genesis 1:14)

The white horse (pestilence) began its ride in 2019/**2020**. As the sacred calendar begins in spring, so did the covid-19 outbreak in the USA. It represents the medical, political, economic and religious chaos and confusion as was seen. We are still seeing it today and it will only get worse! The **bow** and the **crown** are not what most folks think. **"And I saw, and behold a white horse: and he that sat on him had a bow (G5115); and a crown (G4735) was given unto him: and he went forth conquering (G3528), and to conquer (G3528)."** (Rev 6:1) Definitions from Strong's:

*G5115 - toxon - a bow (apparently as the simplest fabric) Derivation: from the base of G5088; KJV Usage: bow.

>G5088 - tikto - to produce (from seed, as a mother, a plant, the earth, etc.), literally or figuratively. Derivation: a strengthened form of a primary teko (which is used only as alternate in certain tenses); KJV Usage: bear, be born, bring forth, be delivered, be in travail.

*G4735) - stephanos - a chaplet (as a badge of royalty, a prize in the public games or a symbol of honor generally; but more conspicuous and elaborate than the simple fillet (G1238), literally or figuratively. Derivation: from an apparently primary stepho (to twine or wreathe); KJV Usage: crown.

>G1238 - diadema - a "diadem" (as bound about the head) Derivation: from a compound of G1223 and G1210; KJV Usage: crown.

*G3528 - nikao - to subdue (literally or figuratively) Derivation: from G3529; KJV Usage: conquer, overcome, prevail, get the victory.

>G3529 - nike - conquest (abstractly), i.e. (figuratively) the means of success. Derivation: apparently a primary word; KJV Usage: victory.

Cotton is a simple fabric made from the fruit (seed bearing) part of a plant. It is now (8/15/21) in bloom in my community. The symbol of honor (badge of royalty) has something twined around it like in a wreath. **Think white cotton cloak and medical symbol!** WHO is subduing whom? Who will get the victory? The red horse joined the white horse in 2020/**2021**. It represents violence/riots/rebellion, which takes peace from the earth and usually leads to all-out war. Been keeping up with world events lately? In 2021/**2022**, the black horse joins them and it represents famine which can have a variety of causes. Who has been buying up massive amounts of farm land? Who has invested heavily in vaccines? Are there those who seek population control? Then in 2022/**2023** the pale horse joins them and it represents death. By the spring of 2024, **The Four Horsemen of the Apocalypse** will have control over a fourth of the earth, which happens to be $2/3^{rds}$ water (seas). [I was in the Navy; I know!] (Rev. 6:1-8) Will there be an election in 2024? Who will be the leader of this nation and what will it be when it becomes a nation under the King of Kings and the saints? (Rev. 2:26, 12:5, 15:4, 16:19 19:15-16, 20:4-6, Isaiah 9:6-7)

THE CONVERGENCE HAS BEGUN!
(Ecclesiastes 12:13-14, John 14:15-21)

Come out of Babylon for her judgement is near!

www.ingramcontent.com/pod-product-compliance
Lightning Source LLC
LaVergne TN
LVHW041711070526
838199LV00045B/1301